THE SIDEWALK COMPANION TO SANTA CRUZ ARCHITECTURE

THIRD EDITION

JOHN LEIGHTON CHASE
EDITED BY JUDITH STEEN

PASATIEMPO CHAPTER BY
DANIEL P. GREGORY

THE MUSEUM OF ART & HISTORY
SANTA CRUZ, CALIFORNIA
2005

Library of Congress Cataloging-in-Publication Data
Chase, John, 1953-
The sidewalk companion to Santa Cruz architecture / John Leighton Chase ; edited by Judith Steen ; Pasatiempo chapter by Daniel P. Gregory.— 3rd ed.
      p. cm.
Includes bibliographical references and indexes.
  ISBN-13: 978-0-940283-14-5 (pbk. : alk. paper)
  1. Architecture—California—Santa Cruz—Guidebooks. 2. Buildings—California—Santa Cruz—Guidebooks. 3. Santa Cruz (Calif.)—Buildings, structures, etc.—Guidebooks. 4. Santa Cruz (Calif.)—Guidebooks. 5. Santa Cruz (Calif.)—History. I. Steen, Judith, 1940- II. Gregory, Daniel Platt. III. Title.
  NA735.S43.C46 2005
  720'.9794'71—dc22   2005015051

Reprinted with corrections, 2007

Book design, cover design, and cover photograph by Michael E. Clark
Cover photograph: 1005 Third Street, Beach Hill, Chapter 1, #17
Maps from 2nd ed. by Michael Banta; revised and supplemented by Michael E. Clark
Financial support provided by the Fred D. McPherson Jr. Publications Fund
Published by:
          The Museum of Art & History
          705 Front Street
          Santa Cruz, California 95060
          (831) 429-1964
          www.santacruzmah.org
The publisher assumes no responsibility for the statements or opinions of the author.
Printed in the United States of America

THE SIDEWALK COMPANION
TO SANTA CRUZ ARCHITECTURE

Dedicated to the memory of

Edna Kimbro (1948-2005)
and
Doni Tunheim (1941-2005)

for their many contributions
to historic preservation
in Santa Cruz

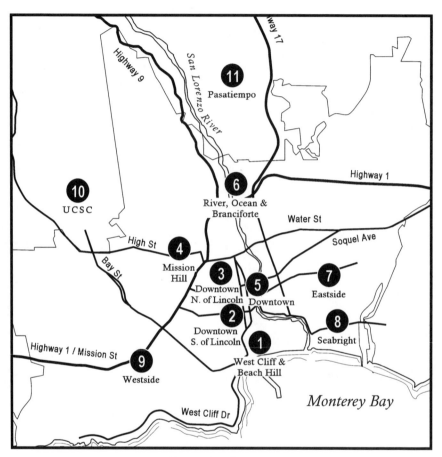

Key to the chapters

CONTENTS

Maps precede each chapter

PREFACE

Santa Cruz is a pleasant place due to an urban fabric composed mainly of small houses set in affectionately cared for gardens. The city's greatest architecture (outside the limits of its University of California campus) was produced during the latter half of the nineteenth century, from the straightforward symmetry and purity of 1850s Greek Revival and Gothic Revival to the gilded swellings and turrets of Queen Anne and Shingle Style buildings of Edward L. Van Cleeck, the city's most accomplished, long-term resident architect.

An affection for the past has encouraged an animated revivalism in Santa Cruz. However, it has also snuffed out the flame of modernism. An example of the local disinterest in domestic modernism would be the entirely needless destruction in 1984 of the premier International Style house in Santa Cruz, the sleek 1939-41 Allegrini house, designed by Wilton Smith. Thacher & Thompson, now an éminence grise in local architecture, continues to produce revivalist work, competent but not always inspired. As in all revivalist work, the question arises whether the result is a watered-down version, an echo of what could have been a more fully developed, detailed, and conviction-filled original. A contemporary Santa Cruz architect who seems to have been able to incorporate recent developments in architecture and effectively advocate tenets of modernism is Mark Primack.

One looks at Santa Cruz architecture because of an affection for the place, a place that is remarkably blessed by climate, topography, natural environment, and history. As a perpetual Santa Cruzan, in my heart if not in residence, I love all things Santa Cruz and find any detail of the city worthy fodder for attention as an element of its ethos, atmosphere, and zeitgeist. As a sometimes sun-kissed banana belt in the mid-California coastal fog zone; as the meeting place of primeval forest and open meadow; as a mission town; as one of the original pueblo settlements of California; as a resort town for a hundred and fifty years and later a university town and spillover territory to Silicon Valley; as the home of lumber, leather, lime, and leisure and of early feminist activists; as a legendary garden spot; as a hippie paradise where the granola never stops flowing and there is no place like a dome home—Santa Cruz is a remarkable environment to live in and relish. I liked it so much that I was loath to sully it by burdening it with my presence as one more inhabitant. I wanted it to be a

Preface

perfect memory—mist dripping from the redwoods; a banana slug creeping across a path at UCSC; the ten-color paint job on Ed and Doni Tunheim's Italianate house, resplendent in the sunshine; Tom Scribner playing the musical saw in front of the now vanished Cooper House; the be-hatted pioneer scion Alice Earl Wilder, citizen-watchdog, vigilant in her umpteenth decade in front of the County Board of Supervisors; the sense of peace and openness from city lots that sat vacant for decades, growing crops of berry vines—these and a thousand other memories I captured at the last stage of arrested late adolescence.

My memories of Santa Cruz are tied to the primal state of innocence in which I existed as an undergraduate at UCSC from 1971-75. As a protected son of the middle-class, living simply by preference, life's hard bargains and the price of serendipity were far from my mind.

Along with everyone else, I was totally unprepared for the destruction wreaked by the 1989 Loma Prieta earthquake, which dealt the final blow to the old Santa Cruz downtown that I knew and cherished. The downtown that I remembered had as its icon the Cooper House, the 1894 Richardsonian Romanesque former County Courthouse that was a poster child for the urban strategy of adaptive reuse of old buildings. There were local department stores, like Leask's and Ford's, and a full, small-town Woolworth's with a lunch counter. You were just as liable to meet the mayor as you were to be panhandled by a flower child who had tripped out once too often. It was a place where the physical, cultural, political, and economic centers all lined up.

But even without the earthquake, large-scale development on the raw land outside and in between the cities of Capitola and Santa Cruz was competing with and eventually took away the original economic function of downtown. Silicon Valley spillover in neighboring Scotts Valley created bigger corporate and office centers than those found in the city. Upper stories of Pacific Avenue buildings that lacked parking and large floor-plates went vacant. But given the resurgence of mixed-use (joint residential and commercial uses in one building) across the state and nation, one has to wonder if the provision of parking garage space might not have made it possible to adapt the upper stories for residential purposes. The big question about the earthquake will always be: did all the quake-damaged buildings that were demolished really have to be demolished for life-safety issues? If there were any errors, they were not on the side of historic preservation. The loss of human life made it more difficult for the preservation community to speak out on behalf of its cause.

For the first years after the earthquake, I couldn't bear to look at, be in, or think about Pacific Avenue. But thanks to a well-coordinated redevelopment effort, the avenue has been resuscitated as a specialty boutique, dining, and commercial center with a significant residential component and a much

Preface

stronger link to UCSC. In terms of human scale, well-crafted detail, and proportions, some of the architecture is as good as, or better than, what it replaced. The University Town Center, by architects Thacher & Thompson, would take first place here. Last place goes to the hopelessly ham-handed, mixed-use building at 1010 Pacific Avenue.

Santa Cruz now has a rare opportunity to take downtown to a new level of mixed-use by redeveloping the original redevelopment district, the area bounded by Water Street, Ocean Street, Soquel Avenue, and Front Street. The efforts of the last redevelopment have become outmoded. The single biggest task facing the city council, city planners, and the redevelopment agency is allowing future Santa Cruzans the same opportunity enjoyed by citizens of yesterday and today—the opportunity to act on their heart's desire and move to a beautiful, vibrant, and historic place without destroying the Eden that beckons them. The only way to accomplish this—while preserving the prized happenstance charm of existing low-density neighborhoods—is to allow mixed use, with housing on commercial boulevards, buildings converted to loft and live-work spaces, and new high-density housing created in districts that do not currently exist as viable low-density neighborhoods, such as the industrial district on the far Westside.

John Chase, West Hollywood, 2005

ACKNOWLEDGMENTS

The author and editor acknowledge with great appreciation those who have assisted in research, editing, review, technical production, photograph selection, map preparation, design, indexing, and in countless other ways. However, responsibility for any errors is, unfortunately, ours.

Our overwhelming thanks to Joe Michalak and Carolyn Swift, who, at every stage in this project, generously contributed their talents, skills, and unconditional support.

To the following individuals and institutions we express our gratitude.

Paul Figueroa, Executive Director, Museum of Art & History for his unfailing enthusiasm and confidence in this project

Members of the Museum of Art & History Publications Committee for their invaluable and continuing review and comments: Michael E. Clark, Steve Lawton, Joan Gilbert Martin, Joyce P. Miller, Allan Molho, Frank Perry, Jill Perry, Stanley D. Stevens

Michael E. Clark, for his book design, computer production, map preparation, and unending good humor and good ideas

Stanley D. Stevens, for his comprehensive indexes, reasoned and patient consul, and leadership of this project

Steve Lawton, for contributing his valuable printing and marketing advice

Daniel P. Gregory for granting permission to reprint his Pasatiempo chapter

University of California, Santa Cruz: Christine Bunting, Head of Special Collections, University Library; Gretchen Dempewolf, Special Collections Assistant; Cynthia Jahns, Map Librarian; Laura Campbell, Maps, Public Services Assistant; Louise Donahue, Public Information; Don Harris, Photography Services; Frank Zwart, Associate Vice Chancellor and Campus Architect

Historians: Charlene Duval, the late Edna Kimbro, Susan Lehmann, Sandy Lydon, Bruce MacGregor, Frank Perry, Marion Pokriots, Phil Reader, Stanley D. Stevens, Carolyn Swift, and Claudine Chalmers, art historian; with a special acknowledgment to the late Donald Thomas Clark, historian and University Librarian Emeritus, UCSC, for his classic reference work, *Santa Cruz County Place Names: A Geographical Dictionary*, and for his commitment to the highest

Acknowledgements

standards of scholarship and his supportive, collegial spirit that continue to inspire

Architects and Designers: Mark Primack, Clarke Shultes, Thomas Thacher, Matthew Thompson

City of Santa Cruz: Joe Hall, Redevelopment Agency; John Ancic, Sandy J. Brown, Nancy Concepcion Boyle, Don Lauritson, Anne Wakefield, Planning Department; Ray Sherrod, Parks & Recreation; Leslie Keedy, Urban Forester

Owners (or former owners) of historic homes: Katherine Beiers, Lisa Brewer, Lloyd Hebbron Jr, Otto Lund, Cynthia Mathews, Melanie Mayer, Ruth Ogilvie, Geraldine Shelley, Brion Sprinsock

Preliminary work on entries or index: Suzi Aratin, Barbara Keeney Clark, Michael E. Clark, Winnie Heron, Ann Hubble, Cynthia Jahns, Steve Lawton, Peter McGettigan, Rachel McKay, Allan Molho, Alverda Orlando, Lucia Orlando, Frank Perry, Jill Perry, Stanley D. Stevens

Companies: Covello & Covello Photography, and especially Eric Fingal; Otter B Books, Steve Lawton; Santa Cruz Seaside Company, Kris Reyes, Director of Community Relations, Bonnie Minford, Archivist

Libraries, Museums, and Organizations: Santa Cruz Public Library, Reference Department; Genealogical Society of Santa Cruz County, collection staffers and indexers, and, especially, Sara Bunnett; University Library, University of California, Santa Cruz; Museum of Art & History, Amy Dunning, Archivist/Research Librarian; Marla Novo, Collections Manager

Special assistance: Gary A. Goss, Architect Reference Files, San Francisco; Nelson "Red" Davis, great-grandson of Charles Wellington Davis, architect; and Brother Larry Scrivani, SM, Archivist, Diocese of Monterey.

About Santa Cruz

The city of Santa Cruz is located at the northern end of Monterey Bay on a raised plateau divided by the San Lorenzo River and its adjacent lowlands. The plateau slopes up to the redwood-forested foothills of the mountains that isolate Santa Cruz from the San Francisco Bay area. On the east, Santa Cruz is part of a continuous urban area extending along Highway 1 to Rio Del Mar. Development to the west of the city has been hindered by the rugged terrain.

Although the older commercial area is concentrated along Pacific Avenue and Front Street, it has infiltrated the residential neighborhood to the west as far as Chestnut Street. Ocean Street is the town's prime example of strip development. In the section from the freeway off-ramp to Broadway, the street offers the typical array of gas stations, fast food franchises, and motels. Other strip developments are concentrated along Soquel Avenue and Mission Street.

Interesting nineteenth-century buildings can be found throughout the west central section of Santa Cruz, from Mission Hill on the north to Beach Hill on the south. Other groups of nineteenth-century structures are to be found along Riverside Avenue, Ocean View Avenue, west of upper Ocean Street, and in the Seabright area. Although the beach area lost its great resort hotel, the Sea Beach, it retains the unique casino and roller coaster.

The city has origins of a dual nature: as the site of the Misión de la Exaltación de la Santa Cruz and as the pueblo of Branciforte. The mission was established in 1791 on the lowlands next to Mission Hill and moved to the top of the bluff in 1793. The town of Branciforte was established in 1797 on the bluff east of the San Lorenzo River. By the beginning of the American period, both mission and town had almost entirely disappeared.

Americans were already beginning to exploit the area's commercial and agricultural potential by the time gold was discovered on the South Fork of the American River in 1848. The start of the Gold Rush and Mexico's surrender of California to the United States that same year resulted in a mild boom for Santa Cruz, which ended in the potato depression of 1854. During this period, the town became firmly established, and its commercial center moved from the Mission Plaza to the flatland to the south.

The early lumber, tanning, lime, agricultural, and seaport industries were

About Santa Cruz

supplemented by the resort trade as early as the mid-1860s. The town's mild climate and proximity to redwood forests and beaches were major attractions. The development of Santa Cruz as a resort peaked around the turn of the century with the construction of the Sea Beach Hotel in 1890 and the casino in 1904.

Another period of change occurred in the 1960s with the advent of the University of California and the growth of Santa Cruz as a counter-culture mecca.

Santa Cruz has an extraordinarily diverse collection of buildings from various periods. The majority date from the latter half of the nineteenth century, although the twentieth century is also represented by a small but significant number of Mission Revival, Period Revival, Bungalow, and Moderne buildings.

Innovations in design were not made in Santa Cruz nor did major architects locate their offices here. The better known architects whose work is represented usually designed only one or two buildings in Santa Cruz. Nevertheless, these buildings were generally among the most prominent locally and often helped introduce new styles.

It is the city's builder-architects who are responsible for the vast majority of structures which have determined the appearance of the town's neighborhoods. Virtually all of these builder-architects received their training in the eastern United States and brought eastern building methods and styles with them.

It is not surprising that there are so many distinguished Victorian-era buildings in Santa Cruz. During the Victorian period the city was a much larger population center relative to other towns in the state than it is now. The fairly steady growth since 1920 has not been of sufficient intensity to overwhelm completely its early architectural heritage.

Nevertheless, many square blocks of nineteenth-century construction have been obliterated in the central areas. Nowhere in Santa Cruz is there a neighborhood unblemished by ugly modern building. Over the years, it became increasingly uncommon to remodel a building for a new use or even to move it to another site. Stiffer fire and building codes made adaptation of older buildings more difficult. Victorian-era buildings were long out of favor in the twentieth century, often pulled down by their owners who preferred a vacant lot to the upkeep of an older building. Attitudes began to change in the 1960s with the opening of the university, the threatened destruction of much of the central area by a freeway, and the perseverance of photographer Chuck Abbott and other like-minded individuals. Efforts to secure legal protection for historically and architecturally significant structures were initially spurred by the impending demolition of a downtown landmark, the 1886 McHugh & Bianchi Building. After an unsuccessful first try at passing a historical preservation ordinance, an ordinance creating a historic preservation commission was approved by the Santa Cruz City Council in 1974.

USING THE GUIDE

The Sidewalk Companion to Santa Cruz Architecture is intended to serve as a do-it-yourself walking guide. It has been written for the pedestrian willing to take the time to experience architecture as well as for the armchair reader. Those who wish to use the book as a walking companion do not have to visit the sites in the order in which they appear. Rather, they may arrange their own tours by using the maps at the beginning of each chapter, selecting contiguous sites along a particular route, and referring to the corresponding entries in the text. Because the peculiarities of Santa Cruz geography defeat the logic of linearity, some consecutively numbered sites are unavoidably far apart.

Some of the buildings listed in the guide have been demolished or completely stripped of all architectural detail. They have been included for their continuing historical and architectural interest. A study concerned solely with surviving nineteenth-century buildings would have resulted in an incomplete picture of that period. Inclusion of a site in the guide does not necessarily mean it is visible from a public street.

Most of the buildings listed are private homes and should be respected as such.

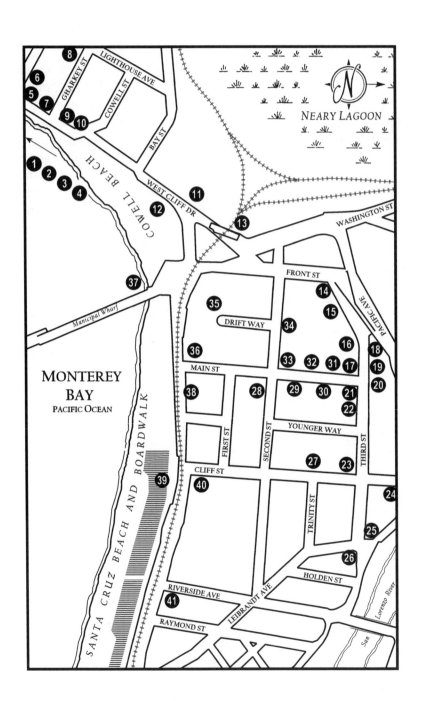

Chapter One

West Cliff Drive and Beach Hill

West Cliff Drive and Beach Hill were once choice locations for large summer homes and estates of the wealthy. The Beach Hill area was a prime resort site with visitors arriving, often by train, to spend a leisurely vacation, enjoying the mild weather, the abundant hotels, and the superb beach. As increased mobility led to shorter stays by tourists, the beach area became oriented to day-trippers. Starting in the late 1970s, large condominium and apartment complexes were constructed on Beach Hill, increasing the scale, height, and density of the neighborhood.

(1) At the bend in **West Cliff Drive** are **Point Santa Cruz** and **Lighthouse Field.** The first lighthouse on the point was constructed by the U.S. government in 1869. The first lighthouse keeper was Adna Hecox, followed by his daughter Laura. The present lighthouse building was erected in 1967 by Chuck and Esther Abbott in memory of their son Mark, who died in a bodysurfing accident at Pleasure Point in 1965. Inside the Mark Abbott Memorial Lighthouse is the Santa Cruz Surfing Museum, which opened in 1986.

Lighthouse Field was owned in the 1860s by butcher A. L. Rountree and later purchased by the Julius and Anna Pelton family. It is best known, however, as **Phelan Park,** the summer estate of the Phelan family of San Francisco, who acquired the property in 1887. James Phelan made his money during the Gold Rush; his son, James Duval Phelan, was mayor of San Francisco from 1897 to 1902 and a U.S. senator from 1915 to 1921. The Phelans remodeled the existing cottages and erected new structures, among them a gazebo with an observation deck. The architect for this work was John Marquis of San Francisco. Statues were installed throughout the grounds, which were designed by Rudolph Ulrich, who was also the landscape architect for the Del Monte Hotel in Monterey. Much of Phelan Park, which was supervised and tended by gardener Louis Doeltz, was covered with a grove of eucalyptus and cypress trees. There was a swimming pool filled with salt water from the bay. The last members of the Phelan family to frequent the estate were Gladys Sullivan Doyle and her family.

By the 1940s, much of the Phelan land had been bequeathed to the Catholic Church. The lighthouse, deemed obsolete, was replaced by a tower. During World War II, the government-owned property became a security post manned by members of the Fifty-fourth Coast Artillery Regiment, an all-black army unit.

(1) House on the grounds of the Phelan Estate
(Special Collections, University Library, University of California, Santa Cruz)

After the war, several of the soldiers returned to Santa Cruz, settling in the Circles area on the Westside. In 1960 the City acquired Lighthouse Point for a park.

A convention center, hotel-motel, and retail shop complex at the field was proposed in 1962 by Peter Pasetta, who then owned the property. For this project William Wesley Peters of the Frank Lloyd Wright Foundation designed an elaborate geometric fantasy, "The Court of the Seven Seas," in the same spirit as the Marin County Courthouse. Santa Cruz was not ready for such a grandiose scheme at the time, and the concept was dropped.

In 1968, however, a Joint Powers Authority Agreement between the City and the County of Santa Cruz set up an agency charged with the development of a convention center at Lighthouse Field. Two years later, Teachers Management Investment Corporation agreed to develop the private facilities needed to make the center profitable: hotel, shops, and condominiums. The final design by the Santa Cruz firm of Stevens & Calender featured a medium-rise complex in pseudo-early-California style.

The loss of the city's last major oceanfront open space to a convention center complex generated widespread opposition. Efforts to halt the project culminated in a two-to-one vote of the electorate against City operation of a center on the property. Shortly before this June 1974 vote, the State Coastal Commission had rejected the project. Battles over the proposed development of Wilder Ranch and the planned expansion of freeway routes through the heart of the city sparked a grassroots political movement that seemed for a time as if it would transform Santa Cruz into the southernmost outpost of Ecotopia.

In 1981 the thirty-six acre area became Lighthouse Field State Beach, a state park unit maintained by the City with County financial assistance.

(2) At **544 West Cliff Drive** is the **Shrine of St. Joseph, Guardian of the Redeemer**, operated by the Catholic order of the Oblates of St. Joseph. Construction of the chapel was begun in 1952 but was left unfinished until 1992, when work on a new design by architect Mark Primack began. Completed in 1993, the building has a prominent Star of David window in the front. Saint Joseph Marello, Bishop of Acqui and founder of the Oblates of St. Joseph, was beatified in that same year and canonized in 2001.

(3) Davis House
(Special Collections, University Library, University of California, Santa Cruz)

West Cliff and Beach Hill

(3) The Prairie/Mediterranean style Davis house, **544 West Cliff Drive**, built in 1912, was designed by architect Chester Miller of Oakland. Francis H. Davis and his brother, Frederick, were, respectively, the plant manager and the superintendent of the Santa Cruz Portland Cement Company plant at Davenport. At the time, Miller was the company's architect. The brackets supporting the entry canopy are missing. The property is owned today by the Oblates of St. Joseph.

(4) Rutherglen Terrace
(Special Collections, University Library, University of California, Santa Cruz)

(4) Rutherglen Terrace, the third building of the Oblates' property at **544 West Cliff Drive,** was designed by Santa Cruz architect Edward L. Van Cleeck for James and Louise McNeil. McNeil was principal owner and president of the Santa Cruz Electric Light and Power Works. "The homelike colonial mansion with its delicate cream color, its broad veranda, its rounded corners and tower, and its steep hipped roof harmonizes admirably with the scene," observed the June 17, 1893, *Santa Cruz Surf,* shortly after completion of the house. Monograms of Rutherglen Terrace, enclosed in a wreath of Scottish thistles, are engraved on the sidelights of the front door.

Adjacent to the McNeil property was the eight-acre William J. Dingee property, later subdivided as Cliff Manor. In 1907 Dingee began plans for a large mansion and estate here that were never completed; however, an elaborate garden planted with full-grown trees was laid out by John McLaren, landscape architect of San Francisco's Golden Gate Park. Dingee was the wealthy owner of several cement plants, including the one at Davenport.

(5) Epworth-by-the-Sea, or **The Breakers,** at **320 West Cliff Drive**, was built for C. C. Wheeler in 1887. It was purchased a year later by Mrs. Elizabeth Fraser Iliff Warren and her husband, Methodist Bishop Henry Warren of University Park, Colorado. Before Mrs. Warren married the Bishop, she was the millionaire widow of John Wesley Iliff, "the early cattle king of Colorado whose herds once roamed from Wyoming to Texas" (*Santa Cruz Surf,* May 29, 1897).

The Warrens added a dining room and veranda and had the rear portion of the house raised up a story. A barn and stable were built at the same time. Local architect Daniel Damkroeger designed both the original house and the additions. Rudolph Ulrich, landscape architect for the Phelan estate, laid out the grounds.

The house has the bent roofline and vertical siding beneath the eaves frequently seen in Eastlake buildings.

(5 and 6) Epworth-by-the-Sea, right, and neighbors *(Carolyn Swift)*

West Cliff and Beach Hill

(6) At **116** and **120 Santa Cruz Street,** to the west of Epworth-by-the-Sea, are two Victorian Revival homes that create a sympathetic streetscape for their neighbor. In 1995 Jim Lloyd designed both Victorians, 116 Santa Cruz Street for John and Liz Turner and 120 Santa Cruz Street for Herman Perez.

Modernist purists would find this kind of effort (which creates the illusion of a series of Victorian houses that never actually existed on this street) a sham; but why deny architecture the delights of fiction and invention that are allowed other arts? Federal standards for rehabilitation, restoration, and addition to historic buildings call for careful avoidance of any replication of historic fabric that is so literal that it confuses the viewer into thinking new is old. But in truth, if one looks carefully, small differences in proportion and detailing reveal that these are Victorian Revival rather than Victorian buildings.

(7) The Warrens' stepson, William Iliff, and his wife, Alberta (Bloom) Iliff, in 1911 built **Rockcrest**, a home on a corner of the family property. Located at **314 West Cliff Drive**, the house was designed by Watsonville and San Francisco architect William H. Weeks. A concrete, Mission Revival style building, it has a sun-porch at the front, Sullivanesque detail on the columns, and finely detailed projecting beams, eaves, and drainspouts.

(8) At **135 Gharkey Street** is a two-story Eastlake style house with spindle-trimmed porch and a lavish display of the familiar sunburst pattern. It is possibly the Dr. John A. McGuire residence, moved to Lighthouse Avenue from West Cliff Drive in 1907 to make way for the never-to-be-completed home of William Dingee (Ernest Otto, *Santa Cruz Sentinel,* February 1, 1942).

(9) 240 Gharkey Street was the second home of Mr. and Mrs. William S. and Alice Goodfellow of Oakland. The Craftsman Bungalow, designed by William Weeks, was built in 1907. At one time, Goodfellow was a member of the prominent San Francisco legal firm of Jarboe, Harrison, and Goodfellow.

(10) At **234 West Cliff Drive** is a well-proportioned Shingle Style Revival house with a generously sized turret surrounded by a half-circular porch. Designed by architect Stephanie Barnes-Castro, it was built in 1997 for Kim and Will Frentz.

(11) Built for Sedgwick and Jane Lynch in 1877, the house at **174 West Cliff Drive** is the finest example of the Italianate style in Santa Cruz. It has split-pedimented gables, squeezed-pedimented window cornices, and two-story slanted bays with pipestem colonnettes. Constructed at a cost of $12,000, it was the second-largest home in Santa Cruz when built. "There are four fireplaces and that portion usually made of wood or marble, consisting of the mantelpiece, mantels, columns and arch, in fact the whole facing is of iron, cast in one piece and painted with a fireproof coloring in most artistic designs, no two being alike" (*Santa Cruz Sentinel,* April 21, 1877). John Morrow was the architect.

Sedgwick Lynch was a general contractor who had been apprenticed to the "house carpenter and joiner's trade" at the age of fifteen in his native Pennsylvania. Arriving in California in 1849, he travelled aboard the steamer *Senator* on the Sacramento River as its maintenance man, along with A. P. Jordan and I. E. Davis, the original owners of what became the Cowell Ranch. The *Senator* was the same ship that had ferried Lynch to San Francisco from Panama.

Before 1850 he had also prospected for gold at Downieville, crossing a six-foot snow pack to get there. "After he arrived at Downieville it commenced snowing and continued for fourteen days, making the snowfall eight feet. He

(10) Frentz House *(Carolyn Swift)*

(11) Lynch House *(John Chase)*

had no shelter but brush and came very near starving before the snow became hard enough to travel on. He opened a claim there and got two and a half pounds of gold per day" (Elliott's 1879 *Santa Cruz County*).

Lynch was a member of San Francisco's Vigilance Committee in 1851 and later helped survey the Colorado desert. He became a general contractor, constructing wharves, railroads, and buildings in various parts of the state and also operated lumber yards and planing mills.

In 2005, the Lynch house is being redeveloped into a bed-and-breakfast inn.

(12) At the intersection of Bay Street and West Cliff Drive looms the ten-story wing of the **Coast Santa Cruz Hotel** (formerly the Dream Inn), a gigantic concrete ice-cube tray. The bulk of the addition effectively blocks the beach below from sight and sun.

The original three-story building dates from 1962. The permit for the slab addition was granted in 1972, before anyone really considered the impact of high-rise construction on the beach in Santa Cruz and before regulations limiting the height of buildings were adopted.

In 2005 plans to replace the hotel with a larger and more expansive facility were defeated.

(13) On the bluff known as Blackburn Terrace, at the site of the Ramada Inn, was **Concha del Mar,** the ca. 1890, rambling, Shingle-influenced second home of prominent San Francisco attorney John R. Jarboe and his wife, author Mary Halsey Thomas. Mrs. Jarboe, using the pseudonym Thomas H. Brainerd, wrote short stories and novels. Daughter Mary Kathryn Jarboe Bull was also a writer.

(14) At **80 Front Street** is the **Kittredge House/Hotel McCray/ Sunshine Villa**, a two-and-a-half-story, mansard-roof building with angled and corner square bays. Originally at right angles to the main facade was a long, two-story wing festooned with vines. Its galleried north side had the warm charm of a Monterey Colonial style hotel of early California.

On this site there have been many historic buildings that are no longer standing. In back of the old main Sunshine Villa/Hotel McCray building were a series of boxy cottages tacked onto a stuccoed, story-and-a-half house with twelve-pane windows. This house, the oldest structure on the property, was built by John Morrow for Dr. Francis M. Kittredge in 1867. Although Kittredge had practiced medicine for twenty years in the East before coming to California in 1849, he did not practice in Santa Cruz. When elected to the state legislature in 1853, he was working as a wharfinger, or wharf manager, for Davis and Jordan.

(13) Concha del Mar *(Francis, Beautiful Santa Cruz County, 1896)*

For a time the house was leased by livery stable- and hotel-owner Albion Paris Swanton. In 1877 Harriet Blackburn leased the property and erected a rear addition to the main building. Philbrick and LoRomer were the architects.

Four years later Pacific Ocean House proprietor E. J. Swift purchased the property from the Kittredge heirs. He began construction of the present front section of the building in 1883, at which time the original Kittredge house was moved back to make way for the new addition. The thirteen-room addition was designed by John H. Williams and cost $5,000. In 1887 it was known as the Peakes House for proprietor James B. Peakes.

The heyday of the main building arrived in 1890, when millionaire James P. Smith, an international food distributor, and his wife, Susan (Crooks) Smith, purchased the property from E. J. Swift's heirs for $24,500. Mr. and Mrs. Smith immediately proceeded to fit out "Sunshine Villa" in the elegant style to which they were accustomed. The place was stripped inside and out and thoroughly remodeled and landscaped. A semi-detached gazebo was added as an open loggia on the second story and a conservatory on the first, and the stone retaining wall on Front Street was built. Competing with the brilliance of the vermilion mansard roof were the "lawns, shrubberies, beds of bright foliage, and the rarest and choicest of plants from all countries" (*Santa Cruz Weekly Surf*, March 22, 1890).

(14) Hotel McCray (*Museum of Art & History*)

On July 1, 1893, the *Santa Cruz Weekly Surf* reported that "Mr. Smith . . . has brought from Japan and China several thousand dollars worth of rare and valuable oriental trees and plants to be put on the grounds of Sunshine Villa." Another improvement was a "magnificent Japanese bronze purchased in Yokohama, which is sixteen feet high and was, of course, correspondingly expensive. It is to be placed opposite the billiard room" (*Santa Cruz Weekly Surf*, June 10, 1893). The bronze, in the form of an immense dragon, was placed in a basin of water filled with goldfish and sprayed with four jets of water. The Smiths were fond of Eastern design for interiors as well and amassed a large collection of oriental curios and art objects. This opulence was the setting for many social gatherings of all descriptions.

Mrs. Smith is also well remembered for her active role in the Venetian Water Carnival of 1895. The San Lorenzo River, which formerly ran nearer Sunshine Villa, was dammed to form a *lagunita* upon which flower-decked floats and tableaux drifted. Electric lights, fireworks, and band programs completed the pageant, during which Mrs. Smith's daughter, Anita Gonzales, was crowned queen and Mrs. Smith, dowager queen.

Later the building became the Hotel McCray. In 1991, after years of decay, the hotel was completely renovated to house an assisted living facility renamed Sunshine Villa. Everything east of the main-entry bay wing, including the original one-and-one-half-story house and the boxy cottages to the rear, was demolished and replaced with large additions surrounding the secondary elevations. Architects were Treffinger, Walz & MacLeod, with Michael O'Hearn.

"According to Santa Cruz lore, the dilapidated Hotel McCray, now the refurbished Sunshine Villa, inspired the Bates Mansion" in Alfred Hitchcock's thriller movie *Psycho*. Hitchcock was often in this part of the city, as he bought fresh seafood at Stagnaro's and dined at Gilda's restaurant on the wharf while he was staying at his Scotts Valley home (Jeff Kraft and Aaron Leventhal, *Footsteps in the Fog: Alfred Hitchcock's San Francisco*).

(15) On **Third Street**, on the site of the parking lot for the Sunshine Villa was the 1867 home of hardware merchant Lucien Heath. Heath's son, Frank, is probably Santa Cruz's best known late nineteenth- and early twentieth-century artist. He specialized in large scale landscapes, which he left on exhibit in San Francisco while he traveled throughout America. After an eleven-year painter's sojourn, he returned in 1895 to his Beach Hill home to paint and to teach. Frank Heath died in 1921, but his artist wife, Lillian Heath, continued to reside at the 1025 Third Street address. Lillian died in 1961, and the house was demolished three years later.

(16) 1017 Third Street is a large Shingle- and Queen Anne-influenced house with some half-timbering and a rounded corner porch supported by Eastlake-detail columns. For many years it was the home of the Lloyd and Malvina Hebbron family. Hebbron was president of Hebbron (later Hebbron-Nigh) Lumber Company, located on Pacific Avenue at the base of Beach Hill.

(17) East of 1017 Third Street were three cottages owned by lumberman Mark Whittle. The middle cottage was Whittle's own home and has been torn down, while the small plain house on the west and the elaborate Stick-Eastlake raised-basement cottage on the east remain. The raised-basement house at **1005 Third Street** was built in 1887 by J. Hart of San Jose.

(18) 1012 Third Street is a Streamlined Moderne house from 1936. The offspring of a toaster and an ocean liner, it has corner and porthole windows without moldings, a curved wall, and pipe railing. The window and door hoods are tied together by narrow, projecting strips. It was built for State Senator Henry Raymond Judah Jr. and his wife, Mrs. Eva (Bowman) Judah.

Mrs. Judah's father, Gustave Bowman, had built a fifteen-room Stick Villa on the site in 1885. Calvin Davis was the contractor for the first house, and Calvin's brother, Charles Wellington Davis, was probably the architect. It was a virtual mirror image of Calvin Davis's own house at 207 Mission Street, although the resemblance was marred in 1891 by the addition of a bulky corner tower similar to that of next-door Golden Gate Villa. The mansion and the iron fence have disappeared, but the fountain and the peaked-roof, iron summerhouse draped with iron vines remain, strangely compatible with the present house.

Bowman, a native of Ohio, had become a successful hardware merchant after fifteen years in the business at Santa Cruz and was the town's mayor from 1888 to 1892.

(19) At **924 Third Street** is **Golden Gate Villa.** The building's variegated surface treatment and proportionately outsized tower indicate Queen Anne influences, while the large, simple masses and the bands of windows are in the Shingle Style.

"The style of the exterior is the modern renaissance of the designs of Queen Anne's time, adapted by the architect to the out-door life which is the great attraction to sojourners in Santa Cruz," commented the *Santa Cruz Surf*, June 3, 1891.

The back of the structure, broken into almost equal areas of wall and roof space descending the hill, is its most attractive facade.

In contrast to the relatively simple exterior, the interior is one of the most lavishly ornamented of any house in Santa Cruz. The entry room has a wood-ribbed ceiling, wainscotting in natural wood, and a staircase with elegant, elongated spindle-railing, popular in the 1890s.

The huge stained-glass window illuminating the landing depicts a classically draped female figure reaching up to admire a branch of a flowering tree. It supposedly represents Agnes McLaughlin, stepdaughter of Major McLaughlin, who built the house.

The room behind the entry originally had a band of elephant-hide upholstery bolted to the wall with large studs. Unfortunately, the elephant hide did not survive the 1989 earthquake.

Chapter One

(18) Judah House *(Carolyn Swift)*

(18 and 19) Bowman House and Golden Gate Villa
(Special Collections, University Library, University of California, Santa Cruz)

(18 and 19) Golden Gate Villa and Bowman House from lower Pacific Avenue
(Santa Cruz, Cal.: Illustrated in Photo-Gravure, 1894)

The house was built for Butte County mining engineer and capitalist Major Frank McLaughlin in 1891 from plans drawn by Australian-born San Francisco architect Thomas J. Welsh. The Major was a personal friend of Teddy Roosevelt and Thomas Edison and an important figure in the state's Republican party.

On November 16, 1907, Santa Cruz was stunned by the news that McLaughlin had shot Agnes and ended his own life with a "potion of cyanide of potassium." Grief over the death of his wife, Margaret, may have been a factor—the incident took place on the second anniversary of her death—so may have been his financial reverses, chief among them his notorious Feather River diversion project. In an attempt to extract gold and platinum from the riverbed, McLaughlin had put together a company that spent the years 1892-96 diverting the river, only to find that the '49ers had done so long before. McLaughlin had drawn a salary from the company but did not own stock in it, a circumstance which cast doubt on his integrity. Although he is said to have killed Agnes because he couldn't bear the thought of her living in reduced circumstances, there was adequate capital in the estate to pay all his debts. Even so, his personal secretary, Miss Anna C. Busteede (whom, it was claimed, he had offered to marry) sued the estate for some $15,000 she had allegedly loaned him. The mystery of why McLaughlin killed his stepdaughter and committed suicide may never be solved.

Before the construction of Golden Gate Villa, the site had been occupied by the picturesque story-and-a-half Gothic Revival cottage of retired sea captain J. J. Smith. This building was moved around the corner to Second Street, where it was later demolished.

(20) At **912 Third Street** was a simple one-story cottage of the 1870s, the last remaining structure of the William and Jane Hardy boardinghouse and cottages. It was demolished because of 1989 earthquake damage; a multiple-unit residential building is currently on the site.

Ernest Otto, newspaper columnist and local historian, described the former appearance of the Hardy house and property: "The lot was large, with the boardinghouse at the rear. A grove of native buckeyes, laurel and oaks grew on the hillside at the back. The long path to the main building was lined by rows of locust trees. The property, which had a number of cottages, was enclosed by a white-washed picket fence" (*Santa Cruz Sentinel*, October 7, 1951).

Captain William Hardy was an English seafaring man who arrived here after a journey round the Horn in 1846. His first house on the property "consisted in part of the hull of a vessel which Captain Hardy had owned, and around this, as a nucleus they built quite a comfortable home" (*Santa Cruz Weekly Surf*, March 21, 1896). When the Hardys became more prosperous, they built a new house on top of the first one, removing the boat hull through the rear of the house when it was completed.

West Cliff and Beach Hill

Hardy had worked for Thomas Larkin as a shipbuilder. In 1846 he also built the first ship on the Santa Cruz beach, working with Jean Baptiste Dabadie for Charles (Carlos) Roussillon and Pierre (Pedro) Sainsevain.

"Mrs. Hardy was the first one on Beach Hill to open a place for summer visitors. The house grew by accretion, and by and by, the demand for accommodations was so brisk, that cottages were built," the *Santa Cruz Weekly Surf* article concluded. By the 1890s the place had fallen into neglect due to the Hardys' old age, ill health, and litigation over the property.

(21) 917-919 Third Street is the Eben and Mary Elizabeth Bennett house, constructed in 1870-71. Originally the building was a symmetrical Italianate structure with quoining and a hipped roof supported by brackets. The Tudor-Revival arched porch and present window frames were added in the 1910s or '20s, when the house was converted into apartments. Bennett, who had arrived in California in 1848, came to Santa Cruz in 1866. He opened the Santa Cruz-Felton toll road in 1868 and operated lime kilns near Felton.

(22) Next door at **915 Third Street** is **Green Gables**, a stucco and half-timber Tudor-Revival house with small pane windows. In recent years it was the home and studio of artists Elizabeth Sanchez and Gene Holtan, who also ran a small press named Green Gables.

(23) 417 Cliff Street is a large apartment house fashioned in a mixture of Queen Anne and Colonial Revival styles by Santa Cruz architect Edward L. Van Cleeck. It was built in 1899 for the family of banker Henry S. and Josephine Deming of Terre Haute, Indiana. It was the childhood home of Dorothy Deming Wheeler, who would later build her own mansion at Windy Hill Farm (see Chapter 4, #78 and also Chapter 6, #4).

The house boasts a pedimented central gable and a circular corner tower capped with a turret. Its Cliff Street facade possesses an almost Baroque demeanor because of the powerful massing of the various elements that thrust forward and backward. The Shingle Style influence is evident in the curved corners and the continuous lines that wrap around them.

(24) Where the large cypress tree stands sentinel at the north end of Cliff Street (formerly **514 Cliff Street**) is the site of the William Rennie house. Rennie was a carpenter and farmer from Scotland.

A large and imposing Stick-Eastlake structure, the Rennie house was designed by local architects Damkroeger and Saunders and built in 1890.

(23) Deming House *(Carolyn Swift)*

"On the northwest corner rises a tower, which is of fine proportions, and several bay windows and projections, together with a hipped roof, give the necessary variety to the outline," reported the *Santa Cruz Weekly Surf*, March 11, 1890. The main floor was finished in redwood with panels of burl; the staircase was made of Spanish cedar. The mansion was torn down in 1970.

(25) 706 Third Street, at the northwest corner of Third Street and Leibrandt (spelling of family name is Leibbrandt) Avenue, is Rennie's earlier home, built in 1870 and moved from the site of his 1890 home to the bottom of Third Street, where it was split into two stucco cottages. The house at 706 Third Street may be one of these cottages (*Santa Cruz Sentinel*, February 1, 1942). Demolished, 2006

(26) 611 Third Street, Rio Vista, is a handsome home of Stick-Eastlake design. The lines of the window frames are extended out to the edges of the facade, and there are strips at the corners and between the floors, creating a half-timber-like pattern. This outlining, plus the strong lines of the corner square bay, pedimented square bay, and pedimented gable on the north side, creates a very crisp, hard-edge design.

West Cliff and Beach Hill

There are ten stained-glass windows in the house, set in frames inlaid with beveled French plate glass. Pewter rather than lead was used to mount some of the windows. There are double Moorish arches inset with spindles over the staircase. The woodwork, by M. F. Clute, is painted and grained in mahogany, where it has not been left in the native redwood.

The house, built in 1890, was designed by LeBaron R. Olive for Mrs. Margaret Barfield, a wealthy Merced widow. It was later owned by piano teacher Josie Tretheway, who installed the hardwood floors over the original redwood ones. The parlor floor is inset with a five-pointed Eastern Star. The exterior of the house is still painted in its original colors of light olive-green and dark green.

(27) At **407 Cliff Street** is **Cliff Crest**, a Queen Anne-influenced residence designed for Mrs. Margaret Ann Elizabeth Perkins by D. A. Damkroeger. The nine-room house was built in 1887 at a cost of $1,500. It was later extensively remodeled by William T. Jeter and his wife, Jennie Bliss Jeter. He was a businessman, lawyer, and banker, active in the Democratic party, mayor of Santa Cruz, lieutenant governor of California, and a leader in the effort to acquire the Big Tree Grove as a park, now part of Henry Cowell Redwoods State Park.

(28) At **413-417 Second Street** is **Beach Hill Court,** a Spanish-style bungalow court straight from one of Raymond Chandler's Southern California detective novels. The overlapping of the gateway and portico arches creates a layering of space like that of the giant arches at Kresge College on the University of California, Santa Cruz campus. The sunblasted film noir aspect has been largely obscured by new planting.

(29) At **316 Main Street** is a simple two-story structure with suggestions of corner pilasters and a split pediment. An incredible number of additions have been added at the rear. According to Ernest Otto, it was built by the Palmer family, who had come to Santa Cruz from the Mother Lode town of Jackson. The house has been used as a cooperative living facility for UCSC students in past years. The COOP, as it is known, was renovated after a 2003 fire.

(30) 332 Main Street is a modest cottage built in 1884 for the widowed Mrs. Eben Bennett, who no longer needed the large family home at the corner of Main and Third Streets.

(31) 333 Main Street is a pleasant shingled bungalow, ca. 1906, with gambrel roof and a triangular bay in the gable. For many years it was the home of Philip B. and Adela Eteson, who were both born in India. Mr. Eteson served in the Royal Engineers of the British Army during World War I.

(28) Beach Hill Court *(Carolyn Swift)*

One of the earliest residents of Beach Hill was Joseph Roberts. In 1854 Roberts lived in the first house constructed on Beach Hill and built the second house, his own residence, on his property located between Third and Main Streets.

Born in Falkirk, Scotland, he was a seafaring man and for eight months was stranded on a South Sea Island, living with the natives (Harrison, *History of Santa Cruz County*). After a partnership in the sea freight business with Captain J. J. Smith, he became a general contractor and housemover.

(32) At **315-321 Main Street**, adjacent to Robert's property, are the **Carmelita Cottages**, a charming collection of six 1870s-1914 cottages tucked away in a green and leafy bower. According to Rick Hyman, who has written a detailed history of the cottages, "Widows, sea captains, relatives, music, jilted wives, and

(32) Carmelita Cottage *(Carolyn Swift)*

long-tenure describe the famous owners…The two front houses, constructed circa 1872, are among the oldest surviving buildings on Beach Hill" (http://www. santacruzpl.org/history/arch/ccot1.shtml). The cottages are now owned by the City of Santa Cruz and are operated as a youth hostel.

(33) 311 Main Street is a large, impressive Colonial Revival and Queen Anne influenced home with a central, recessed porch with rounded-off corners. In the right-front gable is a Palladian window. The porch is supported by raised, composite columns. A stained-glass window lights the staircase, and there is much fine interior paneling.

Built for the A. H. Wilbur family of Marysville, California, its present facade dates from 1897, when the house was extensively remodeled.

(34) At **526 Second Street** is the exuberant Mediterranean Revival **Villa Mar Vista** development, designed by Michael O'Hearn. Earlier it was the site of the 1877 Second Empire style house of lumberman William F. March. The concave, sloping mansard roof atop two stories made the March home one of the earliest three-story houses in Santa Cruz. It was second only to Martha Wilson's ill-fated boardinghouse on Ocean View Avenue, which stood for only one year until it burned in 1877.

The mansard roof was not called for in the original plans but was added as an afterthought by the builder, Mr. Cloud. In the twentieth century the house was divided into apartments, became dilapidated, and was torn down in 1963.

(34) March House
(Special Collections, University Library, University of California, Santa Cruz)

(34) Villa Mar Vista *(Carolyn Swift)*

The only thing to remain from the house is a limestone rock wall along the sidewalk.

In the days before the university made off-campus rentals profitable, the simplest thing to do with an old house in need of costly repairs was to demolish it; "... the land on which it stood had become valuable business property," explained the *Santa Cruz Sentinel*, December 15, 1963. The statement is ironic in view of the number of lots around town, such as this site and that of the Jordan-Fagen house on Mission Street, that remained vacant for decades after the Victorian-era buildings that once stood on them were torn down.

In the block bounded by Second, Front, Beach, and Main Streets were the Joseph Kenney Hotel (ca. 1888), the Seaside Home, and the Sea Beach Hotel.

(35) Along with the Hardy boardinghouse, the Seaside Home was one of the first tourist resorts on the hill. Operating as early as 1865, it was managed by James R. and Anna Marguerita Richards and subsequently by Mrs. Frank Lewis,

(35) View of Beach Hill from the pier, ca. 1877-1887.
From left to right: Seaside Home, Liddell House, and Douglas House
(Special Collections, University Library, University of California, Santa Cruz)

the little Patty Reed of the Donner Party. This property, together with the adjoining Liddell property, was purchased by the Mrs. D. D. Colton family.

Mrs. David Doudy Colton was the widow of the junior partner of "Big Four" railroad barons Leland Stanford, Mark Hopkins, Charles Crocker, and Collis P. Huntington, heads of the Central Pacific Railroad (later, the Southern Pacific

Railroad). Newspapers referred to Mr. Colton as one of the "Big Four and a Half." After her husband's death, Mrs. Ellen Colton released letters her husband had received from Huntington that described the efforts of the railroad to bribe congressmen and influence elections. Her daughter Caroline (the thrice-married Mrs. Cook Martin Dahlgren) and her granddaughters Theodosia Cook (Mrs. Francis Grace) and Katherine Martin (Mrs. Marcel Cerf) all owned property on Beach Hill. The Colton/Grace property became known as **The Cabins** (*Santa Cruz Sentinel*, September 30, 1956); the Cerf home was built on the site of the Sea Beach Hotel. The white house at the rear of the Edgewater Beach Motel at **525 Second Street** is likely to be one of the main cottages remaining from the days of The Cabins. The building is also visible from Beach Street.

(36) To the east of The Cabins was the **Sea Beach Hotel**, the premier hotel of Beach Hill in the days of its greatest glory as an oceanside resort. The Sea Beach had originated in the early 1870s as a two-story building constructed for Thomas V. Johnson. Known as the **Ocean View House**, it was lengthened and made in 1877 into a three-story structure by raising the roof. In 1883, Johnson sold the property to A. H. Douglas, who named it the **Douglas House** and in turn sold it to David K. Abeel in 1887. Abeel, a capitalist from Kansas City, added to the original thirty-room structure a 150-room main building. Harrison's 1892 *History of Santa Cruz County* credits George W. Page as the architect.

Page was the architect of Edenvale, an extraordinary Queen Anne pile constructed six miles south of San Jose for Mrs. Mary Hayes-Chynoweth. For sheer size and complexity, it was a fit rival for the Flood mansion at Menlo Park and the Carson house at Eureka.

A simple, boxy Shingle Style structure, the Sea Beach Hotel opened in May 1890. The rooms, fitted with "closets, fireplaces, and marble lavatories, are furnished in solid oak, carpeted in English Brussels, and are in every way comfortable," the *Santa Cruz Weekly Surf* (May 24, 1890) informed its readers. Many of the rooms had little porches, and there were some particularly delightful suites located in the towers.

Isabel Raymond describes the famous Sea Beach garden in Phil Francis's 1896 *Beautiful Santa Cruz County:* "The broad porches have been fenced in by… a fragrant wall of heliotrope and pelargonium, overhung with a delicate frieze of passion vine, whose red or purple flowers gleam out like stars from the foliage ….In this same Christmas-tide garden are abloom to-day calceolarias, begonias, lobelia, violets, mignonette, the advance guard of a big white army of callas, roses, the rarest Duchesse, Sofrano, Marechal Niel, La France, and a dozen others." Best known of all the plants in the garden were the pelargoniums, which grew as high as fifteen feet tall.

The hotel burned in a spectacular fire at 3:30 in the morning of June 12, 1912.

West Cliff and Beach Hill

(36) Sea Beach Hotel

(Special Collections, University Library, University of California, Santa Cruz)

(36) Cerf House *(Carolyn Swift)*

A portion of the Sea Beach Hotel site is now occupied by the Judge Marcel and Katherine (Martin) Cerf residence, designed about 1916 by San Francisco architect George McCrea, who also designed the Rispin Mansion in Capitola. Katherine was the stepsister of adjoining property owner, Theodosia (Cook) Grace. The Cerf property is presently known as the **Casa Blanca Motel and Apartments.** Although the main house has been altered and the stone terraces of the Cerf house built over, the small house at the rear appears to be largely intact. The house shows an interest in simplified period forms treated in an almost Craftsman-like style, an interest that relates it to the work of Southern California architects like Frederick Roehrig and Elmer Grey. The simplicity, however, has been given a few kinks: the stairways extending out onto the arcade and the chimney with a door in it. The dormers were unsympathetically modified sometime after 1979.

(37) The present municipal pier at the foot of **Washington** and **Front Streets** was constructed in 1914 and is the last of four wharves to be built in the harbor. The first wharf, actually just a short chute for loading potatoes onto ships, was put up by Elihu Anthony in 1849. In 1857 the chute was replaced by a thousand-foot wharf constructed by lime manufacturers A. P. Jordan and Isaac E. Davis.

(38) The Seaside Company's **Casa del Rey Apartments**, today known as **La Bahia**, at **215 Beach Street**, were built in 1926. The William C. Hays design places two- and three-story buildings around the terraced Court of the Laurels and the Court of the Mariners, with a fountain supposedly supplied by a natural spring.

(38) La Bahia *(Carolyn Swift)*

The tiled roofs, the thick concrete walls, and the carefully placed details epitomize the Spanish Colonial Revival style. Period touches, such as the patterned-tile tower dome, the wood balcony, and the columns, are displayed against blank walls.

One newspaper description of the apartments reported, "Castles in Spain were never erected all at one time, but units were added through the years and as the mud dried each time the color differed. And so each unit of the Casa del

Rey apartments differed slightly in shade from its neighbor" (*Santa Cruz Evening News*, July 13, 1928). The Casa del Rey apartments are unquestionably the most successful courtyard development in Santa Cruz.

(39) On the bay side of Beach Street is the **Santa Cruz Beach Boardwalk**, redolent of the odor of roasting hot-dog grease, popcorn, and salt-water taffy.

A capsule history of American popular culture from the turn of the century to the present may be had by wandering through the various games and amusements in the main building.

As early as 1867 a notice appeared in the *Santa Cruz Sentinel* announcing the construction of a "dwelling house for the accommodation of bathers on the beach" by Charles Martelle (*Santa Cruz Sentinel*, November 23, 1867). The next year John Leibbrandt built the Dolphin Baths, which was a combination bathhouse, swimming tank, and entertainment house. In pre-flood-control days, the San Lorenzo River delta area was the most favored spot for bathing.

In 1884 Captain C. F. Miller opened the Neptune Baths, such a successful venture that fifty more rooms were added the following year. Leibbrandt and Miller consolidated their concessions in 1893 and built a bathhouse with an indoor seawater pool.

The Boardwalk as it stands today began to take shape in 1903, when Fred Swanton and John Martin bought the Miller and Leibbrandt bathhouse, forming the Santa Cruz Beach, Cottage, and Tent City Corporation.

Swanton was an imaginative, energetic promoter and entrepreneur who operated a wide variety of businesses during his lifetime. He ran a lumber mill at Felton and opened the splendiferous Palace of Pharmacy in the old IOOF Building on Pacific Avenue. From Alexander Graham Bell he secured the rights to the first commercial telephone system in California, establishing systems in Santa Cruz, Bakersfield, and Los Angeles. In 1896 he opened on Big Creek the first hydroelectric generating plant west of Chicago and started the Santa Cruz electric streetcar system, the second in the state. He also participated in the Alaskan Gold Rush in 1900. At age forty-two Swanton was a millionaire, opening his Neptune Casino "with a blare of music, a blaze of rockets and the boom of bursting bombs" (*Santa Cruz Sentinel*, June 13, 1904). A lacy folly of Moorish inspiration, its onion domes and Venetian ogee arches painted in bright colors rose up like an improbable vision of Baghdad at the foot of Beach Hill. Edward Van Cleeck was the architect of the casino, probably the largest commission he ever had.

The casino burned to the ground on June 22, 1906, at an uninsured loss of half-a-million dollars. While the embers were still smoking, Swanton took his partner and financial angel John Martin up to Beach Hill to survey the ruins and persuaded him to invest a million dollars in a second casino. Work began the day of the fire and was completed a year later, in time for the scheduled opening date of June 15, 1907. John Philip Sousa's band was there, as was Queen Liliuokalani's band, the Royal Hawaiians. President Theodore Roosevelt telegraphed his congratulations.

Originally, the present casino's central, semicircular domed pavilion was flanked by twin obelisks. At either end of the casino were hipped-roof pavilions with bulbous domes. It was designed by William H. Weeks, though Joseph Cather Newsom had been mentioned as a prospective architect in a *Santa Cruz Sentinel* article of June 26, 1906.

Italian artist Michelangelo Garibaldi was hired to ornament the interior with rococo design and statuary. Garibaldi often got roaring drunk on the weekends and would have to be bailed out of jail.

A newspaper story recounted this tale of Garibaldi at work on a statue of Venus: "Suddenly a group of handsomely dressed ladies from the Alisky theater appeared in the doorway, chatting and laughing, strolling aimlessly about on pleasure bent. The stately Miss Alice Douvee was modestly taking the lead. Almost before the gentlemen present had realized the situation, the timid actress was noticed by the gallant Ez (Ezra Goodwill) to blush at perceiving the unveiled Venus. With the chivalry of Sir Walter Raleigh coming to the aid of his queen, he spread his cloak around the soft form of the shrinking mermaid. As a result of Ez's abrupt action, Venus, queen of form and beauty, was very much broken up.

"'Help! Murder! Fire! Police!' cried the infuriated Michael Angelo Garibaldi [sic] in splendid Italian. 'My Venus, my sweet, my lovely Venus is crushed beyond recovery. She has been squeezed to destruction. Oh Bocaccio, Oh Vespucci! Oh Christefer Colombo [sic]. Yet unhardened by the elements of this world, so young and faultless, my Venus is maimed for all time'" (*Santa Cruz Sentinel*, March 18, 1907). When Neptune's Kingdom was built, Garibaldi's cherub and King Neptune panels were taken down and placed in storage.

In 1907 Swanton anchored the barkentine *Balboa* in the bay, beyond the Pleasure Pier, which had been constructed in 1904 as part of the development of the first casino and boardwalk. "The *Balboa* was originally built in Bath, Maine, in 1874 and sailed as the *J. B. Brown*. In 1906 she was refitted in Oakland and rechristened the *Balboa*," noted Chandra Moira Beal and Richard A. Beal, in *Santa Cruz Beach Boardwalk*. Preceding similar ventures in Southern California by ten to twenty years, it was run as a "pleasure ship," providing dancing, gambling, dining, drinking, and "pleasures" illegal on shore.

The Pleasure Pier was torn down in 1962. At the same time, the Boardwalk's plunge was converted to an indoor miniature golf course.

The Boardwalk merry-go-round was moved here from Riverside, Rhode Island, where it had been constructed by the Danish woodcarver Charles I. D. Looff in 1910-11. Looff was a factory worker who became a skilled wooden-horse

(39) Second Casino and Boardwalk, 1911 (*Lionel Lenox Collection, Capitola Museum*)

(39) Casino and Boardwalk at night
(Special Collections, University Library, University of California, Santa Cruz)

carver in his free time. His first merry-go-round was completed in 1875 for New York's Coney Island Amusement Park.

The Santa Cruz merry-go-round is carved from Japanese white pine. It accommodates seventy-three passengers. Musical accompaniment is provided by the Ruth and Sohn band organ, which was made in Germany in 1894 and has 342 individual pipes.

The first roller-coaster on the beach was constructed in 1884 with a five-hundred-foot circumference and a daring top height of twenty-four feet. In June 1908 the L. A. Thompson's Scenic Railway was opened, the longest (1,050 feet) in the United States at the time. It was replaced by the existing roller coaster in 1924. Constructed by Looff's son, Arthur Looff, it has a top height of seventy feet and a one-minute-and-fifty-second ride.

Viewed from close up, it is the purest possible expression of its own structural elements, stick upon stick. By repeating this one element, over and over again, an abstraction of the balloon frame has been created. The oldest full-sized roller coaster on the West Coast, it is a structure of regional importance and a reminder of the unsanitized, pre-Disneyland amusement park. When illuminated at night, it is the electric Eiffel Tower of Santa Cruz, a free-form landmark visible from much of the central city. On sunny days the lights glance off the whitewashed beams, and the structure looks like the bleached skeleton of some prehistoric leviathan that had crawled up on the beach to die.

In 1912, a year after Swanton had completed the Casa del Rey Hotel, the Boardwalk Company went bankrupt during the President Taft-era depression. Swanton later became promotional director for the 1915 San Francisco Panama-Pacific International Exposition under President Charles C. Moore, also a Santa Cruz resident. The year of the exposition, a local syndicate of investors, including Swanton, took over the Boardwalk and reopened it. The business, known as the Santa Cruz Seaside Company, has been a powerful political and economic force in the area for many years. Swanton himself was mayor of Santa Cruz from 1927 to 1933. He was the town's greatest promoter but died virtually penniless in 1940, at the age of seventy-eight.

The section of the Boardwalk buildings that is closest to original appearance would be the facade of the former plunge in the eastern section of the main building facing Beach Street.

(40) George Applegarth was the architect of the 1910-11 **Casa del Rey Hotel**, which was located at **120 Cliff Street.** It was a monumentally simple building with fake, Pueblo-style projecting rafters, known as "vigas," a Mission Revival segmental roofline, and giant, composite entrance columns in a robust classical vein, similar to the Spreckels house that Applegarth designed in San Francisco. The Casa del Rey had the curious quality of impermanence defied, appearing

West Cliff and Beach Hill

(40) Casa del Rey *(Judith Steen Collection)*

as if it existed only in hand-colored postcards and not in reality. The interior courtyards were memorably peculiar; given the regularity of the architecture and landscaping (especially the rows of mauve hydrangeas) and the volume of the space, it appeared to be the exercise yard of a World War I-era sanatorium—where one was unlikely to recover. It did indeed serve as a naval convalescent hospital during World War II.

The Casa del Rey was once connected to the casino by an arched bridge lined with wicker chairs. It occupied the site of the Tent City, a predecessor of the latter-day bungalow courts and motels. Superceding the tents were cottages hardly larger or more elaborate than the tents they replaced. The cottages were painted in such a way that they produced a rainbow effect when viewed from the hills. The Casa del Rey was bought by the Seaside Company (owners of the Boardwalk) in 1984 and converted into a retirement hotel. The hotel, unfortunately, became another of the great landmark buildings lost to the earthquake of 1989.

In 1979, at the time of the last edition of *The Sidewalk Companion,* the low-lying flatland between Beach Hill and the San Lorenzo River was a slightly ramshackle collection of small apartment buildings and former beach cottages, many of them added to haphazardly through the years. The small scale and ad-hoc nature of the construction were delightful. The demolition of the Casa del Rey and some of the more marginally usable buildings, the expansion of Boardwalk parking lots, and the cul-de-sacing of streets to solve the massive traffic influx to the Boardwalk has weakened a cohesive sense of neighborhood.

(40) Casa del Rey entrance *(Carolyn Swift Collection)*

(41) Representative of the area's origins are the simple beach cottages at **208-210 Riverside Avenue** and at the corner of the main beach parking lot. Many of these early cottages were from Cottage City, built about 1907 for visitor lodging and located across from the Casino and Plunge on Beach Street. When the Casa del Rey Hotel was constructed, and again when the main parking lot was expanded in 1941, many of these small cabins were sold for a nominal fee. They were trucked to various Santa Cruz lots, as well as to neighboring cities. Eight of these cottages are located in a courtyard off Soquel Avenue at Pacheco Avenue; another is in Scotts Valley. One, formerly on a lot on Oak Drive in Capitola, has been moved next to the Capitola Museum, where it will be preserved as an example of resort cabins found along the coast.

West Cliff and Beach Hill

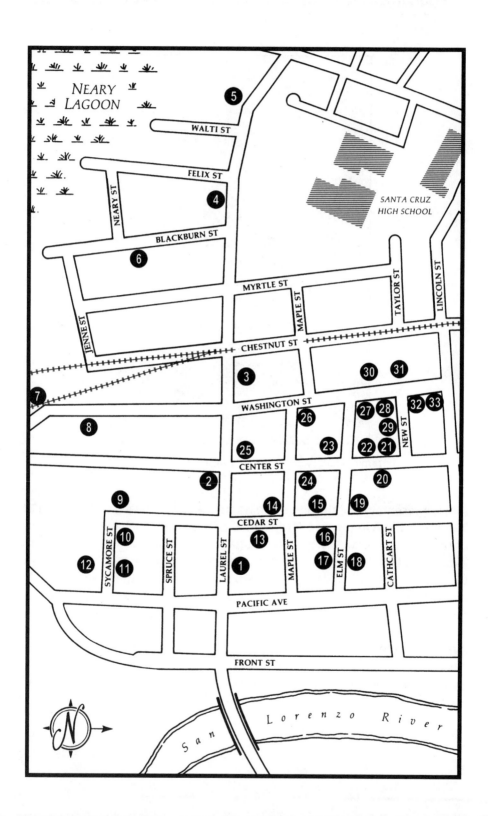

Chapter Two

Downtown, South of Lincoln

Most of the area downtown below Lincoln Street was laid out in the 1860s and 1870s on land once owned by Frederick A. Hihn, William and Harriet Blackburn, Thomas Weeks, and John Dreher.

(1) 216 Laurel Street is a story-and-a-half, clapboard cottage of the 1860s, once occupied by Judge Edgar Spalsbury and his artist wife, Sara Spalsbury. Although the lacy bargeboards are probably original, the curved porch and adjoining rooms were added by Judge Spalsbury in the 1880s. Since 2000, the house has been the Compassion Flower Inn, a bed-and-breakfast that welcomes medical marijuana patients.

(1) Spalsbury House *(Museum of Art & History)*

(2) The **Four Palms Apartments, 319 Laurel Street**, is a tour de force of the scroll saw. The use of a simple background to set off elaborate ornament is the design concept behind this 1887 Eastlake house. A veil-like, Moorish-arched screen of curlicued pattern sawn-wood and Swiss Chalet railing has been placed in front of a square box. These details, along with the bent roofline, are typical of the Eastlake style.

(3) 510 Laurel Street is a story-and-a-half house of the 1860s or '70s and one of several houses moved here by Ed Haggerty when the Laurel School grounds were enlarged. The house is one of three or four buildings in Santa Cruz to have wooden siding scored to imitate cut stone. The balustraded front porch was removed in 1973.

(4) 807 Laurel Street is an impressive Gothic-influenced house of the late 1860s or early '70s. Gothic gables with bargeboards inspired by the stone tracery of cathedrals are combined with the classically inspired balustrade above the porch. Another Gothic detail is the use of cut-out quatrefoils in the porch.

It was built for Titus Hale, a farmer, commission dealer, and vice-president of the Santa Cruz-Watsonville railroad. In the early 1880s, the house was moved from the corner of Laurel and Center Streets to its present site.

(5) From Felix Street northward up **Laurel Hill,** the land was owned by the Feliz family, whose adobe home once stood at the top of the hill. The Mission grist mill, constructed in 1796, was also located in this neighborhood. The remains of the mill were there as late as 1866, having been operated in the 1850s by José Bolcoff and Eli Moore (*Santa Cruz Sentinel,* February 22, 1953).

Part of the area became a tannery, founded by Charles Brown and later purchased by Richard C. Kirby, who greatly expanded the business.

Kirby came to America from Staffordshire, England, in 1842, and led an adventurous life before finally settling down in Santa Cruz. "He worked at the trade of a tanner at New York and in New London for some time and there, the spirit of adventure seizing him, signed on the whaler *Morrison* for a trip around the Horn.

"Tiring of this life after two years he deserted the ship with five companions at the mouth of the Columbia river and after several weeks of adventure among the Indians reached Astoria. Later he went to Sutter's Fort and helped Colonel [sic, that is, General] Sutter with his hides.

"In 1847-48 he came to Santa Cruz at the invitation of Judge Blackburn and worked here as a tanner until the announcement of the gold strike. He went to the diggings and within a few months had secured $10,000. This he lost in a few months of speculation" (Obituary, *Santa Cruz Sentinel,* July 14, 1904).

(2) Four Palms Apartments *(Museum of Art & History)*

(4) Hale House *(John Chase)*

He returned to Santa Cruz and opened a tannery in 1850 at Squabble Hollow (Glen Canyon). In 1854 he moved the operation to the location of the Mission tannery in the area around eastern Escalona Drive. It later became the Boston & Jones tannery.

The grounds of Kirby's third tannery eventually reached all the way up Laurel Street to Mission Street. The old tannery wheel, fed by a flume from a stream that still flows underneath Laurel Street, was located on the north side of the street near California. This landmark was destroyed in 1926 for the widening of Laurel Street. The tannery itself was closed in 1893.

Inspired by the picturesque waterwheel and the woodsy sloping hillside, actress Maybelle Place built the log cabin at **1025 Laurel Street** about 1909. "The Places had their own successful touring stock companies at the time, and played here at the Opera House, Jewel, and Unique or Swain's" (*Santa Cruz Sentinel,* February 22, 1953). In 1911 the cabin was used as a set for the *Danites,* a movie produced by the Selig Company, based on a story by Joaquin Miller.

The building is constructed of logs of varied sizes, chinked in between, and is shingled below the roofline. The balcony is suspended by chains, and there is a clinker-brick chimney. A redwood tree has been left growing through the extensive decking. The original, elaborate interior ironwork by Santa Cruz artisan John Otar, known as Otar the Lampmaker, has been removed. Frou-frou white ironwork, decidedly non-rustic, was added by later owners, Mr. and Mrs. Charles Chandler. Mrs. Chandler styled herself a countess and had a reputation as a self-made grande dame. She also added the stone walls and rock work that held back terraces of fern, daisy, pyracantha, nasturtium, ivy, and acanthus.

The original log structure is now a part of the Babbling Brook Inn. In 1981, three, two-story structures were added to the complex.

(6) 208 Blackburn Street is an unusual pagoda-like bungalow with a steep, concave roof, curved rafters, extra-wide clapboards, and squat raised posts supporting the porch.

(7) 119 Center Street is the site of the old Southern Pacific Railroad Depot. The structure had eaves, wide, grooved, perforated Eastlake bargeboards, fish-scale shingling on the second story, huge curved Eastlake brackets, and small partial gables on the Washington Street side. There was much use of large details on a relatively small building.

Prior to the station's January 1, 1893, opening, the *Santa Cruz Surf* commented, "The new union depot is neither a very large nor a very showy building. It is, however, conveniently arranged and neat in appearance. The ground floor is divided into a commodious ticket office, two waiting rooms, one for the broad and one for the narrow gauge road, and a large baggage

(7) Southern Pacific Railroad Depot *(Covello and Covello Photography)*

room. In the second story there is a room for the telegraph operator and another to be used as a dressing room for employees."

After passenger service to Santa Cruz was discontinued, the building found a new use as a restaurant in the 1970s. A caboose that was part of the Feather River run in 1944 served as the entrance. Trim from the demolished Rennie mansion on Beach Hill adorned the interior. Stained-class panels were placed in the bottom window-sashes of the first floor. There was so much brightly enameled gingerbread that some people felt the building belonged on Disneyland's Main Street as an overenthusiastic imitation of the Victorian period.

After the 1989 earthquake, the damaged El Palomar Restaurant on Pacific Avenue relocated to the depot building during renovations. After the restaurant moved back to Pacific Avenue, the depot building remained vacant; it became a victim of fire in 1998.

The freight depot is the last remaining structure related to rail transportation left on the site. The building was relocated and renovated and is now part of Depot Park.

(8) 344 Washington Street is the 1869 Edward Foster home moved here in the 1870s from a site now under the Cedar Street cut-through.

(9) 101 Cedar Street is one of the few unaltered Greek Revival houses in Santa Cruz. The strong, simple detail, the pillared porch, the wide corner-pilasters, the clapboarding, and the split-pedimented gable impart a look of dignity and solidity to the house. It is now part of the **Blackburn House Motel**.

It was built about 1854 for Judge William Blackburn, a cabinet maker from Jefferson County, Virginia. He immigrated to California by way of Independence, Missouri, settling in the Santa Cruz mountain community of Zayante. He and fellow members of his overland wagon train operated a shingle mill there before joining Frémont's battalion at the time of the Bear Flag Revolt. Blackburn was the first to fire a shot at the Battle of Buenaventura.

Returning to Santa Cruz after the Treaty of Cahuenga, he opened a store on the Upper Plaza that doubled as a sort of "open hotel, for no white man was ever asked to pay for supper or lodging; but anything there was in the house was at the service of the guest, open-handed hospitality being the character of the host and people in those primitive times, here, as elsewhere, throughout California" (Blackburn's obituary, *Santa Cruz Sentinel*, March 30, 1867).

In 1847 Blackburn was appointed *alcalde,* or judge-administrator, by Governor Richard Mason. The judge became known as a dispenser of swift, harsh sentences, sometimes carrying them out before they had been sent to the governor for approval.

(9) Blackburn House *(Carolyn Swift)*

An often-cited example of his jurisprudence is described in his *Santa Cruz Sentinel* obituary:

"A native Californian, to spite another of his countrymen, sheared off all the hairs from his horse's tail and mane, which was considered a great injury and insult, and the case was brought before Judge Blackburn for settlement, the injured man having his friends with him for support and sympathy. After a patient hearing of the case, the Judge, in a solemn manner announced his decision—that he could not find any law bearing in this case, but the old Mosaic law which says 'an eye for an eye and a tooth for a tooth.' 'Take the culprit and shave his mane and tail,' he said. The sentence was literally carried into effect, the native inhabitants enjoying the operation hugely, as the man was stripped and his hair shaved clean to his skin from the crown of his head to the sole of his feet, or as low down as the sentence called for."

After a stint in the goldfields in 1848-49, he returned to become justice of the peace. In 1851 he and his brother, Daniel Blackburn, began farming a large area of rich bottom land in the southwestern central portion of the city. Prices being good during the Gold Rush, the fertile land produced $100,000 worth of potatoes. "From this place the Judge sent samples of potatoes of four lbs. weight (which was a general average) to the Crystal Palace Fair at New York and received a prize for the finest potatoes ever known" (*Santa Cruz Sentinel* obituary).

He planted his famous fruit orchard in 1854. It eventually included apple, avocado, fig, lemon, olive, plum, and peach trees. In back of the house was a small lagoon bordered by willows, water maples, and sycamores. North of the lagoon was a large blackberry patch.

Blackburn's wife, the former Harriet Mead(e), married Blackburn in 1859, outlived him by fifty-three years, and eventually sold or developed much of the property.

(10) Joscelyn House *(Carolyn Swift)*

(10) The hexagonal house at **130 Sycamore Street** is often inaccurately spoken of as the "Octagon House."

"The odd-looking appearance of the building being erected by Dr. J[uliana] A[ldrich] Joscelyn on the corner of Sycamore and Cedar Streets has occasioned some wonder and speculation among those who have noticed the additions made to it each day. The building is hexagon shaped and covered with a three-quarter mansard roof. In the cellar is to be a kitchen and dining room. The first story will contain the living rooms. Upstairs is to be devoted to a business office and a reception room for patients. There is plenty of light and the necessary conveniences in every apartment. Although the residence is not altogether in the general style it is quite comfortable and well-planned" (*Santa Cruz Sentinel,* August 30, 1884).

Sometime between 1892 and 1905, the porch, with its crude circle-and-arch detail, was added, according to the Sanborn Fire Insurance Maps of those dates.

(11) At **116 Sycamore Street** is a simple structure built in 1876 for Joe Rutherford, a transfer man, as a six-room, one-story house. In 1889 the present two-story Stick Style front was added according to plans prepared by LeBaron R. Olive. Since that time, the bottom story had been stuccoed over, and a large bracket in the gable and other trim were stripped away.

(12) At **101-131 Sycamore Street** is the **Sycamore Street Commons,** a generously spirited affordable housing project designed in 1998 by Michael Pyatok, with front yards, back yards, terraces, and lavish internal common landscaped grounds. Pitched roofs, cross gables, bay windows, brackets, and stories differentiated by siding type create a remarkably pleasant place to live without pushing any architectural boundaries.

(13) 310 Cedar Street is a simple story-and-a-half Italianate style house of the 1870s with a one-story slanted bay with a dentil-course cornice topped by a sawn-wood balustrade. There is a suggestion of arches above the pilasters supporting the portico, and the frame siding is scored to imitate stone construction.

(14) 201 Maple Street is a two-story house with bold Stick half-timbering, a corner, angled square bay, and an Eastlake-trim portico. The small porch supported by split pilasters on the Cedar Street side, reminiscent of the Eastlake sunburst motif, is noteworthy.

The rear portion of the house was probably built sometime in the 1870s. The two-story front portion of the house was added in 1887, after the property had been purchased by groceryman Charles M. Collins. Local architect Daniel Damkroeger drew the plans for the addition, which cost some $2,000.

In the 1970s, landscape architect Roy Rydell restored this building for his office.

(15) 411 Cedar Street is a story-and-a-half house of the late 1860s or early 1870s. The windows are double-arched and round-headed, as are the French doors opening onto the porch. The shiplap siding is grooved to imitate stone, and there is quoining at the corners. Bordering the porch are the remnants of what was once a classical balustrade. The slanted bay at the side, with double-arched, Gothic-pointed windows, has had its two side windows paneled over.

It has a dentil course and widely spaced paired brackets underneath the eaves. This trim is slanted at an angle in the gable to match the slope of the eaves. The building was remodeled as the Cedar Street Gallery and Café in 1977.

(16) At **418 Cedar Street** is a one-story, raised-basement, 1886 cottage emblazoned with the legend "Dr. Miller." Originally, this sign read "Dr. Miller, Dentist." The building is now a coffee house called Caffé Pergolesi, which remains a staple of the UCSC college scene.

(17) 117 Elm Street is the simple Mission Revival style **Elm Street Mission Building**, constructed in 1912. The previous Advent Christian Church building on the site had been "an octagon in shape with the roof rising to a sort of cone in the center" (*Santa Cruz Sentinel*, April 17, 1884).

(18) 112 Elm Street is a symmetrical, two-story, stucco apartment house with split-pedimented gables, glassed-in porch, and twin doors opening onto the roof of the porch. This was the home of Granville and Mary Shelby and once stood at the northwest corner of Pacific Avenue and Elm Street (*Santa Cruz Sentinel*, November 14, 1948).

Built in the 1850s or '60s, very possibly in the Greek Revival style, its rear section was enlarged from one story to one-and-a-half stories in 1876. It has since been much enlarged and remodeled.

"Granville Shelby was born in Tennessee in 1825, the son of an MD. He learned the cabinet makers trade in Nashville. He was the town's principal builder, its first furniture maker, and its first undertaker" (Centennial edition of *Riptide*, October 19, 1950).

(19) 210 and **214 Elm Street** are two large, plain, story-and-a-half apartment houses on property once owned by D. D. Dodge. One of them might well be the Dodge home, while the other might be the barn that Dodge converted into "a house to rent" in 1877.

(20) 516 Center Street is a new (larger for the neighborhood than previous development) multiple-unit residence that fits in with, rather than overwhelms, its neighbors. Its bulk steps up from the street, giving it a scale complementary to that of its neighbors. Orchestration of stucco, board-and-batten, and wide siding areas further breaks down the size. The partially hipped (jerkinhead) roof in the front facade gives just enough detail to add charm, while the overall simple massing and window placement give it the same directness as early cottages from the 1850s, '60s, and '70s. This 1995 building was designed by Thacher & Thompson.

(21) The **Progressive Baptist Church** and the **Progressive Baptist Hall and Parsonage,** at **517 Center Street**, were both built in 1902 by Edward Van Cleeck. The church building was originally constructed for the All Souls Unitarian Church during the pastorate of Rev. George Whitefield Stone. The steeple, designed by Michael O'Hearn, was added to the church when it was restored.

(22) At **511-513 Center Street** and **314 Elm Street,** a variety of buildings, new and old, have been cobbled together by Michael O'Hearn to form a lush landscape erupting with vegetation at every turn. What would be space abandoned to the automobile in other more ordinary developments has been recaptured by hedges, vines, and a variety of large and small trees to act as a pedestrian forecourt. Since neither development is gated, passersby have the benefit of being able to glimpse the serendipitous, semi-public spaces through spirited, neo-Victorian spindle entrance arches.

(23) 419 Center Street is the site of the Greek Revival-influenced John Dreher house, built in the 1850s or '60s. German-born John Dreher arrived in San Francisco in 1847 as a member of a regiment of soldiers recruited in New York. He came to Santa Cruz in 1849 and acquired eleven acres of farmland between Lincoln and Laurel Streets and Center and Washington Streets. His wife, Catherine, "served mothers of early days as midwife and nurse; possessed of considerable business acumen and a mind of her own" (Centennial edition of *Riptide*, October 19, 1950).

The two-story structure had corner pilasters, clapboarding, and gables treated as pediments. There was a door opening onto the roof of the porch, which was centrally placed, balustraded with narrow classical spindles and supported by split pilasters. The cornice over the front door was treated as an entablature. An addition at the rear of the house was constructed in 1877, and the house was moved closer to Center Street in 1887. The house was demolished as a result of the 1989 earthquake.

At 311 and 315 Elm Street are the remaining Dreher family homes, built in the 1870s by John Dreher—311 for his daughter Mathilda (later Mrs. Francis Becker) and 315 for his daughter Katherine (later Mrs. Louis Wessendorf).

Following demolition of the Dreher house, the Bowen house, formerly at 346 Church Street, was moved to this site but turned so that its front entrance is at **301 Elm Street**. The structure was built as a double tenement in 1877 by carpenters Alexander and Marsh for Mrs. Rosanna Bowen. The plans were drawn up by C. W. Davis.

It has two square bays slightly mansarded at the top of the first story, fish-scale shingle window hoods, and a flat-roofed portico. The bracketed, square facade conceals the tenement's double-peaked roof. During its renovation in

1974 for use at its earlier site by the City Parks and Recreation Department, the wall between the two tenements was partially removed.

(24) The house at **416 Center Street** was built by Christian Werner in 1877 at a cost of $1,400; carpenters were Butler and Walsworth.

(25) At **301 Center Street** is the **Louden Nelson Community Center**, though it should be the *London* Nelson Community Center, named in the 1970s for the former slave who in 1860 willed his estate to Santa Cruz City Schools. Though there has been much confusion over the spelling of his name, his place in Santa Cruz history is unmistakable. The building was formerly Laurel School, designed by William H. Weeks and constructed in 1930.

(26) 322 Maple Street is a two-story, cube-like Italianate style house. The arched windows are paired and capped by wooden keystones. It has a one-story slanted bay and an outside staircase to the second floor (added after the house was built). The brackets under the broad eaves of the hipped roof are gone, but the arched hood over the front door remains.

The house was the subject of a *Santa Cruz Sentinel*, June 10, 1876, item: "W. G. Alexander, recently of Oakland, a builder and contractor, on the corner of Maple and Washington Streets, is erecting for his own occupation a handsome two-story residence, hip-roof and what is a new departure in architecture from the many barn-like structures that are scattered promiscuously in the valley and on the hills."

(27) This house was at 214 Lincoln Street before it was moved to **616 Washington Street** in 1977 to make way for the addition to the Nickelodeon Theater. It was built about 1890 with Eastlake bargeboards and brackets and oversize lattice work in the gable.

(28) The building at **620 Washington Street** once stood at the southwest corner of Pacific Avenue and Maple Street as the John Werner house. Werner manufactured harnesses, boots, and saddles in his Pacific Avenue shop, located at a site now occupied by the north section of the St. George Hotel.

Werner purchased the home from James Munroe Cutler in 1876. At that time it was raised and remodeled and "improved by having weights attached to the windows, water and gas introduced, a new kitchen added, sitting room enlarged (with bay window adornment) new cornice all around, new steps in front, etc.," reported the *Santa Cruz Sentinel*, June 10, 1876.

In 1905 the house was moved to its Washington Street location to make way for the brick building that Henry Rhein was preparing to erect on the Pacific

Avenue lot. On Washington Street the house was used as the parsonage for the German Methodist Church at 708 Washington Street.

(29) 115 New Street once stood at 202 Lincoln Street and was known as the Cady Building. The symmetrical L-shape is an unusual house form for its time and place. It may have been built in 1876 by Charles D. Holbrook. The porch seems to have been added between 1883 and 1886. For many years it was the home of Jesse and Ellen Cope.

The house became the subject of controversy in 1975 when it was slated to be torn down to make way for a taco and hot-dog luncheonette. Owner Jack Chiorini was persuaded by testimony from members of the Santa Cruz Historical Society to have the building moved off the Lincoln Street lot rather than have it demolished. The idea of historic preservation was already so well accepted by 1975 that the building was saved much more easily than would have been possible a few years earlier.

(30 and 31) 619 and 621 Washington Street *(John Chase)*

(30) 619 Washington Street is a clapboarded 1860s house with corner pilasters, tabernacle-frame front door, and front porch topped by a classical balustrade. The incised bracket and pendant in the gable matches exactly the bracket of neighboring 621 Washington Street.

(31) 621 Washington Street is a tiny boxcar-shaped elf-house, built about 1880.

(32) 702-704 Washington Street is a boxy, story-and-a-half structure stripped of all original trim and window frames. An exterior stairway leads to the first floor above the raised basement.

(33) 708 Washington Street was originally the **German Methodist Church,** the only foreign language church in Santa Cruz when it was built in 1884. Constructed by contractor Calvin W. Davis at a cost of $1,500, it held two hundred people. The original concept called for a belfry, which, if included, has since disappeared. The church, with its narrow lancet windows, is now the Kali Ray Tri Yoga Center.

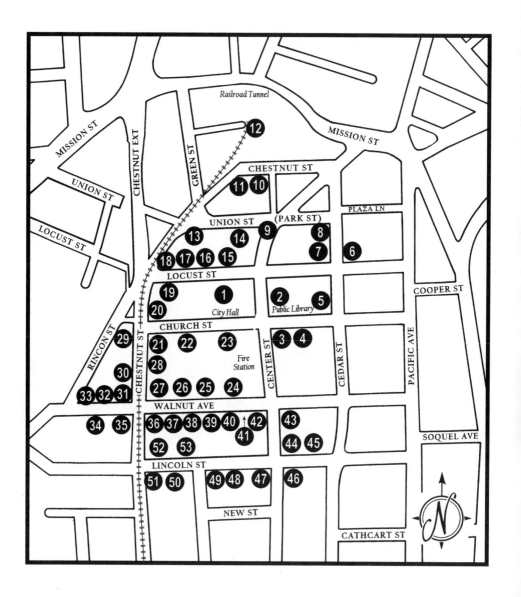

Chapter Three

Downtown, North of Lincoln

Along with other sections of downtown, north of Lincoln Street occupies part of the low-lying flatland through which the San Lorenzo River once ran on its way to the sea. The area later became the site of the Mission farm, which extended all the way from Mission Hill to Beach Hill, bordered by a line of willows along Pacific Avenue.

Preacher, businessman, and blacksmith Elihu Anthony arrived in Santa Cruz the day before Christmas 1847; he delivered this reminiscence in the January 9, 1885, issue of the *Santa Cruz Sentinel:*

"[James] Dunleavy was in possession of all the land west of Pacific avenue, beginning at the foot of Mission Hill and extending as far down as Maple street. The land consisted of about sixty acres and was unfenced. All the farming he did was to raise a patch of potatoes on the spot where the Pacific Ocean House now is [at approximately 1543 Pacific Avenue]. The clover and grass were up when I arrived, and high enough to mow. Dunleavy said to me: 'To-morrow is Christmas. Suppose we go and shoot some geese.' He had no bullets, but used slugs with which to kill the geese, which we found in large numbers on Locust street where James King lives [near the northwest corner of Center and Locust Streets]. All you could see of the geese were their heads, their bodies being hidden by the clover and grass. We succeeded in killing two of them."

The area began to develop in the 1850s, when Santa Cruz was profiting from the Gold Rush. Much of the land was laid out by businessman and developer Frederick A. Hihn, and here many of the more elegant homes were built for members of his family. Santa Cruz's narrow-gauge railroad station and the Opera House were both located in this section of town.

By the end of the nineteenth century, however, this area began to lose favor as a fashionable residential neighborhood. Increased demands by businesses for new commercial space and, later, parking lots resulted in extensive retail and professional construction, as well as the ubiquitous car lots that accompanied such development. Many homes were leveled for projects like the Civic Auditorium and City Hall, public parking lots, Center Street and Cedar Street extensions, and the Pacific Telephone Building. In the last twenty years, this area has once again become a desirable place to live. Individuals and groups, such as the **Downtown Neighbors Association**, have planted trees, restored and maintained historic homes, and created a sense of community.

(1) At **809 Center Street** is the 1937-38 **Santa Cruz City Hall,** designed by Monterey architect C. J. Ryland in the Monterey Colonial Revival style. The original U-shaped building opens onto an elaborately landscaped courtyard and garden. The broad central walk leads to a fountain of blue, red, and turquoise tile surmounted by a fluted urn. Beyond the fountain are the solid Doric columns of the central galleria.

The two side-wings have galleries supported by paired posts raised on a low flagstone wall and are entered through flagstone arches that are repeated at changes of level along these galleries. Robert Stevens & Associates built the 1967 annex.

The building occupies the site of the 1872-73 Frederick A. and Therese (Paggen) Hihn mansion, designed by Charles Wellington Davis. It was the only full Italian Villa style residence ever built in Santa Cruz, as well as the largest, most costly, and most elaborate house constructed in the city, with the possible exception of Golden Gate Villa. "The new residence of F. A. Hihn Esq. in point of architectural beauty and grandeur not only surpasses all buildings in this county, but excels the great majority in the state, ranking nearly every luxury residence extant. It is a chaste and elegant ornament to our city," boasted the February 8, 1873, *Santa Cruz Sentinel.* The "Ionic style" house had a "lofty tower with octagon shaped roofs, 69 feet in height, being easily distinguished from almost every portion of the city. The main entrance opens from a large vestibule–two double doors of solid walnut, traceried carvings, giving admission to the main portion of the house; while to the right and left are broad walnut balustraded stairways to the second floor, while the large heavy piazzas and verandahs have, as also the main house, rich carvings, & etc." In the dining room was a "richly panelled wainscot of native wood, laurel, pine, walnut grown in this country."

The mansion numbered among its rooms a skating rink, wine room, billiards room, conservatory, sky-lighted picture gallery, and gymnasium. Advanced features of the time were the elevator, speaking tubes, hot and cold running water, and telegraph wires from every room.

"The roofs are covered with ornamental shingles and having a number of pediments and being painted in imitation of English tiling or slate has a grand effect."

According to Duncan McPherson, all the turned work came from Hihn's mill and "the fluted columns [were] all solid pieces of timber and came from trees owned by Hihn and finished off at his own mill" (*Santa Cruz Evening News*, July 22, 1920).

Ernest Otto recalled in his *Santa Cruz Sentinel,* December 20, 1942, column that the garlands of flowers and fruits painted under the cornices were rendered

(1) Hihn Mansion, on site of present City Hall

(Hihn-Younger Archive, Special Collections, University Library, University of California, Santa Cruz)

(1) Hihn Mansion, Santa Cruz City Hall wing, and Santa Cruz Public Library
(Hihn-Younger Archive, Special Collections, University Library, University of California, Santa Cruz)

in their natural colors. Surrounding the house was a formal garden of lawns, trees, flowers, and clipped hedges.

The mansion was leased to the City for use as City Hall as early as March 1920 and was purchased outright in 1923. On completion of the present City Hall, the Hihn house was torn down, and Santa Cruz lost one of its greatest Victorian-era landmarks.

(2) Santa Cruz Public Library
(Special Collections, University Library, University of California, Santa Cruz)

(2) At **224 Church Street** is the **Santa Cruz Public Library**, completed in 1968 and designed by the San Francisco firm of Spencer, Lee & Busse. It replaced the previous 1903-1904 Carnegie library, designed by William Weeks.

The walls of the first building were of concrete and Santa Cruz County sandstone with Arizona red-sandstone trimmings and a roof of slate. The squat lines, broad entrance arch, and the rusticated surface of the building suggested the influence of the Richardsonian Romanesque Revival.

The library site was part of F. A. Hihn's large home lot, which he sold to the City on an easy-payment basis. Steel-magnate and philanthropist Andrew Carnegie contributed $15,000 of the total cost of the original library building.

Before construction of this building, the library had been housed in many different structures, including the Williamson & Garrett Building and the St. George Hotel. Minerva Waterman became the head librarian in 1890, the position she held for fifty-one years until her retirement in 1941.

(3) Across Church Street is a large magnolia tree in the parking lot on the site of Wessendorf & Son mortuary, now the Prophet Elias Greek Orthodox Church, at **223 Church Street**. This tree remains from the garden of the Samuel Drennan house, which was built in the 1850s or '60s and sold to Wessendorf in 1941 (*Santa Cruz Sentinel*, May 4, 1941).

(4) Next door was the 1858 Greek Revival style **Congregational Church,** which gave the street its name. Four pilasters supported the pedimented gable and simple steeple. The building's New England appearance was due to the Massachusetts training of its carpenter and architect, John B. Perry.

When they moved into a new building in 1890, the Congregationalists sold their Church Street building to the Methodists. The Methodists moved the 1858 building back, incorporating it into a new church, put up an auditorium, and tore down the pre-1857 Bart Stevens house (*Santa Cruz Sentinel*, August 18, 1940). The Stevens house had been long occupied by the George and Gertrude Otto family and was the boyhood home of *Santa Cruz Sentinel* historical writer Ernest Otto. The Santa Cruz Sentinel now occupies the site.

(5) 903-911 Cedar Street may be considered the last gasp of the Streamlined Moderne in Santa Cruz, dating as it does from 1948-1951. Superior Court Judge and Mrs. James L. Atteridge admired C. J. Ryland's Santa Cruz City Hall and commissioned him to design this combination of ground-floor office space and second-story apartments.

(6) 126 Locust Street is the site of the 1876 George Staffler residence, later occupied by Dr. Benjamin Knight. Staffler had only to lean out of his window and look east along Locust Street to see the Pacific Avenue building that housed his undertaking and furniture business. The building, a false-fronted, two-story structure that had been stuccoed over, was demolished for the City's Locust Garage.

(7) At **1003 Cedar Street** is the two-story **Santa Cruz Hotel,** built in 1877. The plans were drawn by Charles Kaye for owner Robert K. Whidden. In 1904 a cupola with flagstaff was added, but it has since been removed. The result of the latest remodeling is a Streamlined Moderne first story with flattened octagonal windows, a three-level, flat, projecting cornice, and a corner entrance with curved pipe-railings and half-circular stairs. It is now occupied by two restaurants and a cocktail lounge. Don't miss the gallery of Miss California pageant winners in the lounge.

Those interested in the Santa Cruz version of an Edwardian never-never land of stained glass and oak trim, as perfected by contemporary craftsman/designer Michael Bates, should visit the second-story restaurant.

Chapter Three

(8) 1013 and **1015 Cedar Street** are two houses of the 1870s or '80s remaining out of an original row of three identical houses.

With its plate glass window and new concrete and brick porch, 1013 has been the most altered, but both once had gingerbread trim and detailing that has disappeared.

(9) Near the present intersection of Union Street (then Park Street) and Center Street was the **Opera House.** Built in 1877, it was promoted by a shady entrepreneur not unlike the Duke of Bridgewater in *The Adventures of Huckleberry Finn.*

He was A. B. "Budd" Smith, who had "built and owned the Truckee theatre and was once associated in the ownership and construction of the Salt Lake Music Hall as he informs us," reported the *Santa Cruz Sentinel*, July 28, 1877. This "jaunty 36-year-old Kentuckian" set up an auction business in the Ely block. His next project was an opera house, for which "he persuaded F. A. Hihn to sell him a lot on credit. He then induced James P. Pierce to sell him lumber on the same terms" (*Santa Cruz Sentinel*, April 6, 1952). Hard times, however, forced Smith to sell his interest in the fledging Opera House for sixty-five dollars to the partnership of Jarvis and Lay.

Smith retreated to San Francisco and started a bunco scheme with the prestigious sounding name, the Inventor's Institute of California. This seemingly reputable organization was set up to steal the profitable creations of starry-eyed inventors.

One of Smith's most outrageous rackets was his wonderful butter-making scheme, described in an 1887 *San Francisco Examiner* account:

"I first came across A. B. Smith some years ago, when Sam Martin engaged me to draw up some papers for the transfer of a churn patent from Smith to himself, the consideration being $5,000.

"Smith claimed that this zinc churn, placed in hot water, and containing one quart of milk, the yolk of an egg and a half pound of butter would turn out two pounds of 'butterine' or a substance equal to the best butter."

The lawyer and his client visited the Smith home to witness a demonstration of the device.

"We were ushered into the kitchen where madam [Mrs. Smith] boiled four gallons of water down to one gallon, that being one of the mysterious provisos necessary for a successful result. The yolk of an egg, the milk and a half pound of butter were tossed into the churn and the latter deposited in the hot water. Prior to beginning operations madam began rolling up her sleeves in such a manner that my client Martin, who is a rather delicate individual, suggested that we pass into the parlor while the toilet was in progress. In a few minutes the worthy other half of Smith had taken advantage of our temporary absence to slip into the churn an extra roll of butter . . . . The trick had been successfully

57

(9) Opera House *(Covello & Covello Photography)*

played and Martin fell in for $5,000" (Article reprinted in the *Santa Cruz Sentinel*, March 17, 1887).

The Opera House that Smith had started "opened on November 23, 1877, with 'The Bohemian Girl,' sung by the Hitchings-Bernard Opera company, just back from Australia. Santa Cruzans filled the rows of kitchen chairs and watched the pictured Atlas rise on the curtain . . . ." The actors gave a benefit performance of 'Romeo and Juliet' to get fares back to San Francisco.

"Paderewski and his piano appeared on its stage. High school classes graduated there. Boxing matches were put on. 'The Red Stocking Blondes,' for men only, showed. Jack London, Josh Billings and others lectured from its stage.

"ZaSu Pitts, of screen, stage and radio fame, made her start in high school plays at the Opera House. Frederick Warde brought Shakespearean drama. In 1888, Thomas Nast, . . . one of the newspaper world's first great [political] cartoonists, drew pictures there for local audiences" (*Santa Cruz Sentinel*, April 6, 1952). In June 1891 heavyweight boxing champion John L. Sullivan appeared as the "sturdy blacksmith" in a play called *Honest Hearts and Willing Hands* (*Santa Cruz Sentinel*, August 8, 1954).

Participatory theater of the rowdy Elizabethan variety was not unknown to the patrons of the Opera House. "The evening's amusement began when a theatre party, composed of members of the *Pansy and Lily Club,* filed into the house and took the two front rows. Each member wore eye-glasses, a stand-up collar labelled 'dude' on the back for fear no one would know they were dudes, and carried an umbrella and a supply of vegetables. *The Birth of St. Patrick,* by J. Jackson, threw the *Pansy and Lily Club* into a commotion, and they threw turnips and carrots on the stage, but Jackson took no notice of it and even responded to an encore, which earned him more vegetables. By this time the house was in an uproar, many heartily condemning the club's manner of showing their appreciation of a performer's merits."

The purpose of the umbrellas? After the club had "donated a full supply of vegetables. . . the members of the Club had their umbrellas raised, and the boys in the gallery threw beans and vegetables at them" (*Santa Cruz Sentinel*, April 15, 1886).

The architect of the Opera House was William Henry Burrows, who also designed the old City Hall on Front Street and several other buildings all constructed the same year as the Opera House.

The symmetrical Opera House with its Italianate style, arched and paired windows, and half-circle false front was moved to Capitola in 1921 by Harvey West and Henry Peterson. After serving a variety of uses from garage to pottery shop, it was torn down forty years later in 1961.

Downtown, North of Lincoln

(10) At **738 Chestnut Street** is the **Enterprise Iron Works** building, a two-story corrugated metal structure with a wooden-sided false front. The foundry was started by William V. Pringle, a former employee of Elihu Anthony. Anthony was said to have established the first Anglo-operated foundry in the city, which was moved here from the River Street location in 1898 and remained until 1915.

(11) 734-736 Chestnut Street is a raised-basement cottage restored in 1974 by entrepreneur Max Walden. A cupola was added at the top and a new floor inserted at the bottom. Much new decking with exterior staircases was built above the ground floor.

(12) Along Chestnut Street, near Green Street, is the **Mission Hill Railroad Tunnel**, surveyed by Thomas Wright. When built in 1875, it was 900 feet long and measured twelve feet by twelve-and-one-half feet.

When the South Pacific Coast Railroad was taken over by the Southern Pacific Railroad, the tunnel had to be widened and deepened four feet to accommodate the larger engines.

On the Chestnut end of the tunnel was the passenger depot of F. A. Hihn's Santa Cruz Railroad. An adjacent depot building was later used as the offices of the F. A. Hihn Company.

A car-house, engine houses, freight house, and turntable completed the little railroad yard.

(13) 233 Union Street is a one-and-a-half-story-over-raised-basement clapboard cottage of the 1860s. There are flattened Tudor-arch cornices over the windows, and a glaringly new plate-glass window has been installed at the front.

The next three houses, **235, 237,** and **239 Union Street**, were built by F. A. Hihn. According to Ernest Otto: "At the upper end of Chestnut Avenue and Park street intersection was a lot which was used as a playground by the 'Depot Gang,' as the boys from Cherry, Park, and Locust Streets were known. They played baseball on this lot. The baselines were not of regulation length, and due to the small field it was easy to knock the ball over the fence. The kids had to look elsewhere when F. A. Hihn erected three small cottages on the lot."

The three houses are more similar than they appear to be at first glance. All are basically hipped-roof, cube-shaped houses with small front gables and central front doors, but 237 has been stripped of its portico.

235 Union Street may be a recycled older house, for some of its walls are clapboarded.

(14) The first story of the house at **225 Union Street** has narrow siding; the second has random shingling. Paired columns support the Shingle Style-influenced porch, and there are simple brackets beneath the eaves and the full-pedimented gable.

(15) 314 Locust Street is a two-story house with a corner recessed porch held up by short, raised pillars. The shingled second story is slightly corbelled out over the narrow-clapboarded first-story. Repeated in the shape of the Palladian window is the shape of the porch arches. Underneath the Shingle Style gable is a pair of windows in an arched, sunburst-decorated frame with outsize keystone. On the west side there is a small oriel window. At the back are visible shiplap siding and twelve-pane windows that indicate a date some twenty to thirty years earlier than the front section. The old part is possibly the James King house, which once stood on the site.

(16) Next door is **320 Locust Street,** the **Fairfax Apartments.** It has a central, two-story square bay crowned with a tiny mansard roof and dormers. A squeezed-pediment cornice and a bracket-supported door-hood are placed above the central entrance.

The house has been added to several times. The one-story section at the rear could be the oldest, followed by the story-and-a-half section visible behind the bay windows. The rear section may be the J. O. Wanzer house of 1867, which was later owned by Cornelius Cappelmann, who built one of the additions in 1885. George W. Reid, who married daughter Cornelia Cappelmann, built another major addition in 1903.

Cappelmann, a native of Spaden, Germany, operated the El Dorado Saloon on Pacific Avenue across from the Pacific Ocean House.

(17) 324 Locust Street has a stucco, false-front facade, poised to spring like a bulldog, on two tiny, dwarfish arches at each side. At the top of the curve-sided facade is a dab of Spanish tiles. The building seems to press down heavily on its bottom story.

This building was the early home of German native Frederick Augustus Hihn, the chief developer and foremost financier of Santa Cruz. It was built in 1857 on the south side of Locust Street, a street that he had laid out not long before. When his mansion of 1872 was constructed on his homestead property, the older home was moved across the street to this location.

Before coming to America, Hihn's work was gathering and processing medicinal herbs, but he disliked the German form of government and longed for an atmosphere of political freedom. He was planning to emigrate to

Wisconsin, when news of the discovery of gold in California convinced him to change his destination.

Reaching San Francisco in 1848 after a journey around the Horn, Hihn joined a party of six gold miners. Their expedition was a failure; a flood washed away their tools and they were reduced to eating manzanita berries to survive. When the bedraggled party returned to Sacramento and disbanded, Hihn stayed on and worked in a candy factory. In a few weeks, however, the factory was flooded out. After moderate success in the mining fields, Hihn came back to Sacramento to operate two hotels.

From Sacramento, Hihn moved to San Francisco, where he opened a drug store. "The great fire of May, 1851 took nearly all of his worldly goods and the balance was consumed in the June fire of that year. Despairing of ever succeeding, he was passing through the burnt district on his way to take passage for his native land, when he saw one of his friends who had been burned out shoveling the burning coals out of the way. 'What are you doing?' was asked. 'Building a new store.' was the reply. 'What! After you have been burned out twice within two months?' Said the friend, 'Oh some one will carry on business here.' 'I might as well do it as anyone else,' thought Mr. Hihn, and so he remained, this incident changing his mind. New courage pervaded him and he formed a partnership with Henry Hintch [Hentsch] to open a store in some town south of San Francisco, where it was supposed, though money was not so plenty, the danger from fire was less and life more agreeable. In October, 1851, they came to Santa Cruz, where they located at the junction of Front street and Pacific avenue. Soon afterward Mr. Hintch [Hentsch] went back to the city, but Mr. Hihn remained. Having the advantage of a good mercantile education, speaking English, German, French and Spanish fluently, besides having some knowledge of other languages, he soon succeeded in establishing a large and prosperous mercantile business" (James M. Guinn, *History of the State of California,* 1903).

The first flush of Gold Rush prosperity was followed by a depression that caused prices of the chief local products, wheat, lumber, and potatoes, to plummet. Since Hihn's clients couldn't afford to pay cash for the merchandise, he accepted bartered produce and lumber and marketed them wholesale for cash. By 1857 he had amassed a fortune of $30,000, but the attendant stress was bad for his health and he turned the store over to his brother, Hugo.

Hihn then devoted his attention to his real estate operations, subdividing many tracts in Santa Cruz and developing the resort town of Capitola in 1868. Beginning in 1860, Hihn created a water system for Santa Cruz and later supplied much of the county with water. He was also active in the development of the county's roads and railroads and had lumbering operations at Felton and in the hills behind Soquel and Aptos.

(18) 326 Locust Street is a two-story Stick-Eastlake style house built in 1888 for Daniel Williams and designed by John Williams.

(18) Williams House *(Joe Michalak)*

(19) At **333 Locust Street** is the Kunitz house, restored in 1976. Johann Ernest H. Kunitz, a Prussian-born apothecary, was a passenger on the same ship that brought F. A. Hihn to California from Germany in 1849. In 1866, for $4, Kunitz bought this lot in the same block as F. A. Hihn's mansion. The building is a two-story Italianate house of the late 1870s with a split-pedimented front gable bearing paired brackets.

(20) On the northeast corner of the City Hall parking lot was the 1877 Rosanna Bowen house. In 1974 the building was renovated for use by the City Parks and

Recreation Department. After the 1989 earthquake the damaged building was relocated to 301 Elm Street (see Chapter 2, #23).

Mrs. Bowen had purchased this end of the block from Ernest Kunitz, who had formerly operated a soap and glue works on the site. He opened his glue factory in 1857, for a time one of the only two in the state. "An excellent quality of Chemical Olive Soap" was also manufactured, beginning in 1861 (*Pacific Sentinel*, December 19, 1861).

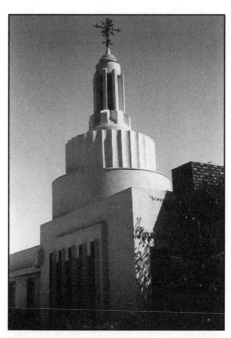

(21) Alsberge Building *(John Chase)*

(21) 343-345 Church Street is a Streamlined Moderne office building constructed for physician R. Carey Alsberge and attributed to Oakland architect F. H. Slocombe. Its most prominent feature is a tiered and fluted wedding-cake tower with a lacy metal weathervane at the top. The tower looks as though it ought to be decked out in whipped cream and cherries. After the first edition of this book was written in 1974, the building was remodeled. Regrettably, the fenestration was altered and tiles were slapped on the cornice.

The building occupies the site of **Cherry Court**, a large one-and-a-half-story-over-raised-basement Stick-Eastlake house built in 1889 for *Santa Cruz Sentinel* editor and later publisher Duncan McPherson and his wife, Amelia Hinds McPherson.

"There are four bay windows, one at each side and end of the building, two stories high," read a contemporary account in his newspaper. "All corners are cut off up to the third floor. The roof is steep, all ridges being on a level, [as are]

(21) Cherry Court *(Harrison's History of Santa Cruz County, 1892)*

all third-story [dormer] windows. Over each bay window is a gable, and there is a very steep roofed one over each entrance. The architect, J. H. Williams, knows of no residence in the state where the main entrance is cut across the corner as this is to be" (*Santa Cruz Sentinel*, January 23, 1889).

McPherson's family moved to Santa Cruz in 1856, after having attempted ventures in the mining and hotel trades elsewhere in the state. Duncan had earned money for his college education by working as a school janitor and had garnered a six-year scholarship as well, but he was compelled to quit the University of the Pacific due to ill health. Switching to work in the open air, he bought three yoke of cattle on credit and went into the "teaming business," at which he was very successful.

(22) 323 Church Street is the site of the **Bret Harte Honeymoon Cottage**. It was so named because of a popular, though undocumented, belief that Bret Harte and his bride, Anna Griswold, had spent their honeymoon here in 1862.

The Hartes did stay at the cottage in 1868, along with Mr. and Mrs. Anton Roman. Roman was the publisher of the *Overland Monthly,* a journal of western literature edited by Harte.

Besides laying plans for the brand new journal, Harte also drafted here his famous short story, "The Luck of Roaring Camp." This tale of a rough-and-tumble Gold Rush mining town suddenly confronted with the responsibility of caring for an orphaned infant was Harte's first big success.

Harte's story was submitted for publication but soon encountered an obstacle. The proofreader was a most moral young woman who took exception to the profanity and to the references to Cherokee Sal's profession as a prostitute. After a conference between the indignant proofreader and the magazine's printer, it was decided to send the proof sheets to Harte and his publisher Roman, who were vacationing in Santa Cruz at the time. When they returned to San Francisco, Roman, who liked the story, supported Harte, and "The Luck of Roaring Camp" was printed.

According to historian Leon Rowland, the house was erected by carpenter Jonathan F. Pinkham (*Santa Cruz Sentinel*, June 11, 1944). It was torn down in 1944. A new building constructed on the site now houses the offices of the City of Santa Cruz Parks and Recreation Department.

(23) The architectural design of the **Civic Auditorium, at 307 Church Street,** is less successful that that of **Santa Cruz Fire Station No. 1,** located around the corner at **711 Center Street.**

The buildings are 1939-40 vintage from the hand of San Francisco architect Mark Daniels. One of the economies that was made in adopting the final plans for the auditorium was the elimination of a 109-foot tower with an open belvedere at the top. The style chosen was nominally early-California in order to fit in with the then recently completed City Hall, but the bulk of the auditorium effectively overwhelms the period details.

A June 21, 1919, *Santa Cruz Sentinel* article outlined the history of the **Walnut Avenue** area: "Sixty years ago where is now being laid the foundation for the Hihn [heirs'] (New Santa Cruz) Theatre at the present corner of Pacific and Walnut Avenues was a pond of water in winter and a spring in summer and an immense sycamore tree standing on the inner side of the depression, and beneath this mammoth native of the forest was a cider press. Many a pioneer crushed many an apple in this mill, gathered in this orchard and then went refreshed on his way, with not a word to say and not a cent to pay. . . .

"This orchard was set out by Isaac Williams, after whom Williams Landing, located up the coast, was named. It was among the first planted in California, about 1854. The orchard extended from Pacific Avenue to the base of the hill and was bounded on the south by Lincoln Street."

(24) The **City of Santa Cruz Fire Department's Administrative Building** at **230 Walnut Avenue** is about as close as architect William Wilson Wurster ever got to the Hollywood Regency style of architects like Douglas Honnold and George Vernon Russell. Only the slenderness of the pipe columns and the sleekness of the metal French doors hint at glamour. The surprise in this 1939 building is the circular entrance space. The building was originally the offices of Drs. Ambrose A. Cowden, Samuel B. Randall, and Alfred L. Phillips. It was completely restored and dedicated in 2001 for use by the City.

(25) 234 Walnut Avenue is a two-story Stick-Eastlake design. The pediment of the top gable is split by a square bay, bracketed out over the first story. The eaves, with their wide, evenly divided moldings, are the most distinctive feature of this house.

The L-shaped porch with its lathe-turned columns has been glassed-in at the side. Framing the interior of the entrance hall is a pair of arches filled in with ball-on-a-stick spindles on top of spiral columns with composite capitals. In 1896 the house had a new front added to it by druggist J. G. Tanner. The rear section was once the Albert Jones house, moved in the 1870s to make way for the Scott and Company livery stable on Pacific Avenue. Jones was a county sheriff and his home was located on the site of the Hagemann-McPherson building at Pacific and Soquel Avenues.

(26) To the west, at **240** and **244 Walnut Avenue,** are two story-and-a-half Eastlake cottages with central turrets constructed in 1892 by M. A. Reese. They have corner overhangs with pendants, stylized dentil-courses under the eaves, strip-like panel decoration around the windows, and shingled upper stories. 240 Walnut Avenue does not match its twin because of fire damage, according to area-resident Richard Cutts. The Triplett sisters, Anita and Pearl, descendants of the early California Pérez family, occupied 240 Walnut Avenue. Photographer M. A. Reese and his family lived at 244 Walnut Avenue.

(27) To the west of the twin cottages was a house built in 1885 for August Hihn and his bride, Grace Cooper Hihn. Torn down in 1965, the Stick-Eastlake house was designed by Charles Kaye.

If the building that is presently on the site has any relationship to its distinguished nineteenth-century neighbors, it has been carefully hidden. Fortunately, it is screened by a majestic row of redwoods reportedly planted by August Hihn.

Downtown, North of Lincoln

(26) Reese and Triplett Houses (*Museum of Art & History*)

(28) 516 Chestnut Street is a symmetrical story-and-a-half Stick-Eastlake house with large Eastlake brackets under the eaves, patterned shingling in the gable, and a modern front door.

A band of molding links the four windows in the second story, and one corner of the building is cut away, with half-timbering beneath it.

(29) 529 Chestnut Street is a magnificent two-and-a-half story Stick-Eastlake composition focused on a two-story, partially recessed, partially exterior porch. The entrance way is an 1880s take-off on classicism. The outward-curving central steps with balustrade and newel posts are all there, but the detail is composed of wooden cubes, spheres, and strips.

The interior retains its Eastlake mantels with their numerous shelves supported by small spindles, the sycamore-block entrance floor, lincrusta walton, and ceiling moldings originally bronzed in different hues.

The house was erected in 1888 for realtor Alfred Joseph Hinds by contractor W. J. Hinds. Santa Cruz architect John H. Williams did the design. The house is listed on the National Register of Historic Places.

(30) 511 Chestnut Street is a story-and-a-half cottage with primitive sawn-wood brackets in the gable, above a small pointed arch window.

(31) 304 Walnut Avenue is a large, simple, hipped-roof Queen Anne house with a two-story, semi-detached, circular bay topped by a dunce-cap roof. There is a dentil course and wide-spaced, oversize, incised brackets under the eaves. A large Bunya-Bunya tree, related to the monkey puzzle, grows at the corner of the lot. The house was built in 1893 for banker William Douglas Haslam and designed by Edward L. Van Cleeck.

(32) 316 Walnut Avenue closely resembles 315 Walnut Avenue, which is across the street. It has large, curved, Eastlake brackets at the corners, and patterned shingling in the top story. The front bay is crowned with a squeezed-pediment effect and has corner cut-aways. The hipped roof is interrupted by large and small gables. Above the slightly mansarded, corner-recessed porch is a band of paneling. The house was built by the F. A. Hihn Company in 1892 for local merchant A. Morey and sold a year later to the Palmer family.

(33) 322 Walnut Avenue is an unusual, steep-roofed, story-and-a-half Craftsman Shingle house. The Walnut Avenue facade is contained within a single pedimented gable; the attic is corbelled out flush with the surface of the eaves. The porch is supported by paired pillars, and there are simple brackets under the eaves and diamond paning in the upper sashes of the windows.

Downtown, North of Lincoln

(29) Hinds House (*Santa Cruz, Cal.: Illustrated in Photo-Gravure, 1894*)

(34) 315 Walnut Avenue is almost the twin to 316 Walnut Avenue, with some slight differences. The shingles in its gables are fish scale instead of polygonal, and there are barge boards as well.

(35) At **303 Walnut Avenue** is the 1927 **YWCA Building**, now the home of the **Walnut Avenue Women's Center**. A story-and-a-half building with hipped roof and small pane windows, it is built right up to the sidewalk. Mr. and Mrs. Salvatore P. and Frances Fachutar constructed it as a musical instrument shop and workshop. Fachutar also made perfume in the little building at the rear.

(36) Across the street on the southeast corner is the Cope house at **249 Walnut Avenue.** It was designed by William H. Burrows for F. A. Hihn as a wedding gift for his eldest daughter, Katherine. She received this Italianate house after her marriage to hardware merchant William T. Cope.

"The lower-floor windows have circular heads, upper-floor windows not over bay windows have segment heads. Composite style of architecture observed," noted an October 12, 1877, *Santa Cruz Sentinel* article at the time of the building's construction. "Were it all two stories it would be a model house" (*Santa Cruz Sentinel*, December 8, 1877).

Its low-pitched, hipped roof is broken by split-pedimented gables above slanted bays. The porch and glassed-in conservatory on the Walnut Avenue side have been removed.

(37) 241 Walnut Avenue is a one-story cottage with cornices matching those on the east side of the Cope house.

(38) 235 Walnut Avenue is a symmetrical one-story Italianate house of the 1870s.

(39) 231 Walnut Avenue is a Colonial Revival design house with hipped roof and wide, bracketed eaves. Colonial swags trim the entablature area above the recessed porch. The porch columns rest on a classical balustrade with curved piers.

(40) 219 Walnut Avenue is a raised-basement, story-and-a-half Queen Anne cottage punctuated by a corner turret. It is sheathed in bands of clapboarding, random fish-scale, and polygonal shingling divided by moldings. There is a Moorish-arched portico below the paneled gable. The front door is inset with a large panel of small beveled-glass panes and surrounded by matching transom and side lights. At the east side is a concrete threshold inscribed with the legend "Oldsmobile forever." It was built in 1895 for District Attorney Carl E. Lindsay.

Downtown, North of Lincoln

(40) Lindsay House *(Joe Michalak)*

(41) 215 Walnut Avenue is a raised-basement, late-Eastlake cottage. The double front door has a pair of half-circle windows, and there are chair-leg porch supports. Curved Eastlake brackets nestle under the eaves, and there is a sunburst of spindles in the random-shingled gable of the tall square bay.

A January 18, 1890, *Santa Cruz Weekly Surf* article describes the interior:

"The hall is ten feet square and forms a pretty little reception room. The floor is of end grain mosaic, blocks of end grain ash finely polished and set together artistically, the border showing a pattern in black walnut. The dado and frieze are a handsome pattern of lincrusta tinted in two tones of pearl grey. The walls and ceiling are in rough sand varnish painted in oil and of a pearl color which harmonizes with dado and frieze.

"The walls [in the front parlor] are tinted a pale olive color which is relieved by the gold and silver bronze of the front frieze of lincrusta. The box window is glazed with French plate and is separated from the room by an arch of Moorish fret-work. . . . From this arch are draped handsome curtains of India silk, while the inner curtains are of fine lace. The arch between the parlors is draped with a chenille portiere. The velvet carpet of the parlors is in colors which harmonize with the prevailing tones of the room, and the furniture is of cherry, upholstered in brocade.

"In the back parlor a fire place is framed in encaustic tiles showing a handsome pattern of cherubs and roses in relief, and above this is a mantel of Spanish cedar with a French plate mirror."

The house, built in 1890 for Frederick Otto Hihn and his wife, Minnie Chace Hihn, was designed by the local firm of Damkroeger and Saunders, and the woodwork, ceilings, and lincrusta were executed by J. Frank Carter. The exterior was originally painted two shades of grey with black trim..

(42) 205 and **209 Walnut Avenue** are two elaborately decorated Stick-Eastlake cottages originally part of a matching trio. Differing from its twin, 209 Walnut Avenue retains its original basement windows and steps.

The houses were built for John Brazer in 1884 from plans drawn by Emil John. The third house, once situated at the corner, was ten feet wider than the other two.

(43) At the southeast corner of **Walnut Avenue** and **Center Street** was the Gothic style **First Baptist Church,** moved here from upper Locust Street in 1887. It had been built by John Morrow in 1867 on a site now occupied by the twin houses at 433 and 435 Locust Street on Mission Terrace (see Chapter 4, #46). In 1910 the church was completely remodeled in the Mission style. It was torn down in 1965, along with its annex at 177 Walnut Avenue.

(44) At the northeast corner of **Center** and **Lincoln Streets** was the **First Christian Church,** built in 1896 and demolished in 1956. A mixture of Shingle and Colonial Revival styles, it was a boxy, steep-roofed church with a corner tower and a huge Palladian window. The random-shingled building incorporated an existing small building which had been a schoolhouse and later a synagogue.

Lincoln Street was first named Trust Street, opened by baker Henry Andrew Trust at the time he built his first house on property east of Calvary Episcopal Church. Both he and his wife, Christina, were natives of Germany.

(45) 208 Lincoln Street is a story-and-a-half house of the 1870s, displaying a not uncommon mixture of Greek Revival and Italianate influences. It was the childhood home of actress ZaSu Pitts (1894-1963).

Downtown, North of Lincoln

(43) First Baptist Church (*Santa Cruz, Cal.: Illustrated in Photo-Gravure, 1894*)

(44) First Christian Church
(Special Collections, University Library, University of California, Santa Cruz)

(46) At **532 Center Street** is **Calvary Episcopal Church**, the oldest church building in the city of Santa Cruz. The church, established in 1862, had no building of its own at first and the congregation had to meet in the upstairs room of the Flatiron Building, which then housed the county courthouse. Later they convened in the Temperance Hall on Mission Street. The peripatetic flock then moved to an "old, flea-infested school house," vacated shortly before by the Methodists, a building which still stands, much remodeled, at 123 Green Street.

A permanent home was finally secured when Mrs. Joseph Boston, a driving force in the creation of the church, donated land for a building.

"The design of the church is a modification of the plan in *Upjohn's Rural Architecture,*" the *Pajaro Times* reported in 1864. Richard Upjohn, architect of New York's well-known Trinity Presbyterian Church, included plans for a small mission church, a chapel, a parsonage, and a schoolhouse in his book; plans were intended to provide a simple, low-cost (approximately $3,000) church for a small parish. Calvary Episcopal resembles several small churches designed by Upjohn in the 1840s and '50s. The similarity is especially apparent in the

(46) Calvary Episcopal Church, left, and First Congregational Church, right (*Santa Cruz, Cal.: Illustrated in Photo-Gravure, 1894*)

diaphragm arch between the nave and the apse, the dark wooden trusses, and the light-toned plastered walls.

The cornerstone was laid June 29, 1864, and the first services were held January 8, 1865, in the still unplastered, windowless church. The November 16, 1867, *Santa Cruz Sentinel* appraised the church as "a beautiful and substantial edifice of wood built upon a firm foundation of brick. The style is Gothic of the early English period. The sections of the roof divide the nave into four bays of sixteen feet each. The sides between the posts are plastered and painted a delicate color of ochre, each bay having a window nine feet in length.

"The chancel, separated from the nave by a lofty gothic arch, is apsidal in form, 21 x 20 feet in depth; the walls are pierced by six lancet windows filled with rich colored glass, containing the principal Christian emblems. The West Gable has a beautiful clustered window of three lights headed by a trefoil, three feet in diameter soon to be filled with glass of exquisite design and workmanship from the establishment of Henry Sharpe of New York, who furnished the windows for the whole church."

More stained-glass windows were subsequently installed, and a belfry was added in 1874. The other church buildings are twentieth century.

(47) On the southwest corner of **Lincoln** and **Center Streets**, where a parking lot exists today, was the second building of the **First Congregational Church,** erected in 1890. Architect Warren H. Hayes of Minneapolis was responsible for the Richardsonian Romanesque design in brick and stone. LeBaron R. Olive was the supervising architect and A. L. Whitney the contractor.

Hayes described the building in a *Santa Cruz Sentinel*, May 20, 1890, interview: "The auditorium ceiling is to be redwood timber work, oil finish, the walls plastered, with redwood joinery and furniture.... In exterior design the building is modern Romanesque, a combination of stone and timbered and shingled work. The main and more prominent features of the exterior are the corner tower, 16 feet square and 96 feet high with open belfry and on either street front of the building the large semi-circular window. . . these with the high-pitched roof, bays, gables, etc. forming a picturesque and pleasing composition quite different from the architecture which we are accustomed to see in church buildings." Indeed, this design was unusually sophisticated for Santa Cruz. The building was torn down in 1958, when the First Congregational Church moved into its new location at 900 High Street (see Chapter 4, #79).

(48) At **317-321** and **323 Lincoln Street** is **Lincoln Court,** a prime example of a California Bungalow court surrounding a green, leafy city oasis. It was built in 1905-20 by pioneer merchant Morris Abrams and is currently under the care of ubiquitous owner/architect Michael O'Hearn.

Downtown, North of Lincoln

(49) At **329 Lincoln Street** is the George Hastings home, built in 1884 and greatly remodeled. From 1890 to 1907, Professor Hastings organized and conducted the Santa Cruz Beach Band. He had first seen Santa Cruz when he was leader of the Montgomery Queen Circus Band. Liking what he saw, he returned to stay, becoming director of an orchestra of fifty or more pieces and an even larger Brownie Orchestra of children. Most of the players in the orchestra were his pupils, and his band played at all the performances at the Opera House and for dances and parades.

(50) **413 Lincoln Street** can claim an unusual, if grisly, distinction. "In the late seventies in this yard were constructed the last gallows used here for hanging a prisoner" (Ernest Otto, *Santa Cruz Sentinel*, March 1, 1942).

(51) **419 Lincoln Street** is a raised-basement cottage with bowler-hatted round bay, narrow clapboarding, and a pedimented central porch supported by raised columns. In the left side of the Lincoln Street facade is a vent detailed as pilaster-supported arches.

(52) The five row houses at **412, 414, 416, 418,** and **420 Lincoln Street** were constructed about 1894 for William T. Cope. The only nineteenth-century row in town, they show an urban building form designed to fit the maximum number of single-family residences together on the minimum of land. Outside of San Francisco, row houses were little used in California, with its formerly wide-open spaces and preference for low-density, sprawling cities.

The basic pattern of each is the same, while the detail differs from house to house.

An unusual feature the houses share in common is the raised stoop, another eastern metropolitan feature. It was not until the construction of UCSC's Kresge College, eighty years later, that stoops were again employed in Santa Cruz.

The row houses were saved from demolition in 1973 by Chuck and Esther Abbott and are listed on the National Register of Historic Places.

(53) **410 Lincoln Street** is a simple saltbox-shaped cottage of the late 1860s or early 1870s. The delicately detailed porch has flattened Tudor arches.

(52) Cope Row Houses *(Carolyn Swift)*

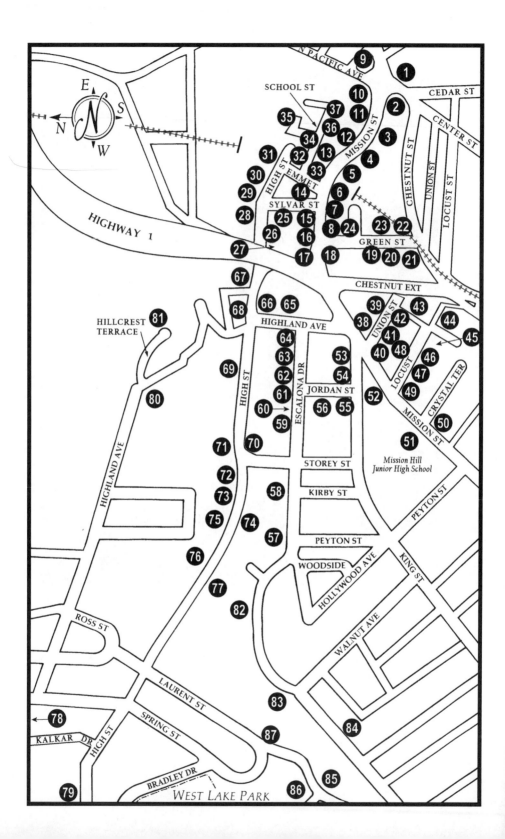

Chapter Four

Mission Hill

In this chapter, Mission Hill is defined as the area bordering Mission Street from its beginning at Pacific Avenue to Peyton Street and including the neighborhoods on the north from High Street and upper Highland Avenue to Mission Hill terrace on the south. Mission Street is one of the oldest streets in the city. It was originally the public road that ran from the Mission Santa Cruz up the coast.

(1) The southeast corner of **Center** and **Mission Streets** was the location of the James G. T. Dunleavy home, later occupied by the Imus family. It was here that the Dunleavys and Elihu Anthony ate the goose they had shot on Locust Street for Christmas dinner in 1847. Dunleavy owned sixty acres extending west from Pacific Avenue to the bluff and south from Mission Hill to Maple Street.

(2) On the opposite corner was the blacksmith shop of William T. Hunter. "It was a rough board-and-batten building with a shake roof, whose rafters were blackened by the smoke from the forges. An outside billboard bore circus and opera posters," wrote Ernest Otto (*Santa Cruz Sentinel*, June 24, 1951).

Hunter's wife was Kate Imus, a member of the Hiram A. Imus Jr. family, who crossed the plains from Illinois, arriving in Santa Cruz in 1850. A later building on the site was a saloon constructed by Antone Cristofanini, after a LeBaron Olive design of 1892. It was replaced by a service station, which in turn was supplanted by a building constructed in 1978.

(3) Further up the hill was the stucco dwelling of Isaac Pierce, built in 1859. Ernest Otto believed it to be the first stucco dwelling in Santa Cruz.

(4) On the brow of the hill is the site of the **Mission Hill Grammar School**, a raised-basement, three-story Italianate structure crowned with a mansard roof. It was erected in 1875 to relieve overcrowded Santa Cruz schools. The original Greek Revival style schoolhouse of 1857, on the same site, had been expanded to three rooms, but it was still much too small for the needs of the growing district.

Mission Hill, view south from Highland Avenue, 1893 *(Carolyn Swift Collection)*

The school property was enlarged through the generosity of London Nelson, a former slave, who was a cobbler and farmer. Even though he could not read or write, his concern for children's education prompted him to will the proceeds from his estate to the school district.

The 1875 building, designed by Levi Goodrich, had a central tower above a pedimented gable, quoining, paired brackets under the cornice, and a Doric-columned, pedimented entrance, unusual for Santa Cruz but often seen in San Francisco.

The mansarded third floor housed the high school before it moved to its own building on Walnut Avenue in 1894. The 1906 earthquake left the schoolhouse shaky and necessitated the removal of the third floor; the entire building was torn down in 1930. The stone steps and retaining wall from the school remain.

(5) 155-157 Mission Street is the site of one of the earliest brick buildings in Santa Cruz, along with the Flatiron Building. It was constructed in 1860 for James Leslie, and it housed a general store. In 1886 it was remodeled with a tower and a battlement on top of the building and a wooden addition in the rear (*Santa Cruz Sentinel, December 29, 1886*).

A year later Frank Alzina, son of pioneer Francisco Alzina, opened a meat, fish, and vegetable market in the lower floor of the building and took up residence with his bride, Lora Effey, on the second story. The building was demolished as a result of damage from the 1989 earthquake.

(6) 207 Mission Street is a spectacular two-story Stick Villa style house with attic. Stick-Eastlake ornament and stylization are applied to Italian Villa form and detail in this hybrid style.

The three-and-a-half-story tower has tiny dormer windows in its mansard roof. At the top of the first story is a continuous cornice, and there is an entablature above the second. Brackets are placed in the gables, and there is much paneling and strip-defined pilasters in the bays.

(6) Davis House *(Museum of Art & History)*

The proportions and detailing of the house have been scaled to make the building appear taller than it actually is, for the second and third stories are progressively shorter than the first.

The interior retains its original wood shutters and cast-iron, tole fireplaces. With a feather, the iron was painted in swirling patterns duplicating those of marble. Another bit of elegant fakery is the imitation oak graining on the redwood doors. In the kitchen door is a panel of red glass patterned with small, opaque, white stars.

The outstanding feature of the interior is the ceiling of the living and dining rooms, painted with trompe l'oeil paneling and designs. Storks adorn the green-and-pink living room ceiling, and cupids run riot in the dining room. One of the cupids is pictured in a snail-drawn chariot, lashing his steed onward; another panel depicts a wolf devouring a lamb.

The house was built in 1883-86 for carpenter-builder Calvin W. Davis. Because of its complexity and sophistication, the design is attributed to Calvin's brother, architect Charles Wellington Davis.

(7) 211 Mission Street is a simple hipped-roof house with cornices matching those of the neighboring Davis house. It was constructed in 1886 as the parsonage for the First Methodist Church, once located next door at the corner. The plan was drawn by Calvin W. Davis and J. S. McPheters.

(8) 217 Mission Street is a Colonial Revival/Queen Anne house. The facade consists of a tower and large square bay tied together with a curving, delicately railed porch. The tower is round at the first story, polygonal at the second, and round again at the dunce-cap roof.

This was the home of Louis Wessendorf and his wife, Katherine Dreher, the daughter of pioneer John Dreher. The house was erected in 1904-5 and is attributed to Edward Van Cleeck. Wessendorf was a German-born upholsterer who went to work in George Staffler's furniture and undertaking parlor, eventually taking over the business, which became Wessendorf mortuary.

The Wessendorf house stands on the site of the first two buildings of the First Methodist Church. The original church was a simple twenty-by-thirty-foot structure erected in 1850; it also doubled as a schoolroom. In 1863 an elegant Greek Revival church replaced the old structure, which was moved to 123 Green Street. There it was converted into a home by carpenter W. W. Reynolds.

In 1890 the Methodists moved from the hilltop to a site on the flat below, purchasing the old Congregational Church building on Church Street. The building they left behind was sold to Holy Cross Church in 1902 and moved to High Street, where it became Montgomery Hall and the gymnasium for the Christian Brothers School.

(9) At the junction of **N. Pacific Avenue, Water Street,** and **Mission Street** were the home, blacksmith shop, and store of pioneer blacksmith, merchant, and Methodist preacher Elihu Anthony.

(9) Anthony Block *(Museum of Art & History)*

The blacksmith shop and store were "one-story high with hewn sills, posts, joists and rafters; the north end of the building was enclosed with shakes and the front with boards.... At the time the building was finished only a few small shanties were located under the hill, the main portion of the town being around the Upper Plaza and along the Coast Road, so that the Anthony building may be considered the pioneer in the now principal business portion of the thriving town of Santa Cruz.... In the winter of 1849 many of the lucky miners wintered in Santa Cruz, and their depot for trade and place of deposit was 'Anthony's store', where their 'dust' was stored, in buckskin bags, with only the name and weight, marked on a tag, for security, or to guarantee a safe return to the owner. ... In later years the building was occupied by other parties, and the first post office and telegraph office were in the building" (*Santa Cruz Sentinel*, April 23, 1870).

Anthony tore down the pioneer landmark in 1870 and replaced it with a two-story, Italianate frame building. On the second floor was a hall fitted out for socials and concerts, which became a rooming house after the Bernheim Building, with its second floor hall, was constructed. The first floor of the Anthony Building held the Moulton and Bias grocery store, a bakery, drugstore, restaurant, and, for a time, Irwin's Nickelodeon.

In 1909 the building was cut in half and moved to a location near the corner of Water and Bulkhead Streets, where it became the Roma Hotel (*Santa Cruz Sentinel*, January 18, 1942). It was razed about 1934.

Next door to the west was Anthony's first home, from which he moved to his subsequent home on the Mission Hill bluff.

Elihu Anthony had arrived in Santa Cruz in late December 1847. "That year [1848] I built a blacksmith shop on the corner of Water street and the Lower Plaza, and bought some goods which I put into the shop. I made bridle bits, spurs, etc., and when gold was discovered I made 7 1/4 dozen picks and sent them to the mines to be sold; this was in '48. I made them of ship bolts which I flattened. They were the first picks taken to the mines. I sent them to Tom Fallon, who took them to the Georgetown diggings. They realized three ounces of gold dust apiece" (Anthony's reminiscences, *Santa Cruz Sentinel*, January 9, 1885). Outside of San Francisco, this foundry was the first one in California.

Anthony's memoirs also include this description of the early development of Santa Cruz:

"There was great opposition to having the town located where it now is. In fact, the idea was laughed at. I purchased the tract of land extending from Neary's lot, on Mission Street [just north of its intersection with Center Street] to Foster & Lake's blacksmith shop [near the intersection of Cooper and Front Streets. The property was bordered on the south by what are now Mission and Front Streets, included part of the tableland on the bluff, and was bounded on the north by the San Lorenzo River.] The residents of the Upper Plaza thought the bottom land was worthless, and I secured it for a mere song—I think just by paying three dollars and sixty-two and a-half cents for filing the papers with Alcalde Blackburn. After the mining excitement had cooled down the country began to fill up, and I readily disposed of the lots."

(10) Across N. Pacific Avenue, then a section of River Street, was the **St. Charles Hotel**, a three-story mansarded structure.

"It was erected in 1867 as a two-story building by William Anthony, a cousin of Elihu. William leased part of his space to Field & Brown for their general store, used part of the ground floor for his own hardware establishment and had a tinsmith shop upstairs" (*Santa Cruz Sentinel*, May 9, 1948).

In 1873 the building was remodeled with a mansard-roofed third story and became the St. Charles Hotel. Charles W. Davis was the architect and John Morrow the contractor. The result was a bracketed Italianate structure with quoining, siding scored to resemble stone, and a porch on two sides, extending out to the street.

The hotel was popular with the actors of theatrical troupes playing in Santa Cruz. It was known as the Waverly at the time it burned in 1919.

(4, 10, 11, and 12) View up Mission Hill. The St. Charles Hotel (10) occupies the foreground, just beyond is the Diesing Brewery (11). At the brow of the hill on the right is Temperance Hall (12) and on the left is the Mission Hill School (4). All the buildings in this picture are gone.

(Special Collections, University Library, University of California, Santa Cruz)

(11) A little further up Mission Street Hill was the **Otto Diesing Brewery**, a Greek Revival structure with a pedimented gable and corner pilasters. It was built by J. D. Bagnall in the 1850s (Ernest Otto, *Santa Cruz Sentinel*, December 19, 1948).

(12) West of the brewery was **Temperance Hall,** dedicated in 1861. This Greek Revival building had a two-story porch supported by pillars and was topped by a cupola. The building was moved to Bulkhead Street in 1893, according to the *Santa Cruz Surf*, May 15, 1893. It was demolished in 1930.

(13) West of Temperance Hall stood the home of William Thompson, also known as William Buckle. Thompson was an early-day lumberman who was granted Rancho la Carbonera, north of Santa Cruz on the east side of the river, in 1838. He was one of the first permanent Anglo settlers in Santa Cruz, having arrived by ship in 1822.

His brother, Samuel, was also an early settler in Santa Cruz. He had set out to find William, who had been missing from home for some years. "Though he did not know where on the globe he might be if still alive yet he thought he could go to sea and make voyages to different parts and somewhere fall in with him, or hear of him" (Elliott's 1879 *Santa Cruz County*). Arriving in Santa Cruz after an unknown number of voyages in search of his brother, he inquired of a captain standing on the beach if his brother was among the captain's crew. The captain suggested he check the men loading hides on the beach. The first man he met was his brother William. According to historian Leon Rowland in his *Annals of Santa Cruz,* "There is some evidence but no proof" that the Buckle (Thompson) brothers were among four Santa Cruzans who had been "soldier-sailors in the privateering fleet of Lord Cochrane, the British adventurer who helped South American countries win their independence."

Thompson's property later became part of the **Sisters of Charity School,** which was established in 1862 in the old Eagle Hotel building on School and Emmet Streets.

An Italianate building had been erected in 1869, but the more prominent of the Sisters' buildings was the large three-story building erected in 1890 in the Stick-Italianate style. It had a square, central tower with pointed roof, a bracketed cornice, and a hipped roof. Thomas J. Welsh was the architect.

The buildings were abandoned in 1941 and torn down three years later to help satisfy the strong demand for building materials during World War II. Only the rock retaining-wall, constructed in 1884, remains.

(14) Bounded by Sylvar, Emmet, Mission, and High Streets is the **Plaza Municipal Park**, also known as the Upper Plaza. It was originally the Mission quadrangle.

An 1854 map drawn for Elihu Anthony depicts Mission buildings around three sides of the quadrangle, with the road later named Mission Street descending the bluff in an S-curve to what became the Lower Plaza.

There were originally no roads around the perimeter of this trapezoidal space, for it was just an unfenced area between buildings. In the early days, quarreling couples were placed in stocks on the Upper Plaza to be jeered at by crowds.

The plaza seems always to have been thought of as public ground. In June 1866 a squatter attempted to homestead part of the plaza by fencing off a plot and erecting a house on it. During the night notices appeared and an indignant citizenry gathered and tore down the fence and dwelling. The victory was celebrated with a bonfire fed by the remains of the short-lived improvements.

In February 1870 what was probably the first meeting concerning the improvement of the plaza was held. At the time the park was described as "a common that is a camping-ground of sick swine, sore-backed horses and braying asses."

It was proposed at the meeting "to lay the plaza out with a street on either side, of fifty feet width, and the park to be fenced with a good and substantial fence, graded, and then to be set out, at regulated distances, to ornamental and shade-trees" (*Santa Cruz Sentinel*, March 5, 1870). The little stream of water, which the Mission fathers had diverted from the Tres Ojos de Agua so that it flowed across the north end of the plaza as the Mission supply, was undergrounded in a flume.

Surveyor Thomas Wright, along with R. C. Kirby and Colonel Albert Heath, laid out the plan for the park. The work was financed by individual contributions, two benefit balls, and possibly the proceeds of a special tax.

By March 1873 the picket fence around the park was nearing completion and trees were being set out under the direction of Thomas Wright. French gardener Albert Routier supervised planting of the evergreens near the outer walks.

Another period of improvement for the plaza occurred between 1885-87. Louis Doeltz, later the gardener at the Phelan estate, built a rockery around the fountain in 1885. Prominent landscape designer Rudolph Ulrich laid out new paths in 1887.

"On the fountain are four large rock vases, which will hold palm trees. A fine piece of rock work is a small rock drinking-fountain which faces Mission Street. Twelve Linden trees have been set out and look well. These trees are popular in Berlin, Germany, and it is the delight of hale old Emperor Wilhelm to sit under der Linden" (1887 *Santa Cruz Sentinel*).

In 1928 the plans for the Upper Plaza, as well as for the East Side Library Park, were reviewed by John McLaren, the man responsible for completing San Francisco's Golden Gate Park.

Mission Hill

(15) Willey House *(Joe Michalak)*

(15) 105 Sylvar Street is a two-and-a-half-story Eastlake house. The basic vertical lines of the house itself contrast with the horizontal lines of the porch, which surrounds it on three sides.

Although the entire porch looks as though it were part of the original plan, [the south-facing portion] was constructed some twenty years after the house was built, designed to match the existing east-facing porch and the porticos.

The hipped roof is interrupted by gables and dormers of various sizes, and there is a wide band of patterned shingling below the eaves. The porch has Chinese railing supporting the multiple lathe-turned columns and the large sawn-wood brackets.

An unusual detail is the large square attic dormer set flush with the eaves and curved out over the second story, its underside embellished with carved anemones and acanthus foliage.

The entryway is lighted by a large, geometric-and-floral-pattern, stained-glass window, and there are stained-glass panels of sea-shell design in the living room. The wainscotted dining-room has a mirrored, bracketed, spindle-supported sideboard, matching pass-through, and a mirrored fireplace mantelpiece with William Morris-like tiles depicting medieval scenes.

This ten-room house was begun in April 1887 for Henry Willey at a cost of $5,000. The plans came from Syracuse, New York.

Willey was a hardware merchant who came to Santa Cruz from Chicago after the Great Fire of 1871 had destroyed his prospects for advancement there. He operated his hardware store in the DeLamater block on Pacific Avenue and was the first president of the People's Bank. Willey owned the house until 1926. From 1943 to 1954 it was a convent for the nuns who taught at Holy Cross School.

(16) 214 and **218 Mission Street** are two clapboarded, story-and-a-half cottages built for Louis Schwartz in 1867. They have Chinese-railed porches across the front and sawn-wood brackets in their gables.

(17) Schwartz House *(Joe Michalak)*

(17) Schwartz lived next door, to the west, in the symmetrical, clapboarded, story-and-a-half house at **222 Mission Street**. The main feature of the design is a steep central gable, containing a pedimented window inset with carving, and a crisp sawn-wood Gothic bargeboard. The original portico has been removed. The front door is similar to that of 207 Mission Street, and there are box cornices above the windows.

Schwartz was a native of Schildberg, Prussia, who had lived in London, New York, and San Francisco. At one time or another, he was a baker, made mackintoshes, and worked in a clothing store.

He arrived in California with seven dollars to his name; only a year later he was able to open a general merchandise store, Schwartz & Brownstone, in the Werner building on Pacific Avenue. In the late 1860s, real estate, lumber, and mercantile interests in San Luis Obispo County became his chief investments, and he closed his Santa Cruz store. He later returned to active participation in Santa Cruz business life, with interests in the County Bank and in his son's dry-goods store, the Arcade.

(18) Downey Apartments *(Joe Michalak)*

(18) 303-307 Mission Street is the Downey Apartments, a two-story, hipped-roof Colonial Revival-style apartment house, ca. 1905-1910, built for William G. and Anna Downey. Sheathed in narrow clapboard, it has simple brackets under the eaves. The partially recessed central porch has a pedimented gable finished with fish-scale shingles. There are grooved pilasters with composite capitals. Matching columns support the two-story porch. Edward Van Cleeck might have been its architect.

Green Street dates from mission days, according to Ernest Otto, and was used for hauling timber down to the beach. Green and Potrero Streets line up and may well have been connected as a through street from one side of the bluff to the other. Probably nameless in those days, it was called the "church street" at the time the Methodist church was built on the corner.

(19) 127 Green Street is a clapboarded, story-and-a-half house with central gable and a classically balustraded porch supported by split pilasters. This house was probably erected in the late 1860s for painter Otis A. and Matilda Ann (Hecox) Longley. Longley had purchased the property, which extended from Mission Street to the bottom of the hill, from the Methodist Church in 1864.

(20) Reynolds House *(Joe Michalak)*

(20) 123 Green Street is a square-fronted, two-story Italianate with low hipped roof. A sawn-wood balustrade of overlapping circles tops the arched porch. The entrance stairway is bordered by a classical balustrade ending in large newel posts. At the south side are a Palladian window and two-story slanted bay with a squeezed pediment cornice. On entering, one is immediately struck by the

Mission Hill

disproportionately large size of the Colonial Revival main stairway, which dominates the parlor like a thrust stage. Notable features of the interior include the wainscotted dining room, Italianate cast-iron fireplace, and the plaster women in the arches of the bay windows.

The house, the first building constructed for a Protestant church in Santa Cruz, was built in 1850 for the Methodists. Originally located at the northeast corner of Green and Mission Streets, it was purchased from the Methodists by William Woolsey Reynolds in 1864 and moved to its present site. It had already been replaced by a larger church in 1863.

Reynolds crossed the plains from Tennessee to California at age seventeen with his father. He "made the entire distance on foot with the exception of three days when he was obliged to ride on account of sickness" (Ed Martin's 1911 *History of Santa Cruz County*). His mother died en route and his party of travelers was in constant danger from Indian attack. A shot fired by an Indian left a lifelong scar on his leg.

After reaching California, father and son Reynolds went to the Mother Lode country to mine. Young Reynolds had been trained as a carpenter and supplemented his mining income by building sluiceways and flumes for other miners.

Arriving in Santa Cruz in 1856, he began his practice as a carpenter and builder "in earnest." For a two-year period he went south to Mexico and erected the old customhouse at Ensenada.

Three years after Reynolds bought 123 Green Street and converted it into a residence for his new bride, Mary Simpson, he sold it to lumberman James Dougherty.

In the mid-1880s the house was purchased by druggist John J. Hug. He doubled the size of the house in 1885 and added the porch and bay windows. Carpenter John S. McPheters supervised the improvements. Another house on the property was sold to Henry G. Insel, who moved it to Washington Street, allowing Hug to expand the gardens around the house.

T. W. Kelly, owner of the Racquet Store on Pacific Avenue, was the next major owner, purchasing the property in the 1890s. He is responsible for the Colonial Revival style alterations, such as the Palladian window.

This property passed through several owners, until it was purchased as a condemned house by Ed and Doni Tunheim in 1964. Among the earliest historic preservationists in the city, the Tunheims carefully restored the interior and exterior of their home. Doni's bold and creative talent as a colorist started the Santa Cruz "Victorian Painted Ladies" trend that continues to enliven the cityscape.

(21) Next door to 123 Green Street was the story-and-a-half home of butcher Wesley P. Young, designed and built by John B. Perry, in 1870.

"There is an abundance of flowers, fountains, croquet grounds, and everything desirable for a pleasant home," approvingly noted Elliott's 1879 *Santa Cruz County.*

The house burned down in the 1920s, but part of the pattern of the paths remains in the circular drive on the property.

(22) 102 Green Street is the site of the two-story, cube-shaped house, with hipped roof and quoining, built for Dr. C. L. Anderson in 1867 by John B. Perry. The stone retaining wall and picket fence remain. The house was torn down about 1950.

Anderson was a physician with an active interest in the natural sciences, particularly geology and botany. He contributed material to Elliott's 1879 *Santa Cruz County*, to Phil Francis's 1896 *Beautiful Santa Cruz County*, and to Harrison's 1892 *History of Santa Cruz County.*

(23) W. P. Young's house (#21) was once occupied by the Leask family, who later moved across the street to **120 Green Street.** The two-story, red-tile-roofed Samuel Leask house was designed by architect William H. Weeks and built in 1922-23. There is curbing under the eaves, and a continuous molding marks the division between the first and second stories. The two sets of triple windows on the ground floor are set in shallow arches with spiral columns. The recessed main entrance is flanked by elongated pilasters supporting an entablature with shield. The design is a subdued version of the Mediterranean Revival, the style so skillfully handled by southern California architects during this period. This has been the home for four generations of the Leask family, who owned Leask's department store on Pacific Avenue.

(24) 134 Green Street is a Bungalow-style house built for Lester and Catherine Wessendorf, ca. 1911. It is set in a shady, manicured garden and bordered by a row of close-clipped sycamore trees along Green Street. Present are the wide eaves, brackets, river-stone chimney, shingling, and clapboarding typical of the style.

(25) 109 Sylvar Street is a clapboarded saltbox of the 1850s, constructed with hand-split lath. Customarily referred to as the oldest frame house in Santa Cruz, it was constructed ca. 1850 by Francisco Alzina and replaced the adobe home of his Gonzales in-laws.

Mission Hill

(23) Leask House *(Joe Michalak)*

(25) Alzina House *(Museum of Art & History)*

"From the time of his arrival here until his death in 1887 he was one of the county's most prominent citizens, first sheriff under state government; prior to the civil war frequently mentioned as a democratic party candidate. He had refused employment on the plantation of Senator John C. Calhoun because of his dislike of slavery and he seems to have broken away from that party at the outbreak of hostilities." Alzina had been born on the island of Minorca, and had stowed away on the ship the *USS Constitution,* when it was in Barcelona harbor, in order to avoid the Spanish military draft (Centennial edition of *Riptide,* October 19, 1950).

In 1848 he married Maria Carlota Gonzales, daughter of Juan Gonzales. The lumber to build the house may have come from Gonzales's ranch up the coast.

(26) 209 High Street has a two-story porch combining lathe-turned columns with a classical balustrade. A new addition has been built below the dormer window. The building originally stood at the southwest corner of High and Sylvar Streets and was constructed in 1872 as the saloon and residence of Jackson Sylvar. It was a simple false-fronted story-and-a-half structure set flush with the sidewalk and ornamented with a balcony across the front. In the gardens Sylvar set out one hundred deciduous and evergreen shade and ornamental trees and installed two fountains.

Sylvar, a native of the Azores, had operated a restaurant and saloon downtown for a time. Perhaps the reason for his location on the Upper Plaza was the proximity to the old stone jail on High Street, for Sylvar became the jailer in 1872.

In 1888 the property was purchased by Oliver H. Bliss of Los Angeles. He remodeled it extensively, removing the false front, adding to the double porch, and enlarging the building.

(27) 215 High Street is a simple saltbox with a delicate spindle railing above the porch. The gables were added sometime after the house was built. It is possible that this is one of the former James Leslie buildings, once located at the corner of Mission and Emmet Streets and moved by Sylvar to his High Street property, where it was fitted up for two residences.

(28) To the west of the Holy Cross Church stood a succession of rectories, the most noteworthy being Edward Van Cleeck's of 1903, torn down in 1964 for the present structure. The second story of this Colonial Revival house was shingled, and the first story was finished in narrow siding. It had a Palladian window in the pedimented attic gable, a corner turret, and a pillar-supported entrance porch topped by a balustrade.

Mission Hill

(29) West of the present church was the second **Catholic Church** building, constructed in 1857 after the partial collapse of the adobe Mission chapel earlier that year. The original plan, designed by architects Waters & Beck, put "four large Gothic windows on each side and two in front; also a large entrance door, all of which will be trimmed with Gothic molding. The roof will be adorned with a belfry of strictly Gothic structure, to contain five bells" (*Pacific Sentinel*, May 23, 1857). A forty-foot tower on each side was added in 1864, and a wide platform and steps were built in 1873. Additional remodeling was carried out in 1877. The building was torn down in 1898, nine years after it was last used as a church.

(30) At **126 High Street** is **Holy Cross Catholic Church**, a landmark because of its hilltop site and tall, whitewashed spire. Designed by San Francisco architect Thomas J. Welsh, it was constructed on the site of the Mission chapel and graveyard.

The first Mission, dedicated on September 26, 1791, was a primitive complex of thatched buildings located about five hundred yards from the San Lorenzo River. The first site was located on the flatland below the Mission Hill bluff and was vulnerable to flooding. The Mission was moved from this perilous place to the bluff, and a new chapel was dedicated there on May 10, 1794, on the site now occupied by Holy Cross Church. After the chapel dedication, a mill, a two-story granary, and a house for looms were built. The mill, located on Laurel Street near California Avenue, was grinding corn by 1796. Three years later the mill was wrecked by a violent storm, as were several other Mission structures.

It seems that the builders were unfamiliar with how to construct adobe buildings to survive wet winters, for the Mission structures continuously fell prey to the elements. The church building itself was badly damaged by rains in 1797, only three years after its completion. By the time the heavy rains of 1824 caused new damages, there were no laborers left to make the needed repairs.

Ten years after secularization in 1833-34, the Mission was abandoned by Father Antonio Suárez del Real in 1843, becoming simply a church. Only the ravages of time and the weather were needed to erase the physical remains of the Mission. Water-logged subsurface soil had already collapsed some of the adobe walls during the wet winter of 1840.

The Mission chapel did not survive long enough for its appearance to be recorded in a photograph or in a painting known to be an accurate representation. Old newspaper descriptions provide our only picture of the structure.

"...The walls were double-tier of adobes; ...The front was cut-stone ornamented elaborately with suitable designs, also the same was on the arch of the sanctuary; the building was provided with sufficient doors and iron locks (no other doors at that time having iron locks, hinges or other fastenings); the

(29 and 30) Holy Cross Church building of 1857 on left; present Holy Cross Church building of 1889 on right *(Santa Cruz, Cal.: Illustrated in Photo-Gravure, 1894)*

(29 and 30) Holy Cross Church building of 1857 with 1891 arches *(Santa Cruz, Cal.: Illustrated in Photo-Gravure, 1894)*

choir gallery was erected inside, over the entrance of the church…." (*Santa Cruz Sentinel*, August 12, 1865).

"The [church's] front was flanked by a massive tower on each side; the walls were lofty, and the building spacious. The sides and ceiling were painted in fresco [in geometric designs of reddish color], and the colors are yet as bright and vivid as when first laid on, although exposed for years to the wear of the elements…A painting covered the whole rear side of the building, from which the mild faces of cherubs peered forth from a dim cloud of glory" (*Santa Cruz Sentinel*, September 28, 1860).

A series of three earthquakes on the morning of January 9, 1857, combined with a wet subsurface, was probably responsible for the partial collapse of the church and complete collapse of its tower on February 16 of the same year. After this disaster a new wooden church was built to the west of the adobe church. What was left of the adobe was given a new front of board siding and a pitched shingled roof. The remaining portion of the church had been the altar room and a room used for teaching music. It was converted into a schoolroom in 1861 and later used as a storeroom and stable. In July 1885 it was demolished to make way for the present Holy Cross Church.

The new church was described in a *Santa Cruz Sentinel* (February 18, 1885) article: "From the tower a wooden spire of octagonal form will rise 64 feet, making the height from the ground 149 feet. The walls of the tower and main building are to be constructed with buttresses to receive the thrust of the roof trusses which are six in number, with one-half trusses next to the chancel arch and tower walls, the buttresses at the four corners rising above the roof and crowned with pinnacles. Over the chancel and sacristy the roof will be slightly octagonal in shape, and of a lesser height than the main building. Inside the front of the church is a gallery. The style of architecture is English Gothic, but will be carried out with due regard to economy and simplicity."

When the church was completed, the *Santa Cruz Sentinel* (September 14, 1889) commented on the interior: "On either side of the high altars are two large statues, one representing the 'Sacred Heart of our Lord,' and the other the 'Sacred Heart of the Blessed Virgin'….Over the high altar is the grand figure of the crucifixion which was formerly brought from Spain for the old church by Father Adam."

In between the ceiling trusses are painted, eye-shaped panels portraying the disciples. They are surrounded by yellow-tinted foliage patterns, which are in turn contained by trompe-l'oeil painted beams and tracery. There is much stenciling in brown, green, and gold tones on the walls. Along the ridge beam of the ceiling are bands of gold and quatrefoils on brilliant red and green backgrounds.

The granite, triple memorial-arch, with its ogee curves and Gothic tracery, was erected in 1891. Designed by Thomas J. Welsh, it commemorated the centennial anniversary of Mission Santa Cruz.

(31) The granite jail of 1864 was a small square building with hipped roof. It had replaced an earlier jail built in 1854 on the same site by John Perry and William Nickerson.

It was in turn superseded by the Front Street jail of 1890. In 1906 the granite jail was sold and dismantled. Much of the stone was carved into headstones by stonecutter John Bilodeau.

(32) Mission replica building of 1931, seen through arches
(Covello & Covello Photography)

(32) Near the corner of **Emmet** and **School Streets** was a building constructed by Thomas Fallon, in 1849, of hewn timbers and heavy boards placed vertically. It was a two-story building with an exterior staircase. Fallon used it as a residence, hotel, and saddlery store. The county purchased it for use as a courthouse in 1852. Afterwards it became the county hospital and was last used to house poor families before it was torn down in 1884.

In 1931 this became the site for the Mission replica, designed by Ryland, Esty & McPhetres. "In the 1930s there was a blossoming of interest in the Spanish period of California history. Santa Cruz area historians [such as Leon Rowland] started delving into the history of local Spanish families and the missions. In Santa Cruz there was just one problem; there was no mission to restore" (Frank Perry, *Lighthouse Point: Illuminating Santa Cruz*, 2002).

Heiress Gladys Sullivan Doyle, niece of James Duval Phelan, paid $9,000 for the replica's construction, and she is buried in the baptistery beneath the floor of the chapel. It is difficult to understand why the effort was made to "replicate" a structure that is somewhat of an unknown quantity. There is no photograph of the original Mission, and therefore no knowledge of what exact forms and details to reproduce. An 1876 painting by Frenchman Leon Trousset "is the only work showing the main Mission and Chapel in its original state and has served as the sole pictorial model for later illustrations" (Santa Cruz City Museum, *Art and Artists in Santa Cruz: A Historic Survey* [exhibit catalog; text by Nikki Silva], Santa Cruz, 1973). Unfortunately, for the sake of historical veracity, the Mission that Trousset depicted was dependent on the memories of local observers, as the original chapel and adjoining wing were so diminished and altered that they were no longer recognizable.

There is also the matter of scale. Mission chapels were generally the tallest and largest single volumes of building and space in Spanish-era California. Making a smaller replica of the original building trivializes the role it played as the center of the mission community. Finally, the replica is not at the exact site of the original.

Despite these shortcomings, the replica is a worthwhile tourist destination. It houses two original depictions of the Mission, the painting by Trousset and a watercolor showing the Mission in ruins after an 1857 earthquake sheared off the front of the building. The chapel and reliquary house mission-era vestments and sacred vessels. In the garden is the stone baptismal font from the Mission chapel.

School Street is a short, dead-end street once bordered on the south by a row of adobe buildings with common walls. A *Santa Cruz Surf* (June 12, 1891) article states that horses were ridden up the hill to the Mission by way of School Street; carts, on the other hand, were driven along a more gradual route corresponding to Mission Street. In 1856 Frederick A. Hihn and Elihu Anthony attempted to open a route from School Street down to Pacific Avenue, but it fell into disuse. They did succeed in building a reservoir for Santa Cruz at the end of the street in 1859. It was fed by the Tres Ojos de Agua streams, which had been diverted to run across the Mission Plaza. The overflow from the reservoir cascaded over the bluff in a waterfall running into the San Lorenzo River, just north of Water Street. In the 1850s the river swung over nearly to the bluff, then curved back parallel to Bulkhead Street, named for the barrier built after the 1862 flood.

(33) At the southwest corner of School and Emmet Streets, the current site of Holy Cross Elementary School, was a two-and-a-half story adobe building once used as the *juzgado,* or legal, administrative, and judicial headquarters for the area. On its Emmet and School Street sides it had double porches, posts, and a spindle railing on the second floor. Simple two-story pillars supported the pedimented gable of this Greek Revival-Monterey Colonial style building.

Historian Leon Rowland stated that the building was granted in 1839 to Job Francis Dye, who sold it to Joseph Majors in 1848. However, a *juzgado* document indicates that Dye assigned title to the property to William Blackburn in 1848 (Starr Gurcke, translator, *Juzgado* Document 582, Special Collections, University Library, University of California, Santa Cruz). Blackburn operated his **Eagle Hotel** and store there and probably remodeled the structure shortly after acquiring it. Alfred Baldwin states in his *Recollections* that he supervised construction at the hotel in 1848, a project that may have added a third floor to the original building.

In 1862 the Sisters of Charity purchased the building from Blackburn for their school. As the school grew larger, the adobe was converted into dormitories and was finally replaced altogether by a new building.

(34) At the west corner of School Lane, at **119 School Street,** is a low one-story building covered in shiplap siding. Probably built in the 1850s or '60s, it was originally sheathed in board-and-batten siding and was the residence of Patrick Johnson. Johnson owned the land from the Mission replica to School Lane.

(35) At the end of School Lane, at **122** and **123 School Lane,** are two houses once occupied by stone carver John Bilodeau and his son-in-law, Seth Blanchard. They have the rough look of frontier, ghost-town buildings, especially 122 School Street with its false front and one clapboarded wall.

(36) Adjoining the Eagle Hotel was a long row of about four adobes with common walls. Two of these, the **Armas** and **Rodriguez Adobes**, are the only structures to survive from the Santa Cruz Mission.

After secularization of Mission Santa Cruz, the east half was purchased in 1838 by Roman Rodriguez and the west half by Felipe Armas in 1842 from two mission Indians, J. Petra and Isidro. Felipe Armas had been a soldier at the San

Mission Hill

(36) Armas-Rodriguez Adobe
(Special Collections, University Library, University of California, Santa Cruz)

Francisco Presidio in 1830 when Kamehameha, King of Hawaii, issued an appeal to California for vaqueros. Felipe was sent over as one of these vaqueros and helped to control the wild cattle that were overrunning the island.

Since they were built, the adobes have undergone many changes. The building was originally seventeen rooms long. It was constructed between 1822 and 1824 by Native American workers and was used as neophyte, or worker, family housing. Wooden floors, doors, and glass windows were added. These items were introduced to California by American settlers around the year 1835. Other major changes were the addition of a second story, the removal of the posts that probably supported the overhanging eaves, and the addition of a shingled gable in the Rodriguez adobe. In 1884 a frame addition of four rooms was added to the Rodriguez section, and in 1890 the westernmost section of the Armas adobe was removed to make room for a driveway from School Street

The Neary family purchased the Armas section in 1864 and occupied it until 1926. The Rodriguez half was inherited by Cornelia Lunes Hopcroft, who had been adopted by the Rodriguez family at age eleven in 1890. Cornelia was a companion to Eloisa Rodriguez and attended classes at Holy Cross School. Cornelia continued living at the adobe and was a dressmaker. At the age of fifty-one she married William Hopcroft, twenty years her senior, and moved into a house on Highland Avenue. Her husband died in 1937, and Cornelia moved back into the adobe.

The State of California gave Cornelia lifetime tenancy in 1957, when it purchased both adobes, largely through the efforts of the Santa Cruz Historical Society and Assemblyman Glenn Coolidge. Mrs. Hopcroft lived in the adobe until her death at age 104 in 1983. Today the adobe structure is part of the Santa Cruz Mission State Historic Park. The remaining seven rooms are a museum showing how the native people lived when they came to the Mission. There is also a model of the original Mission Santa Cruz.

(37) Above the steps to River Street, at the end of School Street, was Elihu Anthony's story-and-a-half home, with Gothic barge-boards, finials, and pendants.

(38) 332 Union Street is a two-story Prairie style house, the only example of the style in the city. The first story is sheathed in wide redwood clapboarding stained dark brown; the top story is treated with a symmetrical plaster and half-timber-like effect.

It was built in 1912 for the Walter C. Byrne family and designed by Byrne's nephew, Walter G. Byrne, who was then a student at the University of California at Berkeley. The house closely resembles the 1913 Salmon house (Beverly Hills, Illinois) by the well-known Prairie School architect, Walter Burley Griffin.

Mission Hill

(37) Anthony House
(Special Collections, University Library, University of California, Santa Cruz)

(38) Byrne House *(Joe Michalak)*

(39) At the end of the bluff-top section of Union Street was the **Gardner-Arana Adobe,** an unusual combination of adobe and frame building types, said to have been built by Manuel Arana in 1849.

In 1874 the property was purchased by Henry E. Gardner, who remodeled the house with a second story in 1888. A story-and-a-half cottage designed by Edward Van Cleeck was constructed adjacent to the adobe in 1894.

It was demolished in 1964, a needless casualty of the Chestnut Street Extension, an insensitively planned gash through the heart of Mission Hill.

(40) Jordan-Fagen House *(Harrison's History of Santa Cruz County, 1892)*

(40) At the southwest corner of Mission and Union Streets, on the original site of the John B. Perry house, was the home of Mary Perry Jordan, the widow of A. P. Jordan, and her second husband, Dr. Pierce Fagen. Before the Fagens built their new house in 1886, the Perry home had been moved to 114 Escalona Drive.

Designed by architects J. C. Matthews & Son of Oakland, the Fagen home was the first Queen Anne style house in Santa Cruz. It was ornamented with tiling, cement work, prominent exterior chimneys, and a corner turret. In 1955 it was razed because of plans for a freeway through the site.

(41) 335 Union Street is a delightful story-and-a-half clapboarded Gothic Revival cottage with sawn-wood bargeboards and split-pilaster supported porches.

(43) Field House *(Joe Michalak)*

(42) 327 Union Street is a story-and-a-half house with a two-story slanted bay in its split-pedimented gable. It has corner pilasters and an Italianate door-hood with pendants.

(43) The portion of the Mission Hill terrace above Rincon and Chestnut Streets and between Union Street and Walnut Avenue was known as Terrace Hill. Of a string of residences that once lined Terrace Hill in the nineteenth century, only the early 1860s Storer and Lucy Ann Field house remains.

Field was a Massachusetts man who arrived in Santa Cruz in 1859 from Wisconsin, where he had been a member of the legislature. He operated a grocery store in the Odd Fellows Building on Pacific Avenue. In 1876 the Fields' daughter, Dr. Lucy Maria Field Wanzer, was the first woman to earn an M.D. degree from a California medical school. She was a practicing physician until her death fifty-seven years later. Their clapboarded Greek Revival house is at **410 Locust Street**. Its split-pedimented front gable sits on a pilaster-supported entablature. Since the Doric-columned porch is placed off center and interrupts the pilasters, it appears to have been added on to the original house.

(44) Farther south was the two-story David K. Abeel residence, erected in 1887 from plans drawn by the firm of Goodrich & Page of San Jose. "The style of the house is Queen Anne... On the front will be two octagon-shaped bay windows; a porch will run around the front and sides of the house" (*Santa Cruz Sentinel*, October 19, 1886).

(44) Pine Place Apartments *(John Chase)*

D. K. Abeel came to Santa Cruz from Kansas City, Missouri, where he was editor and publisher of the *Kansas City Journal.* His major investment in Santa Cruz was the transformation of the humble Douglas House into the one great Santa Cruz resort hotel, the Sea Beach.

Today, the site of the Abeel house is occupied by two International Style apartment houses designed by Edward W. Kress for Mrs. Hettie (Irish) Peters, at **110 and 112 Pine Place**. Taking advantage of their site, he gave them a vertical emphasis somewhat unusual for residential buildings of this style. Artful touches include the slab door canopies, curved pipe railings, and the tall, narrow bands of glass block lighting the staircases. They were constructed in 1937.

(45) 419 Locust Street is a two-and-a-half story Stick Style house built in 1881 for Harrison M. Terry. He had it painted pale brown with the trim picked out in red.

Much sawn-wood Swiss Chalet trim is used in the porch and porch railings and below the windows and eaves. A shallow two-story square bay at the front

(45) Terry House *(Bruce Boehner)*

becomes a polygonal bay below the mansarded roof of the first story. Matching this bay is a similar one in the porch. The most striking feature is the use of bold popsicle-stick brackets in the gables.

(46) 433 and **435 Locust Street** are mirror-image, Stick-Eastlake cottages. Each one is equipped with four Eastlake sunburst-panels in its gable, some half-timbering, and a slanted bay with sawn-wood trim.

They were designed by Daniel Damkroeger for A. P. Swanton at a cost of $1,300 apiece. Swanton purchased the property from the Baptists, who had moved their church building from the site to Walnut Avenue in 1887.

(47) 445 Locust Street is a late Queen Anne Colonial Revival design attributed to architect John Marquis. Paired columns raised on a stone wall support the porch, and the corner turret is capped with a flattened conical roof.

In back of this house is a clapboarded story-and-a-half house of the 1860s, stripped of its doors, windows, and split-pilastered porch. This house, now in need of restoration, was once the Jonathan H. Guild home. The Guild family owned most of the property along the east side of Locust Street in this block and donated the land on which the Baptist Church was built.

The front house was built in 1908 for dairyman and banker Frederick D. Baldwin after he had the original home moved to the rear of the lot.

(47) Baldwin House *(Joe Michalak)*

Baldwin, a native of Massachusetts, had been a teacher and gold miner before he arrived in Santa Cruz in the 1870s and became a dairyman. At age fifty he retired from the dairy business to raise apples. Three years later he became a director and president of the City Bank.

He kept up his work at the bank for many years. "Neighbors on Locust Street were familiar with the sight of the frail old man, age 96, being wheeled in his wicker wheelchair on his way downtown." (Margaret Koch, *Santa Cruz Sentinel,* May 27, 1967).

(48) 434 Locust Street is a Queen Anne Stick-Eastlake cottage with a hipped roof. There are Stick brackets under the eaves, massive oversize pendants in the corner overhangs, and patterned shingling in the front gables.

(49) At **603 Mission Street** is the 1889 Albion Paris and Emily Swanton house, designed in the Eastlake style by Santa Cruz architect Daniel Damkroeger.

It has a turreted, polygonal corner tower and outsize, curved brackets and a band of ball-in-lattice pattern under the eaves. On the east side is a shallow square bay with window frames that extend into the split-pedimented gable to become brackets. A band of mansarding at the top of the first story ties this shallow bay together with the corner tower.

A. P. Swanton had been a butcher and ship chandler before he moved to Santa Cruz from Pescadero. He entered into several business ventures with his son, entrepreneur Fred Swanton, including the Swanton House, the Santa Cruz Electric Light and Power Company, and the Bonner Stables.

(50) 709 Mission Street is an unusual early Bungalow-influenced house. The roof is hipped, with twin shallow pavilions suggested, and there is an Art Nouveau stained-glass window above the portico. Rustic touches are the open trellis work and stone walls of the porch.

(51) A meeting of the International Style with the Constructivist tendencies of California architecture produced the **Mission Hill Junior High School Gym**, just west of the site of the Pope House and across from Crystal Terrace. Monterey architects Robert Stanton and Chester Phillips designed this 1949-50 building. The architect of **Mission Hill Junior High School**, which opened in 1931, was John J. Donovan of Oakland.

(52) At the intersection of Mission and King Streets was the **Pope House**, "the most modern of all the fashionable summer resorts in Santa Cruz" (Elliott's 1879 *Santa Cruz County*). "It is surrounded by ample grounds in which are numerous pretty cottages smothered in trees and flowers."

Often called the first Santa Cruz resort hotel, it had been started in 1862 by Horace Pope. He was a "young Vermont man who had had a year or so of experience in the hotel business operating the San Lorenzo House in 1865 (before its destruction by fire), and the lapse of nearly three years before the completion of the Pacific Ocean House gave Pope's establishment a good start" (*Santa Cruz Sentinel,* 1950).

There were a number of cottages on the site, as well as a two-story main hotel building. A little cottage, ca. 1850, erected for Silas Bennett, who had helped build the famous mill in which gold was discovered on the American River, housed the office, billiards table, and card tables.

The little alley opposite Locust Street separated the office from the hotel. The establishment was patronized by the leading San Francisco families of the time, among them those of James G. Fair and M. H. de Young.

(52) Pope House
(Special Collections, University Library, University of California, Santa Cruz)

Pope died in 1881 and his widow operated the hotel with the help of their two daughters. It became less fashionable through the years, and the last of its buildings was torn down in 1919.

The area from King to High Streets and from Highland Avenue to Kirby and Peyton Streets was the location of the Kirby, Jones & Co. tannery. Richard Kirby moved his tanning operation here from Squabble Hollow (Glen Canyon) in 1854. In 1863 Kirby sold his interest in the business to partners Edmund Jones and Joseph Boston and relocated to his Laurel Street tannery. The Boston & Jones business closed in 1875, and Boston's widow, Eliza C. Boston, subdivided the property. One of the tannery landmarks was a sixty-foot-high chimney that stood until 1885.

(53) 104 King Street is a Stick-Eastlake house with frosted and stained glass panels and a sunburst panel in the front porch. There is Stick Style articulation of some surfaces and an overall Queen Anne effect in the breaking up of the surface area by use of contrasting shingle and half-timbering patterns. Designed by LeBaron Olive, it was built for Dr. H. H. and Matilda Clark in 1889. Dr. Clark was known as one of the most skillful surgeons in the state and was also mayor of Santa Cruz. The house was originally painted in light and dark brown, with a sage green color at the base of the house, accented by black trim.

(54) 110 King Street is an unusual story-and-a-half house of the 1890s with corner overhangs and a porch with low flattened Tudor arches. Next to the porch is an ogee curved window set in a Palladian frame. The bottom of the shingled second story flares out over the top of the clapboarded first story. The second-story roof is brought down low over partial dormers containing doors to the porch roof. The house shows Shingle Style clarity of form picked out with eclectic detail.

(55) Van Cleeck Carriage House *(Joe Michalak)*

(55) 204 King Street is a Colonial Revival-style house which architect Edward L. Van Cleeck built for himself and his wife, Fannie.

There are Shingle Style gables over the rounded, shallow first-floor bays. The recessed corner porch is supported by a single column. Second-story walls flare out at the bottom. There is a dormer over the porch. Lime-rock foundation walls match the retaining wall.

(56) 117 Jordan Street is a clapboarded story-and-a-half cottage of the 1850s with corner pilasters and a slight split-pediment treatment of the gable. An entablature, pilasters, transom, and sidelights, frame the doorway.

It was the home of tanner Richard C. Kirby and his authoress wife, Georgiana Bruce Kirby. The house originally stood on the south side of Mission Street, where the Chestnut Street extension is now. A new wing had been built on either side before R. C. Kirby decided he wanted an all-new house. The old mid-section was moved to its present site in 1888, and a new mid-section was built into the Mission Street house.

Mrs. Kirby "was descended on her mother's side from the celebrated Prince of Condé (Louis Joseph). She left England for Canada when she was about sixteen and subsequently became interested in the Brook Farm experiment and went there to complete her education. At Brook Farm she became acquainted with Hawthorne, Emerson, and Charles A. Dana, the publisher of the *New York Sun*" (Obituary in *San Francisco Chronicle* reprinted in *Santa Cruz Sentinel,* January 29, 1887).

"The Brook Farm Association was the outcome of the advanced religious thought of a number of Unitarian clergymen," Kirby recalled afterwards in her book *Years of Experience*. The preachers organizing this commune "had, one and all, come to the conclusion that preaching Christianity, or the doctrine of brotherly love, was up-hill work, while the entire social fabric was based on the selfish principle of competition. To any reasoning mind it was evident that the good of one was the good of all, and *vice versa;* but our aggressive system, which pitted every man born into the world against his fellow, ignored this *in toto*.

"It was argued that labor, far from being a curse was, and had been, the greatest cause of our continuous development; that it conduced to the health of mind and body, when equally divided among all. But that in our present state, the artisan and laborer were degraded to only one step above chattel-slavery, in order to maintain a few in luxurious idleness."

Affected by the Transcendentalist thought and reform movements of the period, Brook Farm members attempted to eliminate the injustices of society by sharing labor as equals. The members were generally abolitionists, pacifists, and temperance advocates and opposed to orthodox religion and in favor of women's rights.

Kirby left the Farm because "I wanted more space, more seclusion. I was now sure that the world had yet to wait for the millennium." Although the communal movement may not have been the ultimate answer for her, the experience shaped many of her views for the rest of her life.

In *Years of Experience* she theorized, "…as each decade has passed, and I have noted the increasing inequality in social conditions, the growing numbers of the very wealthy, and of consequence the rapid extension of poverty and crime,

Mission Hill

I begin to fear we can only be forced to advance through revolution."

Following her stay at Brook Farm, she was an assistant to Eliza Farnham, matron of Sing Sing Prison, where the two of them instituted great reforms. In 1850 Kirby came west, paying for the journey with funds borrowed from Horace Greeley. In Santa Cruz she helped her old friend Eliza Farnham in the construction of a never-completed many-gabled house in the Potrero area. Doubly unconventional for the period was the idea of well-brought-up women doing construction work and their choice of work clothes–baggy bloomers.

In 1852 she married R. C. Kirby and settled down to live in Santa Cruz, where she retained her idealism and strong opinions.

(57) The George Wood house, ca. 1924, at **502 Escalona Drive**, may have been designed by Wood Brothers Company architect, Lila Sweet Martin.

(58) 316 Escalona Drive is the Duncan McPherson house, moved here in 1955. It is a symmetrical house with grouped window and a central entablature-like portico. The front door is set in a tabernacle frame with elongated pilasters and a dentil course The walls are clapboarded and flare out at the bottom of the second story.

(59) Another landmark, once located between today's 208 Escalona Drive and Storey Street, was a one-story adobe, built by the Castro family. It was "the pioneer dwelling of Santa Cruz. There the first comers resorted and found shelter under its hospitable roof" (*Santa Cruz Sentinel*, September, 1862). In 1862 the tile roof was removed and a clapboarded frame second-story added to accommodate additional tannery workers. The adobe was destroyed by fire in the middle 1890s (*Santa Cruz Sentinel*, January 10, 1954).

(60) 126 Escalona Drive is a two-story Stick-Eastlake house, built and designed by J. S. McPheters in 1887-88. One side of the facade is a vigorous composition of the pedimented entrance portico, the second-story square bay and first-story slanted bay.

Archaeological investigations at this site have verified the presence of a tanning vat associated with the Mission Santa Cruz tannery once located west of the area.

(61) The small Colonial Revival cottage next door at **120 Escalona Drive** was built for C. C. Perry's son, John, in 1905.

(62) 114 Escalona Drive is a board-and-batten cottage with an L-shaped, sawn-wood railed porch. There is an unusual braided-design bargeboard below

(62) Perry House *(Judith Steen Collection)*

the eaves, and curlicue sawn-wood trim at the tops of the sturdy pillars of the porch. The front door is treated as a pilaster-supported entablature with sidelights.

The house was built by Massachusetts carpenter-architect John B. Perry in 1852-53 and moved here in 1885 so that Perry's daughter, Mrs. Mary Jordan Fagen, could build a Queen Anne residence on the old lot at the southwest corner of Mission and Union Streets. After the move to Escalona, it was occupied by John B. Perry's son, Charles C. Perry.

The chimney is likely to be the oldest extant in Santa Cruz, and the front room was used for a school conducted by Perry's daughter.

"John B. Perry came to the west in 1850 and embarked in mining, but the failure of his health caused him to remove to Santa Cruz. Building a house, he sent back for his family, who joined him in 1853. For many years he followed the carpenter's trade in the village and surrounding country. He also drew his own plans to work from" (Ed Martin's 1911 *History of Santa Cruz County*).

Some buildings Perry erected were the 1868 McPherson block on Pacific Avenue, the 1854 County jail building, the 1867 Dr. C. L. Anderson house, and the 1856 Congregational Church.

(64) McPheters House on left, carriage house on right (*Carolyn Swift*)

(63) 110 Escalona Drive is a story-and-a-half Eastlake cottage with sawn-wood trim in its gable and a porch similar to the McPheters house next door. It is possible that McPheters also built this house.

(64) 203 Highland Avenue is the only example of the Second Empire style in Santa Cruz. The second story is mansarded and there is a three-story tower, also mansarded.

There are brackets below the patterned-shingled mansard roof and also below the flat, projecting cornice at the top of the first story. The one-story bay has its own cornice below that at the top of the first story. Above this bay is a strongly projecting, square-topped gable hood inset with a Stick-influence bracket. The house was built in 1882 by carpenter-builder John S. McPheters and was the John S. and Maud McPheters family home. The contemporary "carriage house" was designed by Mark Primack. It is a garage on the ground floor and a library on the second floor. Replication is often looked down upon by architectural critics as unimaginative and by preservationists as rewriting history. But from an urbanist's point of view, this kind of replication could be considered as further enriching the city environment and maybe creating a little enjoyable confusion about what's old and what's new.

(65) 218 Highland Avenue is a Shingle, Bungalow-influenced story-and-a-half house with its top story contained within one large gable. The house has diamond-pane upper window-sashes, a limestone-rock front porch, narrow clapboarding, and small, Shingle Style gables set flush with the eaves.

(66) 222 Highland Avenue is a hipped-roof, cube-shaped Colonial Revival house covered in narrow clapboarding, with simple brackets under the wide eaves.

(67) 246 High Street is a ca. 1890 Queen Anne cottage with half-timbering at the top of the gable and strap-work window framing.

The home was built for George and Mary Bowes. George Bowes was a sawyer who worked in the F. A. Hihn mills.

(68) 260 High Street, Piedmont Court, is a two-story Mission Revival-Moorish apartment building constructed around a central glassed-in court. It was designed by architect William Bray for Pedro Chisem. Construction began in 1912. Chisem had also purchased the Farmer's Union building on Pacific Avenue, on the site of the Bank of America, and had plans for a four-story business block and hotel. But "upheavals in Mexico upset the Chisem silver mining interests," and local investors Frank G. Wilson, Bruce L. Sharpe, and Robert C. Blossom

Mission Hill

(68) Piedmont Court Apartments *(Judith Steen Collection)*

completed Piedmont Court in 1916. The business block was never constructed (*Santa Cruz Sentinel,* May 16, 1954).

At each end of the building is a three-story tower, open at the sides on the third story. The two shallow square bays at the front have segmental-curve rooflines and plaster quatrefoils. On the porch are plaster shields bearing the initials PBC (Pedro B. Chisem).

In the lobby is much intricate tracery work, reminiscent of Arabic script. The unusual lamps, suspended from the ceiling by chains, are metal bowls with colored-glass panels.

"It is a Los Angeles production, something that is all the rage in the city of the Angels," claimed the *Santa Cruz Sentinel*, June 9, 1912, while the building was under construction. "The main lobby will be furnished in correct Moorish architecture with Moorish columns, arches, capitals, corbels and color scheme." Most of the building was of cast concrete, but "the two cupolas [were] built partly of wood and steel, plastered so they [could] readily be removed to add another story to the building, as [was] the ultimate intention of the owner.

"The distinguishing charm of Piedmont Court will be its patio, 42 feet x 63 feet in dimensions, which will be partly roofed with glass around the sides, the center being open to the heavens. A fountain will play at either end of the court and a palm garden will be an attraction. An upper balcony will extend completely around the sides of the patio, which can be used in addition to the veranda on the first floor. Part of the first-floor veranda will project into the patio in circular form, capable of being used as a bandstand" (*Santa Cruz Sentinel*, June 21, 1912). From 1953 to 1962 Piedmont Court was owned by the California Retired Teachers Association and operated as an apartment house for its members. It is now run as a cooperative.

(69) 330 High Street is a story-and-a-half house with twin gables, arched second-floor windows, and a split-pilaster supported porch on three sides. It is set on a half acre of grounds planted to fruit trees, berry vines, and roses.

It is possible that this is the Alexander McDonald house, built in 1867. McDonald's wife was the daughter of John and Sarah Greenwood, who once owned this section along High Street.

(70) 343 High Street (1909) has a mix of Bungalow and Classical influences and is notable for its porch, which has Doric pillars, built-in seats, and carved-and-notched projecting rafters. The house was designed by William Weeks for George Stone.

(71) 346 High Street is a house designed by its owner, architect Lila Sweet Martin.

Mission Hill

(69) 330 High Street *(Joe Michalak)*

(72) 410 High Street is a two-story, 1908, Colonial Revival house sheathed in narrow clapboarding. The Doric-columned, partially recessed front porch is set back of a curving entrance terrace balustraded with extremely delicate spindles. Edward Van Cleeck could be the architect of this symmetrical house, as he often employed the curving porch and frequently worked in the Colonial Revival style during this period.

It was built for Lawrence J. Dake, "an energetic, nervous active young man," according to Martin's *History of Santa Cruz County*. At one time or another Dake was a surveyor (with Thomas Wright), bookkeeper, and court reporter, managed a flour, feed, and provision store, and ran a land title company. He was also the son of Judge W. D. Storey's wife, the former Mrs. Dake, and the brother of artist Lillian Dake Heath. The 1870s Storey home, which was across High Street, was razed in 1944.

(73) Bordering the Dake house on the west is the **Torchiana Estate, Fair View**, a large parcel of land that reached from High Street to Highland Avenue. Once, the house could be reached from High Street by a long, steep flight of concrete steps and pathways overgrown with cerise valerian, myrtle, and periwinkle vines, mimosa, and pine. Toward the top of the seemingly endless stairs there is an open meadow of wild, pink sweet-pea accented with yellow Scottish broom.

On the hill above, the large, white, two-and-a-half story Stick-Eastlake house, at **535 Highland Avenue,** has two-story square bays, corner pilasters of strip moldings, and some bungalow-type early-twentieth-century additions. It was built in 1886 by Kaye, Knapp & Co. for Henry C. Jones at a cost of $4,000 and originally had a mansarded three-story tower. It resembled the Calvin Davis house at 207 Mission Street.

In 1908 the estate was purchased by Henry Albert van Coenen Torchiana, an attorney and Consul of the Netherlands. He and his wife, Catherine, remodeled the house extensively in the Bungalow style.

Among Torchiana's writings were books on Holland and Java and the invaluable *Story of the Mission Santa Cruz,* the most complete single published source of information on the subject.

"When the Torchianas first acquired the place it was hardly to be considered a desirable residence for people of cultivated taste, with a love of nature and a fondness for its worship 'far from the madding crowd,'" wrote Josephine Clifford McCrackin (*Overland Monthly*, March 1912). "They straight-away set to planning how the big but tasteless house could be made over so as to hold a host of friends."

Mrs. McCrackin described the interior, with "flowering vines running up and around the window frames, and inside doors . . . tree stumps from which droop giant fern fronds, rare lilies and choicest palms in pots and tubs." The interior revealed the Torchiana's acceptance of twentieth-century ideas, including the use of materials in their natural state, orientation towards the outdoors, and an emphasis on informality and comfort.

In 1959 state assemblyman Glenn Coolidge purchased the property, and in 1964 it was purchased by the Dominican sisters for their Provincial house. The seven-acre property is again in private ownership.

(74) 525 High Street is the Dr. W. Grant and Amy Hatch house, built in 1922. The *Santa Cruz Historic Building Survey* claims that this is both a Great Lakes style summer home and nominally Spanish Colonial Revival in style. The first assertion seems reasonable; the second does not. The bays, the banded windows, and the treatment of the roof relate more to the Craftsman and Prairie School influences in Midwestern architecture than to Spanish Colonial Revival. The only really Mediterranean aspect of the house is its villa-like siting on the side of the hill. The main facade of the house can just barely be seen from the Escalona Drive sidewalk at Sunnyslopes Court. It was designed by Brust and Philipp of Milwaukee.

(75) West of the Torchiana estate was "the old John Wagner Place, noted for about the finest vineyard within the city limits." (Ernest Otto).

A portion of the Wagner property was purchased by the Appleby family of Minneapolis, Minnesota, in 1889, and they built a house there the following

Mission Hill

(74) Hatch House *(John Chase)*

year. In 1907 the mother, Marie Appleby, was killed when her team of black horses ran away down Mission Hill and slammed her carriage against a pole.

In 1909 the unlucky house was purchased by Samuel H. (Harry) Cowell who thought he might need a large home to which he could bring a bride. Harry never married, however, and consequently never used the house, which was later demolished.

(76) 660 High Street is a large, two-story, hipped-roof house with rustic wide battens in its siding, broad eaves, and small-pane windows.

It is surrounded by sweeping, carefully tended lawns and large trees and has a stream running through the property in a series of ponds and cascades. Like the Torchiana Estate, it is a nineteenth-century estate landscaped and remodeled in a calculatedly rustic Craftsman-Bungalow manner.

Along with the Appleby property, this was originally part of Rancho Tres Ojos de Agua, a rancho granted to Nicolas Dodero in 1844. The rancho received its name from three streams that flowed through it. One of the streams, which also supplied the Boston-Kirby-Jones tannery, the mission, and the Hihn-Anthony reservoir at the end of School Street, operated Dodero's mill.

The property was later owned by Nelson A. Bixby, an early-day shipping man, who sold it to realtor Henry Meyrick in 1877. Evidence indicates that Meyrick built the house that was later moved back to become the caretaker's quarters after Charles C. Moore built his new thirty-room house. Moore acquired the property in 1906.

(76) Interior of the Lounge Building on the C. C. Moore Estate
(Sara Holmes Boutelle)

The new main house was designed by architect Edwin J. Symmes and constructed in 1917. A separate lounge room had been built two years previously by architect Lila Sweet Martin. Sadly, the lounge room has been remodeled since its original construction.

C. C. Moore was a West Coast executive and financier, who was president of San Francisco's Panama-Pacific International Exposition of 1915. After the exposition was concluded, many of the trees and shrubs from the lavishly landscaped grounds were transplanted to Moore's already well-planted gardens. That same year William Jennings Bryan was a guest at the Moore home and helped plant a redwood tree dedicated to peace.

Also on the grounds were Moore's personal golf course, tennis court, swimming pool, and three lakes, fed by a stream which originates in the Louis Dodero (later Kalkar) limestone quarry just below the UCSC campus off Spring Street.

In 1912 Mrs. Josephine Clifford McCrackin penned the following description for the January *Overland Monthly:*

"The clear swift-flowing stream sings and calls and beckons with its rustic bridges, its cascades and waterfalls, and its rare nymphae lilies floating where the water is calm, above the falls. But we must see these rondels first, brilliant and fragrant, with gaudy lilies, with old-fashioned stock, with fuchsias and asters in all colors. The long flower borders edged with the blue lobelia, and built up tier banked on tier of gayest hued snapdragon from dwarf to giant, of chrysanthemum, of oleander, of dahlia of the most wonderful varieties and colors. More wonderful still is the reproduction of the rosarium in the Crystal Palace Gardens."

Much use was made of redwood logs with the bark remaining. They were employed for the garden pergola and for one of the guest cottages. This cottage had "only wooden bolts and buttons for door fastenings," according to Mrs. McCrackin.

(77) 665 High Street is a one-story house with low-pitched shed roofs and large square windows divided into six panels. Built in 1954 for Norman and Mabel Powell, it and the Russell Giffen house by William Wurster at Seabright are two of the few residential buildings of architectural significance from the 1950s in Santa Cruz. It was designed by Dallas Steele.

(78) The Tudor Revival house at **650 Spring Street** is **Windy Hill Farm**, designed by Sidney B. Newsom and Noble Newsom for Mrs. E. Forbes Wilson (Dorothy Deming Wheeler) in 1921. This sophisticated and understated mansion as English cottage is the most successful period-revival in the city. The outbuildings are equally delightful, and the garage is suggestive of the projects of Berkeley architect Thomas Gordon Smith.

Several newer houses have been constructed on the property with a central driveway leading in off Spring Street. Windy Hill House is located on the right side of the driveway, partially hidden by the impressive garage.

(79) The **First Congregational Church/United Church of Christ** at **900 High Street** is a Wrightian extravaganza from 1958. Bates Elliot, who was practicing in Santa Cruz at the time, was the architect.

(80) 515 Highland Avenue is a steep-gabled story-and-a-half house constructed for retired farmer Moses B. and Martha Jane Bliss in 1877. It is not visible from the street.

(81) Hillcrest Terrace runs through the onetime estate of Judge James H. and Catherine (Murphy) Logan. The two-story Italianate house, built in 1880, was designed by John Williams. The upper story of the house was covered in sheet iron processed to look like brick (*Santa Cruz Sentinel*, December 21, 1947).

Logan was an amateur plant hybridist. In 1881 he crossed the Texas Early blackberry with the wild blackberry, a cross which bore fruit (the Mammoth blackberry) the next year.

In 1883 the Judge found a strange berry plant growing in his garden, apparently the result of a cross between a wild blackberry and the Red Antwerp raspberry. "The thought occurred to plant the seed of these berries for the production of something new in the way of blackberries. The Judge obtained fifty plants and set them out by themselves in the spring of '84. Most of them grew quite vigorously. The Logan berries had meat that was rich but not juicy. They are just the berries for shipping. The flavor is tart and similar to the wild blackberry" (*Santa Cruz Sentinel*, May 23, 1885).

Logan removed the redwoods, oaks, buckeyes, and wild thimble bush on the hillside above Evergreen Cemetery and terraced and planted it to his loganberry. Although his "mammoth blackberry" that he had deliberately hybridized was never a commercial success, the accidentally created "loganberry" did become popular, particularly in Oregon.

The estate was purchased in 1903 by Chicago magnate Theophilus Noel, who had made his fortune marketing a patent medicine called Vita Ore. It was largely due to the efforts of Noel and *Santa Cruz Surf* editor A. A. Taylor that the Santa Cruz Portland Cement Company was prevented from locating a dust-belching cement plant on Escalona Heights near Walnut Avenue.

The Logan house was torn down in 1948 to make way for a subdivision.

(82) 622 Escalona Drive has enough broad eaves and projecting rafters to clothe several average bungalow houses of the early twentieth century. It was designed for Daniel Ballen and Kurt Burtin by Dennis Britton in 1978.

This full-blown, latter-day bungalow works because of the consistency of design on several levels, from massing to detailing. Appropriate bungalow windows and details such as narrow lath wainscotting have been used. The building needs more room than it has and lots of trees to poke its eaves through.

Mission Hill

127

(81) Logan House (*Harrison's History of Santa Cruz County, 1892*)

(83) The Dr. Alfred L. and Thelma Phillips house at **662 Escalona Drive** was built in 1933 and designed by William Weeks. Don't miss the gargoyles on the beam ends.

(84) John Carl Warnecke designed **745 Escalona Drive** about 1949 for Clarice and Fred D. McPherson Jr. using the Bay Area version of the International Style as domesticated by architects like Gardner Dailey and William Wurster.

(85) Allegrini House *(John Chase)*

(85) One of several houses designed by Wilton Smith in the neighborhood was the 1939-41 International Style house at **1010 Laurent Street**. It was built for Dr. Anthony E. and Estelle Allegrini. It was Allegrini who laid out the sixty-acre subdivision known as Allegro Heights. The area was purchased by Allegrini from the C. C. Moore estate in 1938.

The house's long low lines were accentuated by its below-grade site and the rows of clipped hedges bordering the yard. Two thick, horizontal slabs separated by bands of windows made up the basic form. Some of the window bands were connected with grooved-wood panels painted aqua. These panels were treated in a manner more suburban ranch-style than International Style. The rear of the house had a curved wall, and there was a patio wall ending in a spiral. A stylish detail was the use of projecting corner windows set into the indented corners of the house.

The landscaping of the formal garden, with its maze-like, low, clipped hedges, magnolias, hydrangeas, and fuchsias, was by Thomas Church. The bottom hillside had been left in its natural state, and the manicured upper portion had a natural bridge over the creek that runs through the property.

The house was needlessly demolished in 1984 to make way for a new house.

(86) 1025 Laurent Street is the Dr. Enrico Raffanti house built in 1941 and designed by Wilton Smith. It is obviously influenced by William Wurster's work of the 1930s, such as his 1939 Raas house at Palo Alto.

(87) 1116 Laurent Street is a wide-clapboarded, plaster "Stockbroker's Tudor." It has small-pane windows, a one-story bay window, partial dormers in the second story, and a mock-rustic touch of assorted-size chimney pots. It is the Dr. P. T. and Ruth Phillips house by William Weeks. It was built in 1933, a period when architects thought nothing of putting steel beams inside a building and half-timbering outside, which is exactly what Weeks did here.

The house is located down a steep, curving driveway amidst lush landscaping with a creek and waterfall running through the property.

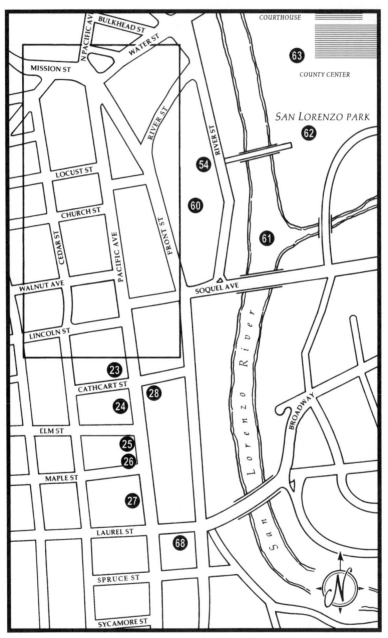

The boxed portion of this map appears in detail on page 134

Chapter Five

Downtown

Pacific Avenue began as a path following a line of willows that bordered the mission farm on the flatlands to the west. "The willow trees stood about ten feet apart. Strips of raw cowhide were stretched between them to form a fence" (1860 *Alta California*). The trees were cut down in 1861, and the name of the street was changed from Willow Street to Pacific Avenue in the Foreman and Wright survey of 1866.

The original, one-block-long downtown business section was located on Front Street (then known as Main Street), between Water and Cooper Streets. It declined as a business district during the late 1860s and early '70s, partly because the primitive buildings were no longer suitable for their prosperous owners and partly because Front Street could not be extended. Consequently, there was a building boom on Pacific Avenue in the late 1870s, and commercial buildings began to replace the gardens, orchards, and homes that once fronted on the avenue.

Pacific Avenue became the focus of commercial activity in the city. By the 1950s, however, the importance of the central business district began to decline, fueled by the geographical dispersion created by the automobile. A recommendation that a mall be created in the downtown area was first made in a 1958 analysis of the central business district and was repeated in the City's 1963 General Plan. The idea was not pursued seriously until photographer Chuck Abbott became convinced that the answer to a decaying commercial core was a mall and began to publicize the idea with slide lectures. A mall committee was formed in 1967 to study and implement the idea. A year later, over seventy percent of Pacific Avenue property owners agreed to join a special assessment district.

The Pacific Garden Mall was a semi-mall, constructed in 1969-70 from the plans of architect Kermit Darrow and landscape architect Roy Rydell. Cross traffic entered via one-way streets, while through traffic was slowed by a single winding one-way traffic lane with frequent crosswalks for pedestrians. The winding sidewalk, with its use of both tile and concrete, varied plant material, and geometric shapes, gave the mall botanic diversity and a lively appearance. The concept was that plants were necessary in order to buffer and mitigate the canyon-like effect of continuous buildings that form a "street wall." However, the raised planters and lush planting took away space from pedestrians on the sidewalk and were essentially anti-urban.

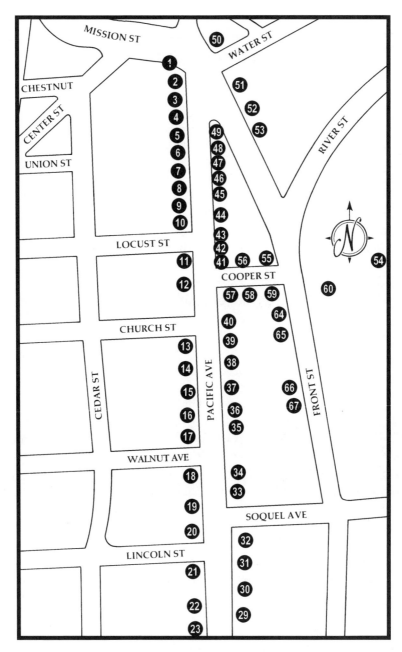

Inset from map on page 132

Fire, building, and zoning codes discouraged mixed use and restoration of older buildings; as a result, many second and third stories stood vacant prior to the Tuesday, October 17, 5:04 p.m., 1989 Loma Prieta earthquake, a fifteen-second quake (6.9 moment magnitude; 7.1 surface-wave magnitude) centered about nine miles northeast of Santa Cruz in the Santa Cruz Mountains. Twenty-nine structures, most of them historic, suffered earthquake damage and were subsequently demolished. The most prominent were the Trust Building, Cooper House, and St. George Hotel. Life-safety concerns were paramount, as the earthquake killed three people on the mall. Perhaps more buildings could have been saved, but the risk of further injury caused by collapse from aftershocks hastened demolition. Two hundred and six businesses—half the downtown core—were homeless. During the three-year wait for replacement buildings, forty-seven businesses moved off Pacific Avenue into a series of tents called the Phoenix Pavilions.

With the rebuilding of downtown came a mix of new shops, offices, and housing and renewed pedestrian traffic, requiring a simplified streetscape. The current street trees, sycamore on one side and cherry on the other, do not overwhelm the buildings and allow more activity and cafes with outdoor seating. Twenty-seven new buildings have been constructed since the quake.

(1) At **1551 Pacific Avenue** was the **McHugh & Bianchi Building**, an Italianate structure designed and built by contractor-architect LeBaron R. Olive for San Francisco developer and liquor merchant Anson Parsons Hotaling in 1886-87.

Two other buildings had previously occupied this site: Charles Eldon's general store building, constructed about 1850, and Briody & Peckner's 1867 fruit store and saloon, designed by architect Thomas Beck.

When first opened, Hotaling's building housed a barbershop, A. B. Cannon's Eureka candy factory, a stove and tinware store, A. Crocker's furniture store, the shop of gun- and locksmith H. G. Insel, and furnished rooms in the Arlington, a rooming house upstairs. For a time, there was a Temperance Coffee Parlor downstairs, and LeBaron Olive had his office upstairs.

The year the building was completed it came very close to igniting from the intense heat of the Swanton House fire across the street. The Hotaling structure was drenched with water and covered with wet blankets.

From 1894 to 1923, C. D. Hinkle operated his Cash Store at the site. In 1898 he installed plate glass windows in the ground floor, and in 1904 bestowed a black and yellow paint job on the building. Lease & Wettstein owned the grocery store from 1923 to 1946, when it was purchased by the last owners, Richard McHugh and Ernest Bianchi.

Downtown

(1) Hinkle's Cash Store, later McHugh & Bianchi Building
(Special Collections, University Library, University of California, Santa Cruz)

Controversy over the building began in 1971, when Golden West Savings & Loan Association (now World Savings & Loan), of Oakland, California, purchased the building with the intent to demolish it to make way for a modern branch office. As news of the building's pending demolition spread and Santa Cruzans began to realize what the loss of the building would mean to Pacific Avenue's historic and aesthetic identity, a grassroots campaign arose to save the building. Resolutions by various historic and preservation groups, a flood of letters to Golden West, and ample press coverage stayed the wrecking crane temporarily. In 1972 volunteers gathered over 2,200 signatures on a petition urging preservation of the building. That same year, the building became the second in the city included on the National Register of Historic Places, "the official schedule of the nation's cultural property that is worth saving."

The threatened demolition of the building was also largely responsible for a temporary moratorium on all demolition in Santa Cruz while a proposed preservation ordinance was under study by the City Planning Commission and the City Council. Although the ordinance was killed by the council, it did increase the public's awareness of the architectural heritage of Santa Cruz.

A new twist in 1973 was a California State Supreme Court ruling requiring environmental impact reports on actions likely to have a significant effect on the environment. In order to avoid having to apply for a new building permit,

(1) Hinkle's Cash Store, interior
(Special Collections, University Library, University of California, Santa Cruz)

with the attendant difficulties of filing such a report, Golden West chose to keep its permit good by periodic token demolitions.

Following passage of resolutions by the council and the County Board of Supervisors urging preservation of the building, the council formed in 1973 an advisory committee with representatives of the council, Golden West, and the public. The firm of Esherick, Homsey, Dodge & Davis was hired to study alternatives to demolition.

The architects recommended demolition of the McHugh & Bianchi Building and construction of a new building. Preservationists took Golden West to court in an effort to prove that the firm's demolition permit was invalid, as demolition of the building itself had not yet begun in earnest. The preservationists lost the case and did not have the funds to file an appeal.

The controversy did not, however, end with the demolition of the building on August 20, 1974. The first design for the new structure, submitted by Esherick's firm, was rejected in the City's review process. Joseph Esherick was a distinguished architect, instrumental in the evolution of San Francisco Bay architecture. It should also be noted that Herbert and Marion Sandler, the founders and longtime owners of Oakland-based World Savings, have made a point of hiring distinguished firms to work on their buildings. However, good architects can design mediocre buildings, and this is simply one of Esherick's less successful designs, stripped and impoverished compared, at the time, to the level of detail on downtown historic buildings, and the overall composition still seems awkward.

The exterior appears to be concerned with two main problems—turning the corner and relating the new building to other structures. A brick veneer was used on part of the Pacific Avenue facade at the insistence of City officials, and there was an attempt to make the fenestration jibe with nearby buildings. That ordinarily delicate staple of vernacular building–latticework–is heavy and "architectural." Over time, vines have done much to soften the impact of the building.

The irony is that had the McHugh & Bianchi Building been preserved, it would doubtless have survived the Loma Prieta earthquake, since it was a frame building with no unreinforced masonry.

Something positive, however, did occur because of the loss of the building. The City Historic Preservation Commission was created in 1974. In 1976 the *Santa Cruz Historic Building Survey* was published. It was based on information "drawn from existing sources, primarily . . . *The Sidewalk Companion to Santa Cruz Architecture,*" published by the Santa Cruz Historical Society in 1975.

(2) 1549 Pacific Avenue was a Streamlined Moderne building with half-circle door-hood and second-story, half-circle windows. It housed the Santa Cruz

Coffee Roasting Company when the 1989 earthquake struck. Falling bricks from the adjacent structure collapsed the building, killing two employees. The undeveloped site is now owned by the City of Santa Cruz.

(3) At **1547 Pacific Avenue**, demolished as a result of the 1989 quake, was a two-story brick Italianate building, with cast-iron columns on the first floor of its facade. The building was constructed in 1899 for the grocery firm of Williamson & Garrett, which had started out in a store on the corner of Walnut and Pacific Avenues. The second floor once housed the public library. From 1969 until 1989, it was home to Bookshop Santa Cruz. As of this writing (2005), sixteen years after the Loma Prieta quake, the site is still a hole in the ground with a plank bridge across the old basement.

The 1974-75 buildings at the rear are from basic designs of owner Ron Lau (who also owned the Williamson & Garrett/ Bookshop Santa Cruz building) and working drawings by Ifland Engineers.

(4) At **1545 Pacific Avenue** is **Lulu Carpenter's**, constructed in 1866 for Alfred Baldwin, a member of Frémont's 1846 expedition to conquer Los Angeles. The second floor of the brick building was planned as a hall to be used in conjunction with the then neighboring hotel, the Pacific Ocean House. Chief of Police Robert H. Majors, son of pioneer Joseph Majors, was shot by an acquaintance in front of this building in 1890. Majors died from his wounds the following year (*Santa Cruz Sentinel*, March 6, 1949).

When the building was remodeled for use as a bar in the 1970s, the first floor was set back, making the second-story brick facade appear insufficiently supported. This setback was necessary to reduce the size of the first floor, thus eliminating the requirement for an impossible-to-provide second exit. The facade still incorporates three cast-iron pilasters from the Atlas Foundry. Gary Garmann was the architect of the 1970s renovation. Michael Bates's interior was a splendid example of 1970s woody-goody nostalgia. Much of it was removed by later businesses in the space. Lulu Carpenter's coffeehouse is named for the clothing store of the 1920s and 1930s, "Lulu Carpenter's Dress Shoppe," which was located here.

(5) Next door to the south, at **1543** and **1541 Pacific Avenue**, is the site of the **San Lorenzo Hotel**, constructed in 1852 by a three-hundred-pound Carolinian named Henry Rice. Just before the hotel burned in 1865, a third story and piazza were added.

The year of the fire, on the same site, construction started on a new brick hotel, the **Pacific Ocean House,** in a style termed "Grecian composite" (*Santa Cruz Sentinel*, September 16, 1865). William H. Moore and Amasa Pray were the

Downtown

(5) Pacific Ocean House
(Special Collections, University Library, University of California, Santa Cruz)

proprietors, George Bromley the lessee, and A. C. Latson of San Francisco was the contractor and possibly the architect.

The hotel was renovated and re-opened in 1873 with a grand ball attended by 150 participants who danced for three hours, ate a midnight banquet, and then resumed dancing until early dawn (*Santa Cruz Sentinel*, October 4, 1873). The hotel was long a social center of the city, hosting many events, chief among them its annual reopening for the summer season.

In the rear of the one-hundred-room hotel building were extensive grounds containing swings and croquet lawns. After an 1878 remodeling, the porch roof had thirteen hundred square feet of covered surface, used as a dance floor. "With music at one end and Luna overhead it will be hard to keep the lovers of the giddy dance from tripping the light fantastic on this ample promenade," observed the *Santa Cruz Sentinel*, March 23, 1878. "[The Pacific Ocean House] is the chief hotel of the city," stated Elliott's *Santa Cruz County* in 1879.

The carriage for the hotel had been manufactured in Paris and was drawn by a team of horses that once belonged to a New York City millionaire. Each carriage part was individually numbered, so that it could be replaced with duplicates sent from abroad (*Santa Cruz Sentinel*, April 14, 1885).

A third story of wood, wire, and stucco was added in 1892, and the porch was removed in 1900. The hotel had already lost its fashionable reputation by the time a major fire in 1907 necessitated the removal of the third story. The last remaining section of the hotel was torn down in 1966.

(6) South of the alley, which marked the end of the Pacific Ocean House, was a structure erected in 1873, at the site of today's **1537** and **1539 Pacific Avenue**, for Amasa Pray. A. C. Latson was the supervising architect of this Italianate-style building. "The front is in iron sills, piers and plates cast at the New Foundry,"

(7) Pray Building
(Special Collections, University Library, University of California, Santa Cruz)

reported the *Santa Cruz Sentinel*, October 4, 1873. For many years it was S. A. Palmer's drugstore and known as the Palmer Block. It was demolished after the 1989 earthquake. The replacement building by Helm/Boyd, built for Eric Stolzberg in 1995, houses Plaza Lane Optometry in 2005.

Downtown

(7) South of the Pray building, at **1533 Pacific Avenue**, were the **San Lorenzo Stables** and the **Drennan Block**, a long clapboarded structure erected in 1866. In 1906 the second Drennan building was erected. These buildings were destroyed in the 1989 quake.

(8) At **1521-1523 Pacific Avenue** was a double building constructed in 1868-69, half by Frederick Hihn and half by "Alphabet" DeLamater for his dry goods and grocery store. Lynch and Gragg were the contractors. The building was badly damaged in the earthquake of 1868 and had to be partially reconstructed. It was demolished after the 1989 earthquake. The building's last occupants were Chi Pants and Santa Cruz Hardware. In 1991, the Wenzel Building, which replaced Chi Pants, was constructed at 1521 Pacific Avenue for Robert Wenzel. The Henry Willey Building at 1523 Pacific Avenue, replacing Santa Cruz Hardware, was built for Louis Rittenhouse.

(9) To the south of the Hihn-DeLamater Building, at **1517** and **1519 Pacific Avenue**, was a two-story Italianate building erected in 1873 for Robert Whidden by builder Charles Kaye. After much remodeling, it was torn down exactly one hundred years later to make way for the present building. With its fake second story and two-thirds scale relative to its neighbors, it is an ersatz cousin of the buildings that line Disneyland's Main Street.

(10) At **1515 Pacific Avenue** is a Neo-Classical Revival building with stone Corinthian pillars supporting a massive entablature adorned with lions' heads. There are bound sheaves of grain cast into the bronze window frames, and the interior has a coffered ceiling embellished with shields, foliage, and rosebuds. The building was constructed in 1910 for the **People's Bank** and designed by William Weeks. It took the place of a frame building erected in 1866 for Robert Whidden. It is often referred to as the **ID Building** for later occupant Integrand Design.

(11) At **1415** and **1411 Pacific Avenue** is the Mission Revival style **McPherson Building**, constructed in two sections, one having a segmental curve roofline, the other consisting of flat-roofed, bracketed, stepped levels. The segmental curve roofline of the southern section is an "inflected" design element leading the eye up and out of the building; it has an incomplete quality.

The building was constructed, and doubtless designed, by John Perry for Duncan and Alexander McPherson in 1868. During construction it was damaged by the earthquake of that year and had to be reinforced with iron bolts.

First occupants included Cohn and Michalowsky's New York Cash Store, dry goods and groceries, the *Santa Cruz Sentinel* offices, and the Odd Fellows

(10 and 11) Pacific Avenue at Cooper Street, looking north, ca. 1880. McPherson Building, left, at Locust Street; across Locust Street, Whidden Building, later site of People's Bank *(Special Collections, University Library, University of California, Santa Cruz)*

meeting hall. J. N. Rosenberg had a dry goods store, which carried "embroideries, laces, collars, Bishop and other lawns, jaconets, Cross-Bar, Swiss and dot, Muslins, Linens of all grades and a general assortment of ribbons and dress trimmings of the best and latest styles." Ads for E. P. Butler's second-floor photographic Pioneer Gallery boasted "No Cheap John work done at this gallery." Mr. Butler declared himself ready to produce "all kinds of photographs, ivory, tintypes, sun pearls, and ambrotypes."

(12) Leask's Seaside Store *(Judith Steen Collection)*

Later occupants included the *Santa Cruz Courier* newspaper, Lucien Heath's hardware store, the William H. Bias and John B. Moulton grocery, and Jesse Cope's clothing store. In 1877 iron columns were installed, followed by the addition of a bay window and iron cresting in 1882.

Sometime after 1910 and probably before 1920 the building was remodeled and the third story added. It is now occupied by Noah's Bagels and Pacific Avenue Pizza.

(12) Most of the remainder of the 1400 block of Pacific Avenue was the site of **Leask's,** the historic Santa Cruz department store. In 1892 Samuel Leask, a transplanted Scot, purchased the **Seaside Store**, the dry goods business of George W. and James L. Place at the corner of Pacific Avenue and Church Street. In 1906 Leask built a new Colonial Revival structure with rounded bays, designed by William Weeks. The building was remodeled and the business expanded over the decades, absorbing other structures on the block. In the 1980s, Gottschalks acquired the store, where it remained until the 1989 quake. The building was demolished and Gottschalks moved to the Capitola Mall. Today most of the block is dominated by the Cinema 9 building designed in 1995 by Kenneth Rodrigues & Associates, of San Jose. Cinema 9's dramatic neon sign was designed by Michael Leeds and crafted by Brian Coleman.

(13) Across Church Street, at **1387 Pacific Avenue** was the much remodeled 1873 **Lucien Heath Building**. This low, brick Italianate structure housed Heath's hardware store and by the late 1930s, Horsnyder's Pharmacy. The building was demolished after the 1989 quake.

(14) At **1375 Pacific Avenue** was the **Bernheim Building**, erected in 1875 for Jacob Bernheim, a native of Prussia, who had established a dry-goods business eleven years earlier on Front Street.

The first story of this Italianate structure had an "iron front" consisting largely of glass and cast iron pilasters. The second story had arched double windows under broken pediments. Bay windows were added by contractor John Williams in 1882. Removal of the bays and pediments gave the building the look of someone with his hair and eyebrows singed off. Later known as the **Rittenhouse Building**, it was destroyed by the 1989 earthquake. In 2005, the site of the Heath and Bernheim buildings, owned by Louis Rittenhouse, was still vacant, but the billboard located here depicts a three- and four-story, full-blown Beaux Arts style building to come.

(15) At **1345 Pacific Avenue** was a one-story building constructed prior to 1883 and first occupied by Dr. James F. Christal's drugstore, later by J. H. Horsnyder's drugstore. The cornice was subsequently hidden beneath an awning, but the cast iron columns, manufactured at the Pacific Avenue "Santa Cruz Foundry," could still be glimpsed. It was demolished after the 1989 quake. It is occupied today by the Paper Vision Building, at 1347 Pacific Avenue.

(16) Next door to the south, at **1335 Pacific Avenue,** was the **Jackson Sylvar Building**, originally constructed at the corner of Laurel Street and Pacific Avenue in 1877 as an oyster saloon and lodging house. It was the first major commercial building in that area and proved to be located too far away from the center of business at the time. Consequently, it was moved to its site next to the Christal building and turned on its side. Although the front was stuccoed over, the north side, which once faced Pacific Avenue, retained its beautiful bracketed cornices. It was razed after a 1972 Christmas Eve morning fire that destroyed four other stores to the south. The site is now occupied by Starbucks.

Downtown

(17) At **1301 Pacific Avenue** is the **New Santa Cruz Theatre** building designed by Reid Brothers of San Francisco, who also designed the huge 1888 Hotel Del Coronado at San Diego and the original 1903 Fairmont Hotel in San Francisco. The theater's February 12, 1920, opening night included a showing of the Mack Sennett comedy *Back to the Kitchen*.

(15) J. H. Horsnyder Building
(Special Collections, University Library, University of California, Santa Cruz)

In 1939-40 the theater underwent a major remodeling by architect Alexander A. Cantin, and the entrance was moved from the corner to the Walnut Avenue

(17) New Santa Cruz Theatre
(Special Collections, University Library, University of California, Santa Cruz)

side. To give this entrance more prominence, the Moderne tower with its cut-out stars and moons was added. It was a piece of stage design meant to be seen at night, lighted from within, in concert with the neon tubing which outlined the building. On opening night, which featured a double bill of *Reno* and *The Millionaire Playboy,* gardenias and cigars were given away—for an admission price of thirty cents.

The theater closed on the night of December 22, 1955, when floodwaters from a rampaging San Lorenzo River poured into the lobby.

A second remodeling occurred in 1976-77, when architect Paul E. Davis modernized the building, removing the tower in the process. Replication and replacement of the missing tower would restore the structure's architectural integrity.

(18) Alta Building
(Special Collections, University Library, University of California, Santa Cruz)

(18) Across the street to the south, at the corner of Pacific and Walnut Avenues, was Frederick Hihn's **Alta Building**, erected as a two-story structure in 1889 from plans drawn by John Williams. A third story, designed by Edward Van Cleeck, was added five years later and contained a boardinghouse. The building was torn down in 1938 to make way for the J. J. Newberry store, designed by William Wurster and later occupied by F. W. Woolworth's.

In the 1860s to the 1870s, when the site was occupied by the two-story, clapboarded parsonage of Congregational minister S. H. Willey, the first Santa Cruz **Chinatown** lay directly to the south.

With the exception of the parsonage at one end and the Waterman blacksmith shop at the other, "the entire block was of a number of one-story shacks with a wide dirt sidewalk, as well as a dirt street in front. Along the edge of the walk was a row of Normandy poplars.

(19) F. W. Woolworth Co. *(Covello & Covello Photography)*

"In this Chinatown were a couple of stores where Chinese groceries and clothes were sold. There was also a laundry and a cigar factory.

"The buildings were of rough redwood finish, most of them of wide board-and-batten. The first structure was the most prepossessing of the lot. It was the temple of worship known as the 'joss house.'

"It was also the headquarters of the Chinese Freemasons, supposedly a patriotic organization against the ruling Manchus. In the rear in the center of the altar was an alcove for the picture of the gods, a group of several. Hanging from the center of this shrine was an ever burning light in a brass holder, and on either side were tall pewter holders for large decorated red candles and the tall punks.

"There was not a touch of the orient in Santa Cruz on the buildings, except the signs over the doors or along the sides. Usually these were Chinese characters on China-red paper, spattered with gold, and the one over the door was usually bordered with a festoon of red cloth with the ornaments on each side, triangular in shape with a golden background with paper flowers" (Ernest Otto, *Santa Cruz Sentinel*, July 30, 1944). The Pacific Avenue Chinatown moved to Front Street in the 1870s.

(19) Much of the block south of the Alta Building was also developed by Hihn. In 1884-85 he constructed a three-story building there with a mansard roof. It was designed by Emil John. The 1929 F. W. Woolworth store at **1213 Pacific Avenue** was designed by MacDonald & Kahn. It was replaced after the 1989 earthquake by the Gap clothing store.

(20) At **1201 Pacific Avenue** was the **Medico-Dental Building**, a two-story brick building with curved Eastlake brackets and dentil-course cornice at the top of the first and second stories. It had widely-spaced pilasters and a polygonal corner bay, which was once topped with a polygonal steeple. The roof was slightly mansarded. It was so similar to the addition to the Alta Building that it, too, was likely to have been designed by Edward Van Cleeck. The building was erected in 1894 by F. A. Hihn and suffered heavy damage during the 1906 earthquake. It was demolished altogether after the 1989 earthquake. Gloria Hihn Welsh, great-granddaughter of Frederick A. Hihn, built a new structure, designed by Thacher & Thompson. It now (2005) houses Cottontails.

(21) At the southwest corner of Pacific Avenue and Lincoln Street, today's **1129 Pacific,** was the 1878 **Duncan Block,** erected for Duncan McPherson and designed by John Williams. The Italianate building housed Henry Meyrick's Real Estate Exchange. Its successor was the **Morris Abrams** store, remarkably intact until an unfortunate recent remodel. The Moderne structure was designed by C. J. Ryland and built in 1937.

(22) At **1119 Pacific Avenue** is the **Logos Building**, constructed in 1992 for John Livingston. All the elements of this building are overblown and over-scaled. This landmark used bookstore kept the book-collecting spirit alive after the 1989 earthquake, when customers bundled up to shop in the store's temporary site at the Union Ice Plant.

At **1111 Pacific Avenue** was the **Hotel Metropole,** built about 1908. Kate Handley's Millinery Shop was on the ground floor for a number of years. She was known as the dean of Santa Cruz businesswomen, having operated her shop from the 1870s until the 1940s. The hotel had forty-eight rooms that originally rented for fifty cents a day. Its windows were paired, with squeezed pediments over those on the third floor. It occupied the site of architect and builder John Morrow's home. The building was demolished after the Loma Prieta earthquake in late 1989. The last occupant was Plaza Books.

(23) The 1946 **J. C. Penney Building** by William Wurster was located on the site of the **Grand Central Block** at **1101 Pacific Avenue.** The first building on the lot was the 1856 cottage of architect Thomas Beck. In the 1870s Peter Wilkins purchased the property, moved the house over, and constructed a two-story

(23) University Town Center *(Carolyn Swift)*

hotel. Eventually, the hotel was added onto until it fronted directly on the street. It was torn down in 1941. After Penney's closed, the building became Ford's department store. It was damaged by the 1989 quake and demolished shortly thereafter.

The site is now occupied by **University Town Center**, designed by Thacher & Thompson in 1999. It was built for and by Barry Swenson, a partner in ownership with the Seaside Company, owners of the Boardwalk. The building houses UCSC extension offices, classrooms, and fifty-four units of student housing. The building is divided into alternating bays of brick piers, recessed windows, and metal bas relief panels. The top two stories are set back and the top story consists of dormers inset into the roof.

(24) At **1011 Pacific Avenue** is **The Catalyst,** challenging the flat rooftops of the avenue with its huge shed roof.

Once located in the ground floor of the St. George Hotel, the Catalyst originated as a co-op run coffeehouse in 1965, planned as a meeting place for the various groups in the community.

The scale of the old quarters, especially the intimacy of the Garden Court, was the perfect background of throwaway, old-fashioned charm for the parade of seers, poets, bums, street people, students, attorneys, and other more conventional characters who passed through its swinging doors and paused at its irregular tables. The current structure has a more institutional atmosphere and resembles nothing so much as one of the large college dining halls at UCSC.

Former owner Randall Kane conceived the basic design for the building, originally the ca. 1930 Santa Cruz Bowl, and Ralph Rapattoni drew the plans; it was constructed from 1974 to 1976.

(25) Across the street to the south was F. A. Hihn's building of 1888, first occupied by **Adams Star Grocery.** Designed by Edward Van Cleeck, while he was still a member of Kaye, Knapp, and Company, it had been stuccoed over and greatly remodeled by the time it was torn down in 1973.

(26) 931 Pacific Avenue, now the location of the **Eagles Lodge**, was once occupied by the three-story frame **YMCA Building** of 1888. Designed by D. A. Damkroeger, it had double and triple windows beneath squeezed pediments inset with sunburst carvings. It burned in 1932.

(27) The **Jonas Block, 813 Pacific Avenue**, is a Mission Revival building with segmental roofline and a tiled hood joining the four bays on Pacific Avenue. In between the bays are large scrolled brackets. It was constructed for David Jonas's clothing store in 1908. Jonas had come to Santa Cruz from Placerville in 1879, opening a store near the Pacific Ocean House in partnership with three brothers. The business was later housed in A. P. Hotaling's St. George Hotel building.

(28) The **1010 Pacific Avenue Building** will help cement the status of downtown as a desirable environment in which to live and work. However, the architecture is another story. The 2004 building has clunky proportions and detailing. It is reminiscent of other New Urbanist projects throughout America in its use of devices such as calling out a corner (Pacific Avenue and Cathcart Street) as a separately articulated block. However, there is no integration of this block with the rest of the building. The contrasts in the color scheme of this building create only a cosmetic sense of variety in the building rather than a meaningful breaking down into parts. The architect of this urbanistically correct, but aesthetically deficient, project is R. L. Davidson of Fresno.

(29) At **1114-1116 Pacific Avenue** is the site of the 1906 **Heard Building**, which housed the **Colonial Hotel** and the **Cameo Theatre**. The three-hundred-fifty seat Cameo was the last of the local small movie theaters, opening in 1925 and closing only five or six years later. The building was demolished after the 1989 earthquake. Today it is the site of the 1992 Gularte Apartments designed by Robert Corbett of Watsonville.

(29) Heard Building and Cameo Theatre
(Special Collections, University Library, University of California, Santa Cruz)

(30) At **1124 Pacific Avenue** is the **Theatre Del Mar**, a Zig-Zag Moderne building. Architect for the Del Mar was J. Lloyd Conrich. The interior was designed by noted theater decorator William Chevalis. The facade, divided into three sections bordered by grooved piers, is focused on its tall sign and projecting marquee. On the marquee are neon stars and seashells. Beneath the zig-zag, bas-relief border are bare-breasted maidens. The ceiling of the lobby, between the large red beams, is corrugated and painted in shades of beige, aqua, and gold, with motifs of crossed arrows, swags, seashells, and crudely depicted goddesses. The lamps are of clear and frosted glass, adorned with large stars and bound sheaves pierced by arrows. The facade closely resembles the facade of the Cascade Theater in Redding, California.

The Del Mar opened its doors as a cinema palace on August 14, 1936, with the world premiere showing of Warner Brothers' *China Clipper,* starring Pat O'Brien. "Six usherettes, all blondes, in attractive red uniforms, and three ushers in white sports coats showed the guests to their seats," reported the *Santa Cruz Sentinel.* Page Joe Franks was dressed in imitation of the bell boy in a Phillip Morris ad. In deference to this overwhelming splendor, the New Santa Cruz Theatre dropped the "new" from its title and the Unique closed down altogether.

(30) Theatre Del Mar, 1936
(Special Collections, University Library, University of California, Santa Cruz)

Because of dwindling movie-goers, the Del Mar closed in 1999. The following year it was purchased by the City of Santa Cruz Redevelopment Agency, which leased it as a joint-venture between local developers George Ow Jr. and Barry Swenson Builders. The Nickelodeon Theatre, a local, independent company, sub-leased the Del Mar. Together with community support, the theater has been restored. Restoration was by Lerner + Assoc., Architects, of San Francisco. A grand re-opening was held on March 2, 2001.

(31) Swain's Theatre/Unique Theatre
(Special Collections, University Library, University of California, Santa Cruz)

(31) To the north of the Del Mar was the **Unique Theater**, which opened as a seven-hundred-seat vaudeville house in August 1904. "Three years later Mack Swain and his company took over the theater and turned it into a playhouse of live drama, with *Sidewalks of New York* as their first production. Mack Swain

Downtown

later went on to become Charlie Chaplin's 'partner'—Mack being the huge hulking character always 'haunting' the diminutive Charlie. Perhaps his greatest popularity was reached with Chaplin in the silent film comedy *The Gold Rush,* produced in 1925" (*Santa Cruz Sentinel*).

The Unique was later transformed into a movie theater. In 1936 it was demolished, to be replaced by the present Moderne building.

(32) 1134 Pacific Avenue is the 1929 Zig-Zag Moderne **Bank of America Building** (originally Bank of Italy), with a low-pitched hip roof. The Pacific Avenue facade has four faceted pilasters, the two in the center bearing bas-relief plaques of Hermes-like figures. The cornice is in a zig-zag pattern. Henry A. Minton was the architect.

In 1977 the Bank of America building became the second building in the city, after the McHugh & Bianchi Building, to become the center of an important preservation battle. Fortunately, this building was saved. The Bank of America building was adapted for the New Leaf Market by Thacher & Thompson in 1995.

The bank replaced the **Farmer's Union Block**, constructed in 1884 from plans by John Morrow. The Farmer's Union had been an early day attempt at cooperative buying. Much of the stock was held by the Grover family.

Upstairs was the pressroom of A. A. Taylor's *Santa Cruz Surf* and a multi-purpose hall. Among groups using the hall were dancing teachers, spiritualists, the African Methodist Episcopal Church, and a "Buddhist" church, presided over by a fortune-telling English cockney, Swami Mazzanandi.

(33) At the northeast corner of **Pacific** and **Soquel Avenues** was the **Trust Building.** It was erected for Len Poehlman in 1910 and named in honor of his wife's family, the Andrew Trusts, who once owned the corner. The three-story Colonial Revival building was designed by Edward Van Cleeck. There were simple brackets under the broad eaves and rounded two-story bays with fluted bases. An entablature-like band below the eaves was garnished with colonial garlands and a dentil course. It was demolished after being damaged in the 1989 earthquake. Permitting Borders bookstore to locate on Pacific Avenue was controversial because it is a large chain business. The Borders building, 1200 Pacific Avenue, was built in 1999 for Redtree Properties and designed by Tanner Leddy Maytum Stacy Architects (TLMS) of San Francisco.

(34) Next door to the Trust Building, on the north, was the **Hagemann-McPherson Building**, erected at the same time and to the same design as its neighbor, also attributed to Edward Van Cleeck. For many years it was the Hotel Waldo and later became the Elks Building. Like the Trust Building next door, it

(33) Trust Building *(Judith Steen Collection)*

was damaged by the earthquake and subsequently demolished. Borders bookstore extends to this site as well.

(35) At **1220 Pacific Avenue** was the **Masonic Hall Building**, constructed in 1887 from plans drawn by Charles W. Davis for a brick building and modified by John Williams for construction as a frame building. In 1907 it was remodeled by William H. Weeks, and in 1927 it was badly damaged by fire.

At the time of its construction, the *Santa Cruz Sentinel* commented, "The design is modeled after an ancient castle, modernized to an extent compatible with good taste and beauty. The general style of finish is Gothic, although here and there traces of the Roman are noticeable, especially in the arches over the bay windows. Nearly everything in the way of ornamentation is as near out of center as possible" (*Santa Cruz Sentinel*, February 4, 1887).

It was surmounted with a ten-foot-square tower of Gothic detail with octagon corners. The interior, designed by lodge member Dr. O. L. Gordon, boasted a silver-plated fountain with a marble base and ceiling centerpieces embellished with Masonic symbols.

From 1908 to 1920 the bottom floor housed the **Jewel**, a movie theater. The buildings between the Masonic Temple and the Palomar Hotel were razed after being damaged in the big 1955 flood. In 2005, the site is occupied by Rosie McCann's Irish Pub and the Costa Brava restaurant.

(36) Just north of the Masonic Building was the **A. Mann Building** of 1891, designed by D. A. Damkroeger. It had a "New York front" of cast iron, which the *Santa Cruz Sentinel*, August 15, 1891, claimed was the only one of its kind in the city.

(37) At **1344 Pacific Avenue** is the WPA-Moderne **Hotel Palomar**, with its large, bulky volume divided by vertical ribbing and strewn with gold-and-red-painted busts of conquistadores. The squat pillars in the second story are similar to those of the neighboring Neary Building.

The main dining room has a ribbed barrel-vault ceiling stencilled in dark reds, greens, and browns, tiled balconies, and a massive chimney. Notable also is the Spanish room with its massive over-sized ceiling beamwork.

William H. Weeks designed the building, which was constructed in 1928-29 and formally opened a year later. Rising six stories above the heart of the town, the city had its first "skyscraper." Real estate promoter Andy Balich, who had been one of the partners in the corporation that built the hotel, took it over and ran it until his death in 1933. Buildings torn down to make way for it include the William Ely Block No. 2 and the Legassick and Brownstone buildings, the latter two both constructed in 1877.

(38) At **1362 Pacific Avenue** is the Romanesque Revival-influenced **P. Neary Building**, by Edward Van Cleeck, ca. 1906. The ground floor retains its cast-iron columns; the second story, its rusticated stone surface and Colonial Revival garlands below the cornice. Santa Cruz architect Van Cleeck had his offices in this building for a time. It is the home of Artisans, a gift shop that relocated to the pavilions after the quake, then returned to its former site.

(39) 1386 Pacific Avenue was the **IOOF Building**, in its last incarnation marred by anodized aluminum grills, plate glass, and a gold-finish metal awning over the sidewalk.

Chapter Five

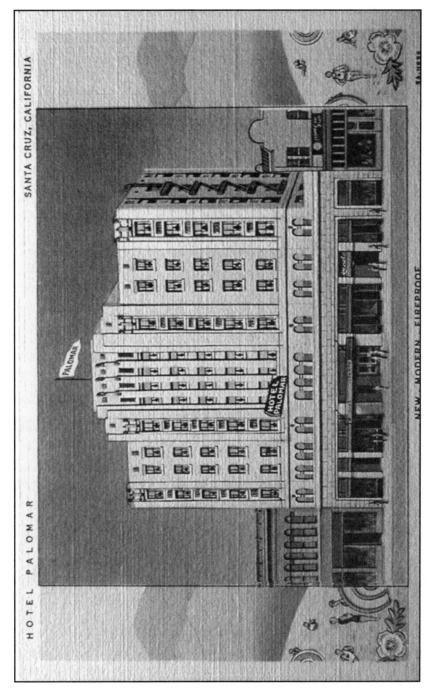

(37) Hotel Palomar *(Judith Steen Collection)*

Plans for the first IOOF Building on this site were drawn up as early as 1868 by John Williams, but construction of the mansarded structure was not begun until 1873.

"The outside of the building is to be covered with rustic, and blocked, to represent stone. The cornice consists of mouldings, console and dentils; the entire cornice is Corinthian, two porticos in front of the building with railing below and above in the Corinthian order" (*Santa Cruz Sentinel*, May 9, 1868).

In 1896 the building had its moment of glory: it was illuminated with six hundred incandescent light bulbs, a display signaling the successful completion of Fred Swanton's power plant on Big Creek.

The building survived the Great Fire of 1894 only to succumb to flames in 1899. It was replaced by a brick structure, which itself survived two fires. It originally had a three-story center section, flanked by two-story sections with square bays. At the top was a mansarded clock tower.

The clock tower was removed in 1964 when the building was renovated. Its chimes had been stilled in 1929, when residents of nearby hotels complained about the noise. The building was demolished after being damaged in the Loma Prieta Earthquake, and a section of the new "Cooper House" now occupies the site. (See entry #50 for the relocation of the clock).

(40) North of the IOOF Building was the **Ely Block No. 1**, constructed for William Ely in 1875 by contractor Calvin Davis, with a facade similar to that of the Bernheim Building.

(41) At **1502 Pacific Avenue** is the Renaissance Revival **County Bank Building**, showing some of the Romanesque-Queen Anne touches of its former appearance.

The ground floor is built of tan sandstone, with banded Doric pilasters and pillars flanking the entranceway. In the brick second story, double and single windows alternate between supported arches. The building once had a corner entrance below a domed cupola. It was constructed after the 1894 fire had destroyed Mike Leonard's two-story brick saloon on the site.

The interior was finished with dark mahogany and with marble from Tuolumne County; the director's room was paneled in oak. Architects for the 1910 remodeling and enlargement were Ward and Blohme of San Francisco.

Before Leonard built his saloon there, the site had been one of the vacant lots used for tent shows featuring attractions such as glass-blowers or Millie Christine, the Double-Headed Woman. "[Her] two mouths would talk and sing, one was a soprano and the other an alto. They could talk and recite. Crowds thronged the tent at 25 cents a head" (Ernest Otto, *Santa Cruz Sentinel*, April 16, 1944).

(39) Pacific Avenue and Cooper Street
(Special Collections, University Library, University of California, Santa Cruz)

(41) Pacific Avenue and Cooper Street, after 1989 Loma Prieta Earthquake. Santa Cruz County Bank Building facade in center; Leonard Building on right
(Mark Primack)

Listed on the National Register of Historic Places in 1982, the facade of this building was saved after the 1989 earthquake. Barry Swenson Builder undertook the reconstruction, which involved demolishing the entire structure behind the two walls facing Cooper Street and Pacific Avenue.

(42) According to *Santa Cruz Sentinel* reporter Ernest Otto, "Just north of Leonard's building on part of the site of the present bank building was a two-story structure erected for the **Pilot Hose Company**, which moved down from a one-story frame building where the Pacific Avenue Purity Store stands [in 1948, at 1532 Pacific Avenue]. It had space for the hose cart, with showers in the rear for the athletes who ran in the tournament. All the boys knew each member of the team by name, the fastest leads, the fastest runner, the hose man, and the nozzle man, who were the great men of the town.

"On the second floor was the meeting place, used as a club room and for society dances which the hose company gave. The building burned in the 1894 fire and was replaced by the present bank structure" (*Santa Cruz Sentinel*, January 25, 1948).

(43) 1510 Pacific Avenue was the **George Staffler Building**; part of its Eastlake cornice still remained until the building's demise due to the 1989 quake. It was erected in 1894 after Staffler's previous buildings had been destroyed by the fire that burned his undertaking parlor and furniture store.

(44) At **1520 Pacific Avenue** is the **St. George Hotel** redivivus, replacing the white plastered confection of Spanish Colonial Revival design that was damaged in the 1989 earthquake, later burned, and was subsequently demolished. It is devastating to think of the original primal set of Santa Cruz buildings, patched together and many times remodeled and awash in motley charm, vanishing from the face of the earth. But in 1992 architects Thacher & Thompson exhibited a true understanding of the cockeyed charm of the original architecture, replicating key details such as the open turret. The main differences between the old and the new are that the new has parking below and a driveway entrance, doesn't have the funky mirrored room where the Catalyst coffeehouse used to be, and opens up to the street with areas of outdoor dining in a way the old building never did, something that is an urban design asset.

San Francisco developer and liquor merchant Anson P. Hotaling owned the Hotaling House on this site in 1889. In 1892 he hired San Francisco architects Kenitzer & Kollofrath to design a new brick hotel to replace the first structure. By 1893 its three stories housed the People's Bank, Tanner's Drug Store, Jonas Brothers' clothing store, and Mrs. Howard Antrim's rooming house. The structure was destroyed in the fire of April 14, 1894.

Hotaling replaced the building with a new hotel that was named the St. George. It "was not planned at one time by the owner or architect, but was a growth, the extent of the building being increased three times during the course of its erection" (*Santa Cruz Weekly Surf*, January 16, 1897). The Pacific Street facade was of red pressed-brick, with black pointed mortar and stone lintel caps over the windows in a design similar to that of the first building.

To make the hotel appear to be a single building, three years later the interior was rearranged by San Francisco architect Hermann Barth. The open Garden Court was roofed over, and the rooms once occupied by the Superior Court were converted into the dining room, kitchen, and pantry. Marble steps to the second floor were installed, along with a solid oak office counter and bar. The mosaic floor in the lobby was laid, and a hydraulic elevator was installed, "the first and only one in Santa Cruz" at the time.

The St. George occupied the site of fifteen buildings once housing twenty-seven businesses. Southernmost on Front Street was the story-and-a-half, clapboarded William Vahlberg bakery constructed in the 1850s and the home of the *Santa Cruz Sentinel* for a time. To the north was a house of ill repute, known as No. 10. When two of the inmates of this brothel appeared in court, the *Santa*

Downtown

163

(44) St. George Hotel
(Special Collections, University Library, University of California, Santa Cruz)

Cruz Sentinel noted they were "gaudily made up, heavily veiled and would not capture a prize in a contest for beauty." Further up Front Street the Bernheim Brothers clothing store occupied a two-story building before it moved to Pacific Avenue. The second floor "was a hall with a stage at one end for dances and local entertainment. At one time it was given over to a beer hall and variety show with girls serving the liquor to the patrons." At the upper end of the site was the Workingman's Saloon, and behind it was the board-and-batten tinsmith shop of Richard Williams. Williams's shop later became the first meeting place of the City's Pilot Hose Company (Ernest Otto, *Santa Cruz Sentinel*, June 22, 1947).

Palm Room

(44) Palm Room, St. George Hotel *(Carolyn Swift Collection)*

Like the Palomar Hotel, the St. George was distinguished chiefly for its interior. The glass-roofed Palm Room, or Garden Court, was built around a fountain. An airy quality was given to the room by its latticework walls and ceilings, all the beams and supports being thin and delicate. The latticed walls were filled in with mirrors, aiding the illusion of the room as a freestanding gazebo in a garden.

On the walls of the room next door to the Garden Court, gauze-draped nymphs cavorted in leafy bowers framed in gilt molding. In 1978 the murals were "restored," suffering an untimely death by airbrush. These modern maidens would have looked more at home on the side of a van. Some interior sections of the building had gorgeous stamped-metal ceilings in quatrefoil designs, Corinthian pilasters, bracketed cornices, and garlanded Art Nouveau seashells.

The exterior of the hotel was remodeled by San Francisco architect Albert H. Larsen in 1929. Two bay windows were supplied with finials, turned columns, and bas-relief plaques depicting helmeted conquistadores. The overall effect on the Pacific Avenue side was somewhat vernacular in character, since several Victorian buildings had been combined and cosmetically resurfaced as a Spanish Colonial Revival building. Until its demolition, the Front Street side retained the original facade of "cut-brick" Italianate.

(45) During its reconstructions, the old St. George Hotel incorporated three earlier buildings on Pacific Avenue—the Werner, Jarvis-Simpson, and Pease buildings. The southernmost of these was the **Werner Building**, constructed in 1876. John Werner rented out the first floor to the Francis and Willey hardware firm and the second to Mrs. Sophia Harris for her rooming house. The building was completely gutted in the 1894 fire, and only the walls, within the St. George, remained prior to the 1989 earthquake (*Santa Cruz Sentinel*, January 2, 1949).

(46) To the north was the **Jarvis Building**, a two-story brick building erected in 1876 for George M. Jarvis's wholesale liquor store. The large Jarvis family lived in the rear of the store after leaving their winery on Vine Hill, and the upper floor housed the offices of the *Weekly Courier-Item* and, later, a rooming house. The building was designed either by Charles Wellington Davis or his brother Calvin W. Davis. The Jarvis Building was later known as the Simpson Building.

(47) North of the Jarvis Building was the 1891 **C. B. Pease Building,** originally a three-story structure with bay windows on the second and third stories. Designed by LeBaron R. Olive, the brick building had terra cotta and galvanized iron trim. There were twenty-eight office and lodging rooms in its upper floors until the 1894 fire necessitated the removal of the third floor. Edward Van Cleeck supervised the post-fire remodeling of the Jarvis and Pease buildings, both of which were acquired by the Hotaling family by 1920 and incorporated into the St. George structure (*Santa Cruz Sentinel*, January 24, 1920).

(48) At **1534 Pacific Avenue** is a wood frame building constructed between 1867 and 1877 for Hugo Hühn. Hugo, the brother of Santa Cruz pioneer Frederick A. Hihn, retained the German spelling of the family name. The brick wall at the south is a remnant of the demolished Pease Building, which protected this wood structure from the 1894 fire that destroyed the rest of the block to the south.

There has been a food-selling business here since 1929, when Plaza Grocery moved in. Robert O. Zoccoli purchased the grocery in 1948. The business is now run as Zoccoli's delicatessen by his son-in-law (Charlene Duval, "History of 1534 Pacific Avenue," prepared for the City of Santa Cruz Inventory Update, Dill Design Group, 2005). Next door, to the north, the Hihns built a second frame building. North of this second frame building, in 1866-67, Hugo F. Hühn erected a brick building supported by six-ton pilasters cast at the Kirby and Martin foundry. In 1867 Hühn returned to Europe, settled in Switzerland, and never returned to America. Brother Frederick handled Hugo's business interests.

(49) Flatiron Building
(Special Collections,University Library, University of California, Santa Cruz)

Downtown

(49) At the northern end of the block was a brick building erected in 1860 by Hugo Hühn, known as the **Flatiron Building**, originally a handsome two-story structure. With its "freestone" finish, shutters, cornice, and projecting iron veranda roof, it would have looked at home in New Orleans's French Quarter. The first floor was occupied by Tanner's drugstore; the upper floor was the County Courthouse from 1860 to 1864. For a time there was a basement saloon in the building, but it closed in 1878 because underground bars had gone out of style. Both this building and the adjacent brick building underwent many changes, including the installation of "iron fronts" in the first stories and a complete modernization in the 1940s or '50s. After the Loma Prieta Earthquake, the City gave permission to demolish the damaged Flatiron Building. "It's better than sex," commented building owner Louis Rittenhouse, about what it was like to see the Flatiron's demolition (quoted on the front page of the *Santa Cruz Sentinel*, October 7, 1992). As far as Rittenhouse was concerned, downtown's oldest building was "a liability."

With the demolition of the Flatiron Building, the city needlessly lost a second major building on a site equal in importance in the city only to the Mission Plaza. The Hühn brick buildings were replaced by a more massive building, designed by Santa Cruz architect William Bagnall for owner Louis Rittenhouse in 1995, in a pop neoclassical revival style. Classical architecture is a symphony, a division of a building into starting, stopping, and supporting pieces, beginning, middle, and end. Here the elements of cornice and column are piled

(50) Town Clock *(Carolyn Swift)*

on top, exaggerated and overstated. Even so, at least the building has articulation in scale with other downtown structures and creates a strong "street wall" that helps to define Front Street and Pacific Avenue. And call them cornball, but the metal bears in its topmost cornice have a certain charm.

With your back to the site of the Flatiron Building, look to the northeast to see the single most civic panorama in the city—the Town Clock, the 1928 Veterans Memorial statue, the Post Office, and the Veterans Memorial Building.

(50) The **Town Clock,** at **Water Street** and **Pacific Avenue**, once stood atop the IOOF Building and was taken down in 1964 and put in storage. It was then purchased by the City, which intended to erect it at the City Museum on East Cliff Drive. In 1966 James Kruger and Sydney Stiles came up with the idea of placing the clock where it is now. In the 1970s Robert Darrow spearheaded the Citizens Committee on Community Improvement drive to finance and build the tower. Kermit Darrow was the architect of the brick base and Roy Rydell was the landscape architect. It was basically completed in time to qualify as a U.S. Bicentennial year project.

The 1900 Seth Thomas clock is all mechanically run, except for the electric motor that winds the clock. Obviously designed and sited to be a landmark, the tower is a success in this role and an excellent model for the re-cycling of building fragments. The base of the tower is not so felicitous, however, being neither contemporary nor in the nineteenth-century Italianate style of the original clock-housing tower-top. The flat ceiling underneath the tower, which seems to really want to be a groin vault, is especially unsatisfying. The fountain at the base of the tower looks as though it was shoehorned in. The promoters of the clock tower had to accept the presence of the Morris Memorial Fountain already on the site, and the present roadside grotto effect is the result. But the appearance of the tower from a distance is striking, nonetheless.

Front Street was already in existence by the early 1850s. It was the principal business street and fittingly known as Main Street, until the Foreman and Wright survey of 1866 changed its name. Hotels and saloons flourished here, and horse races were held in the street.

"There was business everywhere along Front Street. It never would have died had it ended anywhere and been of any length. It could not be pushed beyond the lands of Mrs. Williams and others for want of enterprise and funds. Then all the shipping was by water, and as Pacific Avenue was opened to the water front, the beach travel gravitated to this avenue" (*Santa Cruz Sentinel*, February 24, 1883).

Because of the greater attractiveness of Pacific Avenue, no effort was made to improve the Front Street buildings. When more space or a more appealing building was wanted, merchants relocated on Pacific Avenue.

An idea of the rough-and-tumble nature of the street can be gained from this 1867 *Santa Cruz Sentinel* description of one of its "low dens": "About two weeks ago a midnight row was enacted at the place referred to in which double-

Downtown

barreled shotguns figured conspicuously, growing, we are informed out of a contention for the patronizing smiles of one of the . . . 'beer jerkers.' On last Saturday night a poor laborer from the redwoods–a foreigner who could just speak English to tell his story came into town with his little savings, and unfortunately for his happiness in his peregrinations fell into the clutches of the females who infest this den. The remainder of this story is an old one. By filling him with their double extract of nitro-glycerine tarantula juice, which they peddle over the counter in a bottle labelled 'whiskey,' they were enabled to relieve him of his mite [sic], after which he was brutally beaten by the landlord and thrown into the street" (*Santa Cruz Sentinel*, November 23, 1867).

Ernest Otto stated that there were four brothels and twelve saloons in the one-block section of Front Street from Water to Cooper Streets. Three of the saloons had stages, and young girls served the drinks (*Santa Cruz Sentinel*, February 9, 1947).

Also plentiful on the street were washhouses, offering one of the few jobs open to Chinese. These laundries were operated twenty-four hours a day by men working in twelve-hour shifts. Accommodations for workers were provided by the management—space to sleep under their ironing board while the other shift was at work.

The fire of 1894 destroyed the Front Street **Chinatown** and finished the area as a business district. After 1894 the dwindling Chinese population moved to two new locations. One was a row of cottages constructed by Harriet Blackburn on what is now Jenne Street and the other was Birkenseer's Chinatown on **"the Island"** in the San Lorenzo River.

(51) 850 Front Street is the main **Santa Cruz Post Office,** a Renaissance Revival building constructed in 1911. The post office is patterned after Filippo Brunelleschi's Foundling Hospital of 1419 in Florence, Italy. Its cross-vaulted arched portico is supported by Tuscan columns and flanked on either side by an enclosed pavilion.

The cross-vaulted ceiling of the lobby is supported by composite pillars and pilasters. In four of the arches above these pilasters are WPA style murals by Henrietta Shore. They represent artichoke and brussels sprouts pickers, quarry workers, and fishermen mending their nets.

Oscar Wenderoth and James Knox Taylor were the architects of the building, and John F. Campbell was the supervising architect. He termed the style "mixo-composite of the Florentine school."

Utah sandstone was used for the exterior; the panels over the entrance are of Portola marble, similar to that used in the County Bank Building. The interior has narrow slabs of Vermont oriental and Tennessee grey marble as baseboards. Much "Eastern marble" was called for in the original design, but some of it

(51) Swanton House
(Special Collections, University Library, University of California, Santa Cruz)

was eliminated in response to protests that too much of this "imported" item had been specified.

The first building to occupy the post office site was the blacksmith shop of Lucius Sanborn, constructed in 1852 by fellow blacksmith Elihu Anthony. The two had worked together in Coloma. A year later Sanborn sold the property to Steve Meek, a '49er who had had good luck at the mines. The butcher shop he opened in the building is said to be "the first in Santa Cruz operated by an American" (*Santa Cruz Sentinel*, March 26, 1950).

In 1884 Albion Paris Swanton commenced construction of a three-story hotel, the **Swanton House**, on the site over and around his Bonner Stables. An Italianate structure, the hotel had two-story slanted bays with bracketed cornices above the broad piazza of the first story. Constructed by carpenters Kaye, Knapp, and Harmon, it was destroyed by fire on May 30, 1887.

Besides destroying the hotel, the fire consumed a Chinese washhouse, the Santa Cruz House, Joe Capelli's saloon, and what was left of the Franklin House, already damaged by an earlier fire. In addition, the fire threatened the Anthony block, A. P. Hotaling's new business block (McHugh & Bianchi Building), and the buildings between it and the Pacific Ocean House. The lot stood vacant until the construction of the post office and was owned for a time by Senator James Fair.

(52) Next door to the post office, at **844 Front Street,** is the 1932 **Veteran's Building** by architects H. Y. Davis and J. W. Pearce of Stockton, in the Hollywood Spanish genre. Adjoining its squat tower is a metal balcony with four decorative panels in martial motifs: flag and cannon, anchors and wreath, drum and bugle, and crossed rifles. Above the building is a weathervane designed as a group of charging soldiers.

It occupies the site of the **Santa Cruz House** (called the Union House until 1853), the first major hotel "down on the flat." Pioneer Elihu Anthony remembered its date of construction as the year 1851. Originally built of split redwood, it was later rebuilt as a two-and-a-half-story structure of sawn clapboards. Along the Front Street side was a covered, two-story porch hung with pots of red geraniums.

(53) Adjoining to the south was the **Franklin House**, an 1859 hotel with an appearance similar to the Santa Cruz House. It was operated by Henry Harris.

(54) Garibaldi Villa Hotel *(Carolyn Swift Collection)*

(54) South of the Franklin House was the Garibaldi Hotel, owned by John and Delfina Costella, which was destroyed in the 1894 fire. It was rebuilt as the **Garibaldi Villa Hotel**, located east of Front Street on "the island," a raised patch of ground in the marshy lowlands of the San Lorenzo River. The Garibaldi Villa Hotel was a triple-gabled building with a two-story sawn-wood railed porch across the front. It was demolished in 1958 as a part of the heavy-handed, post-1955 flood redevelopment project. Several other hotels were located in this area bordered by Water Street, Front Street, and the San Lorenzo River, including the Toscano (later Antonelli), D'Italia, Swiss, and Universale hotels.

In the 1870s, according to Ernest Otto, "on the island were several homes of the early California adobe type. The places belonged to the well known Refugia Cordova family, Charles Alarcon, and Lino Ortiz, who came here from Mexico [or were Spanish language families]" (*Santa Cruz Sentinel*, October 22, 1939).

(54) Chinatown
(Special Collections, University Library, University of California, Santa Cruz)

Around the island "the marsh was covered with green plants with yellow blossoms and back of Chinatown in the dampest part grew China lilies. To reach the island pedestrians had to cross by a foot bridge from the end of Cooper Street" (Ernest Otto, *Santa Cruz Sentinel*, October 22, 1939).

Birkenseer's Chinatown, the fourth and last Santa Cruz Chinatown, was located on the island on a short street called Bellevue Place (later, China Lane), which ended at the San Lorenzo River. The community consisted of small, wooden homes as well as the Congregational Chinese Mission building, which was torn down in 1920, and the Chee Kong Tong hall, which was dismantled in 1950. Beautiful photographs and text portraying and describing life in Birkenseer's Chinatown are found in *Chinatown Dreams: The Life and Photographs of George Lee*. Lee, the son of Chinese immigrants, lived with his family on China Lane. For a detailed description of all four of the Santa Cruz Chinatowns, see Sandy Lydon's *Chinese Gold: The Chinese in the Monterey Bay Region*.

(55) At **115 Cooper Street** is the two-story **Michael Leonard Building,** constructed in 1894 from the designs of Edward Van Cleeck. Above the bracketed cornice is a slight mansard roof with small gambrel gables. At the corner is a bowler-hatted round bay. Short pilasters with Romanesque-influence capitals support the arched, paired windows between the larger set of arches above them. Bas-relief grape vines laden with fruit decorate the second story. The grapes are appropriate, for Leonard kept a saloon in the bottom floor of his building. He moved here after his old building, previously located on the site of the County Bank Building, had been destroyed by fire in 1894. That fire had also destroyed the building that stood where Leonard's existing building is now. This was the Cooper brothers' store.

The four Cooper brothers had arrived in the early 1850s and all engaged in merchandising, Thomas S. and James A. in Watsonville and John L. and William F. in Santa Cruz. The Cooper family came from Gettysburg, Pennsylvania. They were related to author James Fenimore Cooper and, further back on the family tree, descendants of James Cooper of Stratford-on-Avon, who arrived in America in 1680.

John Cooper, known as "Fatty," was "a good-natured if somewhat straight-laced man," according to the Centennial edition of *Riptide*, October 19, 1950. William was known as a friend of the mission Indians and in 1876-78 was the first mayor under the reorganized municipal government.

The two brothers opened their general store in Santa Cruz in 1850 with materials transported across the plains by William. The store was a one-story structure with green shutters. The chief feature of its interior was "a huge box stove about which the men gathered to talk politics" (*Santa Cruz Sentinel*, July 23, 1944).

(56) 109 and 111 Cooper Street are two delightful tiny buildings. At 109 Cooper Street, solid and open elements interlock in a playful composition. The building and the courtyard behind it were designed by Mark Primack and landscaped by Janet Pollock. 111 Cooper has a clever use of metal elements with metal webs used as detail and articulation (Thacher & Thompson, 1991). They replace

(55) Leonard Building *(Carolyn Swift)*

a double building, constructed in 1894 for F. A. Hihn and George Staffler, which was destroyed in the 1989 earthquake.

(57) 110 Cooper Street was the Richardsonian Romanesque Revival style **County Courthouse** building constructed in 1894, after the fire of that year had claimed the previous courthouse on the site.

The walls were of ochre-colored brick, above the rusticated, blue Plumas County sandstone of the foundation and entranceways. Although the clustered columns common to Romanesque buildings were absent, the characteristic terra cotta ornamentation of sculpted heads and spiky, twisting foliage was employed. Typical of the style were the building's squat proportions and general air of weight and bulk. The interior had been finished with much fine woodwork.

During construction of the building there was a running feud between architect N. A. Comstock and construction supervisor Thomas Beck. Beck complained to the Supervisors about Comstock's haphazard execution of the specifications for the building. Brick piers appeared where brick piers had not been called for, underweight steel beams buckled, and substitutions and deletions were made without notice to the Supervisors. Eventually, Comstock was fired, and it was found he had been embezzling from the county. Beck took Comstock's place and Edward Van Cleeck became construction supervisor. Comstock also designed the Villa Montezuma in San Diego.

Perhaps Beck was not able to undo all the damage wrought by Comstock, for the 1906 earthquake damaged much of the building. It was rebuilt, with a lower tower, under Beck's direction.

He had also designed the original 1866 courthouse on the site. It was a square Italianate brick structure with two-story pilasters separating the tall arched windows. Above the bracketed cornice were small, pedimented gables in the low-pitched hipped-roof. At the top was a domed, two-level cupola. At the time of its construction, the style was termed a "mixture of the Italianate and the Romanesque."

The land for the courthouse was donated by the Moores and the Coopers, with the stipulation that the entrance must always be on Cooper Street. The County later acquired the rest of this end of the block to complete its holdings.

In front of the courthouse was a fountain, fourteen feet tall, "surmounted by three gas jets, and is made of bronze. There are troughs for dogs and horses to drink, besides places where the thirsty passenger can quench his thirst" (*Santa Cruz Sentinel*, June 10, 1884).

Max Walden purchased the building in 1970, when it was destined for oblivion as a parking lot. He imaginatively restored it as a collection of shops and restaurants called the **Cooper House**.

Cooper House became the soul of the city. The sidewalk café featured the swirl of Rainbow Ginger's colorful costumes and John Thomson's bongo playing accompanying Don McCaslin and Warmth's "Girl From Ipanema." When the sun got too hot, the customers retreated to the Oak Room bar, resplendent in stained glass, ferns, and oak, some of it newly created by Michael Bates.

The Cooper House was damaged in the 1989 earthquake, and demolition began nine days later. This building was considered the icon of Pacific Avenue, and its demolition symbolized the loss of the historic character of downtown.

(56) 109 and 111 Cooper Street, after the 1989 Loma Prieta Earthquake
(Meyer, U.S. Geological Survey)

(56) 109 and 111 Cooper Street and Leonard Building, 2005
(Joe Michalak)

Downtown

(57) Santa Cruz County Courthouse, 1866-1894
(Covello & Covello Photography)

(57) Santa Cruz County Courthouse building, 1894-1989
(Cooper House, 1970-1989) *(Covello & Covello Photography)*

In 1996 it was replaced with a new "Cooper House" building designed by DES architects of Redwood City for owner Jay Paul. Part of the appeal of the original Cooper House was the materials of which it was made, brick and stone. The new building is simply an undertaking of a different order, with a more limited budget and material palette. It is also much larger; while it is articulated into bays, it is not spatially segregated from its neighbors, nor does it have the high pitched prominent roof of the original Cooper House.

(58) Abbott Square is the courtyard between 110 Cooper Street and the Octagon Building. The original square, designed by Roy Rydell, was destroyed in the 1989 earthquake. The square is dedicated to Chuck and Esther Abbott, nationally known photographers, in appreciation for their gifts to the community and their leadership in preserving and beautifying the urban and natural landscape. (The Abbotts' photographs of the urban development of Santa Cruz and other American cities are in the Visual Resource Collection of the University Library, UCSC.)

(59) At **118 Cooper Street** is the octagonal 1882 **Hall of Records,** designed by Oakland architect J. W. Newcum. It is an Italianate structure with a small, pedimented gable in its hipped roof, corner pilasters, and iron shutters over its windows. Above the sidelighted doorway is a broken pediment with a small urn. A boxy, brick addition was added to the Octagon sometime in the early nineteen hundreds but removed during restoration of the building, which became the Santa Cruz County Historical Museum in 1972. It is now the Museum of Art & History store.

(60) In the area bounded by Soquel Avenue and Front, Water, and Ocean Streets is the 1956 **Redevelopment District,** consisting of land leveled after the destructive flood of December 22-23, 1955, had submerged much of this land under several feet of water. As a flood damaged area, it became eligible for federal urban renewal funds. One hundred twenty-six residences and thirty-nine nonresidential buildings in the then run-down district were cleared in anticipation of the shining city of progress that was to spring up under the touch of the wrecking ball and bulldozer. The San Lorenzo River and Branciforte Creek were transformed by the U.S. Army Corps of Engineers into rubble-sided flood-control ditches. Eagle Street, Willow Alley, China Lane, Short Street, Garfield Street, Burnett Street, and a section of Cooper Street disappeared under the straight edge and compass. Colorful older structures such as Adolph's Place, the Garibaldi Villa Hotel, and the Chinatown buildings were razed.

The project followed the recommendations of consultant Harold F. Wise. **Longs Drugs** and **Albertsons** (now **Trader Joe's**), on Front Street between Cooper and Soquel, date from 1964-65 and were designed by Ernest Kump and

Downtown

179

(59) Hall of Records, Octagon Building *(Covello & Covello Photography)*

Associates. The San Lorenzo Parking Garage on River Street by George Knolte Designs and Construction of San Jose was built in 1972. Its free-standing trellises could be compared to those frizzy cellophane-wrapped toothpicks that coffee shops stick into sandwiches.

The first sales of property came in 1960, for the sites of the Dakota Avenue professional offices and the Villa Nueva Apartments (on the east side of the river), and these set the low standard of design for the district, which eventually filled up largely with undistinguished buildings. The redevelopment area between Front Street and the San Lorenzo River is a humdrum collection of parking lots and characterless shopping and office buildings. This site should become the city's densest mixed-use development, with every advantage taken of the twin exposures to the San Lorenzo River and to downtown Front Street and Pacific Avenue.

(61) Bisecting the redevelopment district is the **San Lorenzo River**, first described by Father Juan Crespí of the Don Gaspar de Portolá party in 1769: "We came to a river of water, which we crossed. It was about fifty-four feet wide and in the middle the water reached the bellies of the animals. In its beds are many

(61) San Lorenzo River, with towers, left to right, Courthouse, County Jail, Mission Hill School, Leonard Building, Holy Cross School, before 1906
(Special Collections, University Library, University of California, Santa Cruz)

poplar and alder trees, and it has very good patches of land that can be sown and irrigated." The river then had a much wider and more irregular channel than it does today.

In 1948 Ernest Otto summarized the transformation that had taken place in the river: "Sections that were a part of the river bottom with beaches of sand, forests of willows, alders, maples, and sycamores and open spaces are now automobile rows along Front street; bulb gardens, cherry and other orchards, and walnut groves are now auto camps, motels and cottages on River Street" (*Santa Cruz Sentinel*, July 25, 1948).

The river bottom offered good foraging and hunting, with rabbits, quail, and turtle dove among the game. Fishing was excellent; trout could be caught with primitive poles fashioned out of reeds cut on the spot. Salmon were speared with modified pitchforks.

An 1885 account makes it clear that fishing in the San Lorenzo is not what it used to be. "While crossing the covered bridge Thursday morning C. S. Coolidge heard a noise made by a salmon coming down the river. He ran down to the river, took off his shoes, waded in and caught the salmon, which weighed eight pounds" (*Santa Cruz Sentinel*, March 20, 1885). To supplement the main course, boys would "make fires on the banks and from the orchards they would pick apples, dig potatoes, and take corn and roast the corn and potatoes in the fire" (Ernest Otto, *Santa Cruz Sentinel*, July 25, 1948).

Swimming was popular in the many secluded swimming holes up and down the river, each hole with its own name and special qualities.

(62) Across the river is **San Lorenzo Park**, created by pushing back the levees so that the land flows down to the river in two terraces. A basically suburban park, "naturalistic" in a very clipped, mannered fashion, it relates more to its riverside site than to its location in the center of the city. It was designed in 1963 by the firm of Royston, Hanamoto, Mayes & Beck. The park features a duck pond and a lawn bowling green that has been popular since its inception.

In or near the southern end of the park might have been the location of the bull and bear fight arena during the 1860s. But in recent decades, the benchland has been filled by throngs of folks celebrating everything Santa Cruz—whether it be the early days of the Duck Island Theatre with Bruce Bratton and Gail and John Walters, Earth Day, Spring Fair, peace, gay pride, bluegrass music, crafts, poetry, food, or face painting.

A pedestrian bridge connects the park to downtown.

(63) Dominating the northeastern section of the redevelopment area is the 1968 **County Governmental Center**, designed by Rockwell & Banwell in the

Brutalist style. Brutalism is usually characterized by what critic Robert Venturi termed the "distortion of program and structure" to create a building that is itself ornament, rather than a functional building to which ornament is applied. In this case Brutalist paraphernalia has been applied as a three-dimensional skin to a simple cube.

Brutalism, when employed in this manner, is a spiritual successor to government buildings designed in the Beaux Arts Classical and WPA Moderne modes.

The styling gimmicks include exposed natural concrete, exposed ducts, and the treatment of the building as a collection of separately articulated parts. The fixed windows are an incredibly misguided feature in the mild Santa Cruz climate.

(64) The ponderous WPA Moderne former **Santa Cruz County Jail** at **705 Front Street** was designed by San Francisco architect Albert Roller in 1936. The best detail of this jail is the cut-away corner at the back. The building was gutted and rehabilitated in 1993, in concert with the construction of the new Museum of Art & History at the McPherson Center. Both the remodeling and the new building were the work of noted Bay area architect William Turnbull. Mary Griffin was the lead architect.

(65) To the south was the 1877 Italianate **Santa Cruz City Hall,** with its pedimented gable, small cupola, and arched, double windows in single arched frames. It was designed by William Henry Burrows. Both the City Hall and the earlier jail of 1889 were torn down in 1937.

(66) South of the jail and halfway between Front Street and Pacific Avenue was the first Eli Moore house, said to be the second house erected outside the immediate Mission area, constructed during the winter of 1847-48. The flooring came from Captain Isaac Graham's mill; the studding material was of "split stuff." It was torn down in 1894 (*Santa Cruz Surf*, May 2, 1894).

(67) The second Eli Moore house was constructed about where the lobby of the Palomar Hotel is today. A story-and-a-half house with Gothic bargeboards, it was moved to Front Street in the early eighties when the William Ely Block No. 2 took its place on Pacific Avenue. During preparations in 1928 for the construction of the Palomar Hotel, the house was again moved, this time to Short Street (where Longs Drugs is now). It was torn down around 1952 to make way for an auto repair shop.

Downtown

(66) Buggies lining Front Street, west side, looking north to Leonard Building
(Special Collections, University Library, University of California, Santa Cruz)

(67) Eli Moore House
(Special Collections, University Library, University of California, Santa Cruz)

(68) O'Rielly Dodge Plymouth (later Buick) Showroom *(John Chase)*

(68) 105 Laurel Street, constructed in 1947 as **Bill O'Rielly's Dodge Plymouth Showroom**, reflects the streamlining mania of the 1930s in its semi-circular showroom. Santa Cruz architect Lynn Duckering was the designer. The car dealers have long gone from downtown Santa Cruz, having migrated to Soquel Avenue and the Capitola Auto Mall off Forty-first Avenue. In 1995 the building, which now houses Kinko's, was remodeled by Thacher & Thompson. The interior of the lively teen center next door is by Mark Primack.

Downtown

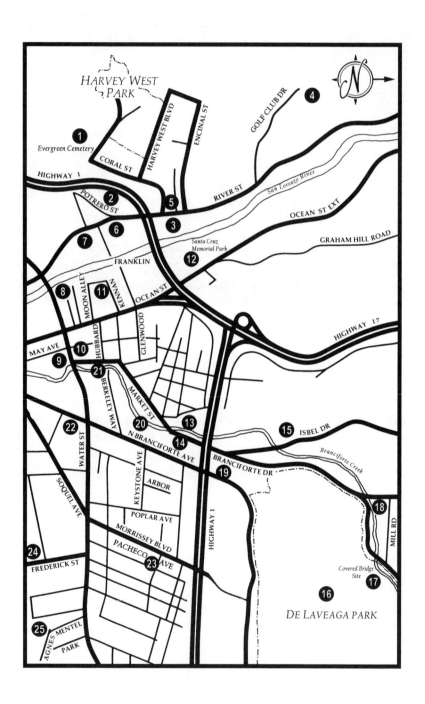

Chapter Six

River–Ocean–Branciforte

The land in the River Street area was originally the Santa Cruz Mission potrero, or pasture, and orchard. The orchard extended from the base of the Mission Hill bluff to Potrero and Mora Streets.

Following secularization of the Mission, the land was granted to José Arana as part of the Rancho Potrero y Rincón de San Pedro de Regalado. Part of the territory was patented by Thomas Russell, who operated a still in the nearby hills. It was in this area that feminist intellectual authors Eliza Farnham and Georgiana Bruce Kirby built Farnham's five-gabled house. The house, never completed, was torn down in 1868. The area was subdivided beginning in 1875.

(1) On the south side of Evergreen Street is the pioneer **Evergreen Cemetery**, covered with a towering mass of foliage climbing the slopes of several steep canyons.

It is always cool in the green depths of the eight-acre cemetery, with its wrought-iron fences, toppled obelisks, gaping crypts, and tilted tombstones. Parts of the cemetery are overgrown with dense shrubs, myrtle, and wild, pink sweet pea. Unlighted at night, partially fenced, and not clearly visible from the street, the cemetery has fallen easy prey to vandals, who break, tip over, and carry off tombstones.

The first person to be buried in the cemetery was Harry Speel, who in 1858 fell over the cliff at what is today Cowell Beach. A month after Speel had been buried, the first 241 lots were sold by founders Samuel A. Bartlett, Richard C. Kirby, William F. Cooper, and Francis M. Kittredge.

A few of the burials have dates prior to the establishment of the cemetery. It is likely that they were moved here from the only previous known Protestant cemetery in Santa Cruz, the vanished Methodist Episcopal yard at the corner of Green and Mission Streets.

The cemetery is divided into five sections, the Grand Army of the Republic, the Freemasons, the main section, the Evergreen extension, and the Chinese, who were allotted the most inaccessible site of all. Remaining in this Chinese section is a

(1) Gravestone, Evergreen Cemetery *(John Chase)*

concrete replica of a large brick oven, where the clothing of the deceased was burned during funeral ceremonies, and the wooden platform on which the ceremonies were conducted. Each grave was marked with a wooden headstone, and a brick scratched with the deceased's name in Chinese characters was placed in the coffin. After five years, the bodies were exhumed and shipped back to China.

The 1884 funeral of Lou Sing, who was murdered (see Sandy Lydon, *Chinese Gold,* p. 269-270), is described as follows: "On reaching the grave the brethren marched around it several times while the band played. A bunch of firecrackers was thrown in the open grave to scare away evils which might be there. The coffin was lowered with music [sic] by the band and the sound of firecrackers. Three roast chickens were placed on the coffin in case Lou Sing should get hungry. If he were wealthy a roast pig would be placed there also." After the coffin was lowered there was a farewell piece by the band to scare away lingering evil spirits, and punks and water were sprinkled over the ground. Small papers pierced with holes had already been scattered along the route of the procession (*Santa Cruz Sentinel*, September 13, 1884).

Often, tramps or small children would sneak in after the ceremony was over to feast off the ritual offerings of food.

The cemetery is now owned and maintained by the Museum of Art & History, which conducts tours for school groups.

(2) 303 Potrero Street was a ca. 1906 wood turning mill owned by John Sinkinson and sons from 1910 to 1925. A 35 h.p. steam-boiler engine turned a line shaft and a counter shaft running almost the length of the building. The various machinery was linked to the line shaft by belts. Boxes, door sashes, and shingles were manufactured here (Monograph by Dan Kaufman). Adjacent to **415 River Street** is the **Farmers Exchange Building.** The restored redwood mill buildings, connected by board sidewalks, and many new structures are now known as the **Old Sash Mill**, a community of shops, offices, studios, a winery, cafes, and other services, businesses, and live-work apartments.

(3) Salz Tannery *(John Chase)*

(3) 1040 River Street is the **A. K. Salz Tannery,** the oldest complex of industrial buildings in the city. A tannery on the site had first been established in 1856 by William Warren and James Duncan. It was destroyed in the flood of 1862, making it unlikely that any buildings constructed prior to the flood remain. The next major owner of the property was Prussian-born Jacob Kron, whose family owned the tannery until 1915. Remaining from this era is the beam house, where hair was removed from the hides, and north of that a building that housed the redwood tanning vats. In the rear was the leach house, where the tanning fluid was leached from the tanbark.

Also built during this period was "Mr. Kron's fine residence at the tannery" (*Santa Cruz Sentinel*, November 23, 1869). In 1882 Jacob and Anna Kron's second home, a large structure designed by John Williams, was built on the west side of River Street, near his tannery. Pogonip Creek flowed through the property and was dammed to form a large pond. The Krons kept a small menagerie of animals, including "Australian monkeys, emus, Kangaroos, and Australian bears" (*Santa Cruz Sentinel*, October 4, 1885). The home was later occupied by members of the Leask family and was torn down in the 1960s.

In the same vicinity was a small rancheria, where the last of the mission Indians lived.

The tannery went into receivership in 1915, following a series of deaths in the Kron family, and was purchased three years later by the Kullman and Salz Company. Temporarily closed in 1929 by the dissolution of the firm, it was reopened that same year by Ansley K. Salz. Norman Lezin succeeded his father-in-law as president of the company, the position he held from 1947 to 1990.

The Salz Tannery closed in 2001. The City Redevelopment Agency is currently (2005) planning an artists' village at the tannery site, with live-work housing, studios, and performance space, while retaining most of the historic buildings.

(4) At **333 Golf Club Drive** is the **Pogonip Clubhouse**. The two-story, brown-shingled Craftsman building was designed by Lee D. Esty in 1911. It was built as Fred Swanton's Casa del Rey Golf and Country Club. In the 1930s it became the Pogonip Polo Club, founded by Dorothy Deming Wheeler, who owned the adjacent Windy Hill Farm. It was during this period that Wheeler, a champion polo player, formed the U.S. Women's Polo Association. The polo grounds attracted many famous polo players. During World War II, the association, led by Mrs. Wheeler, trained mounted troops for the Red Cross.

There have been two opinions of the meaning of the word *pogonip*. One story is that the *po* is from polo, *go* from golf, and *nip* for a drink. However, Donald Clark, in his *Santa Cruz County Place Names*, says, "Humbug!" Citing several scholarly sources, he believes that the word is a Shoshonean term used in Nevada referring to a type of ice fog that sometimes forms in mountain valleys in winter.

In 1989 the City of Santa Cruz acquired the building, which is on city-owned greenbelt property. Plans are to rehabilitate the clubhouse.

(5) 801 River Street is a narrow-clapboarded, Colonial-Revival, raised-basement cottage with pedimented gables and composite columns in the porch. In the gables are unusual applied-wood designs of a cross and quatrefoil.

(6) 602 River Street was the second home of mill operator John Sinkinson, built as a log cabin in the early part of the twentieth century. It has been demolished and replaced with a shopping center.

(7) 240 River Street is Petroff's Steam Heated Motel, a Streamlined Moderne motel with curved glass-brick front and a row of identical cottages equipped with porthole windows, slab door-holds, and a continuous double band below the roofline. It was built in 1939.

(8) 271 Water Street is a story-and-a-half house of the 1870s with a one-story slanted bay. It was long occupied by members of the Rhodes family.

(9) 550 Water Street is a group of doctors' and dentists' offices constructed by Bogard Construction Company in 1962. It was designed in a neo-Wrightian style by Aaron Green of the Frank Lloyd Wright Foundation. The subjection of the plan to programmatic geometry places the offices in a circle around an overscaled, central pharmacy building. Individual buildings have wide eaves, hipped roofs, and panels of sawn-wood cut-outs backed by gold plastic. The most Wrightian feature is the prow-like front, with a pitched roof that angles upward and floats on the corner windows directly below the eaves.

(10) The original house at **121 Market Street** is a raised-basement Stick-Eastlake house with a porthole in its corner, square bay. There is a large sawn-wood bracket in the gable, and sawn-wood trim is used in the porch. It was constructed for Marko Zaro in 1889 at a cost of $2,500, carpenters Kaye, Knapp & Co. doing the work. Surrounding the nineteenth-century home are Victorian revival houses, built in 2004.

(11) 141 Kennan Street is a two-story Italianate house. It differs from other Italianates by its controlled use of detail and larger plain surface area, which together with its height, gives it great dignity. The house has pipestem colonnettes in its slanted bays, quoining, and bracketed, split-pedimented gables. It was constructed in 1877 for J. H. Brown on Ocean Street. It originally stood on five acres that had once been part of the Frank Ball farm and was later moved to its present site.

River—Ocean—Branciforte

Chapter Six

(11) 141 Kennan Street *(John Chase)*

(12) At the northern end of Ocean Street is the **Santa Cruz Memorial Park**, formerly the IOOF Cemetery. In 1870 the IOOF, or Independent Order of Odd Fellows, lodge established the cemetery here on land that borders the San Lorenzo River. The riverbanks are lush and natural and give one an idea of the river's pre-flood control appearance.

Santa Cruz Memorial Park is much larger than Evergreen Cemetery and has more elaborate, generally later, gravestones. Many pioneers, such as early feminist Georgiana Bruce Kirby, African-American-rights activist Joseph Smallwood, and businessmen Frederick Hihn and Elihu Anthony, are buried here.

Motifs widely found in both Evergreen and Santa Cruz Memorial Park cemeteries include wreaths, mason's symbols, recumbent lambs, weeping willows, logs, bibles, roses, lilies, and hands pointing toward heaven. Atop the Jacob Kron family marker is a draped female figure leaning on an anchor and looking across the river at was once the Kron tannery.

The chief glory of the cemetery is unquestionably the 1928 Egyptian Revival **Mausoleum** and **Chapel** by Oakland architect Bernard J. S. Cahill Sr. (1866-1944). It has a gorge-and-roll cornice, an entrance flanked by tall pylons, and a bas-relief, pyramid-and-eagles plaque. English-born Cahill was "a specialist in mausoleum design and mortuary architecture." The plans specified "De Luxe tombs, couch crypts and corridor crypts" (*Santa Cruz Sentinel*, March 24, 1928).

(12) Santa Cruz Memorial Park Mausoleum *(John Chase)*

Don't miss the wax reproduction of the Last Supper on display in the mausoleum. The life-size wax figures were created by Harry Liston, plaster artist, and a team of wax artists from Los Angeles, completing the work in 1950, after five years. The reproduction was on exhibit at the Santa Cruz Art League until 1990, when it was moved to the mausoleum. The figures may be viewed by appointment only.

(13) Formerly at **505 Market Street** was Hammond's Overbrook Farm, hidden by foliage and reached by a private drive bridging Branciforte Creek. The Hammond family had owned the property since 1883, until it was subdivided as "Brookside," a private housing development.

(14) Also located on Market Street was the **Santa Cruz Mountain Wine Company** winery, established in 1887. It took advantage of the soft rock here to run three 120-foot tunnels into the bluff for the purpose of storing 200,000 gallons of fermenting wine. These tunnels did not leak, did not need the support of any beams, and never varied more than three degrees in temperature.

There was also a three-story building where the wine was bottled and labeled. The mash was dumped into Branciforte Creek, with odoriferous results.

In 1899 the winery was sold to the Ben Lomond Wine Company after the original partners could no longer work together.

"Grapes were hauled from Ben Lomond vineyards not far from the Pacific Gas and Electric powerhouse along the Empire Grade," wrote Ernest Otto (*Santa Cruz Sentinel*, May 14, 1941). "The Ben Lomond company wine products were displayed at the World Fairs and exhibits and were always prize winners even at the Paris exhibition."

The bluff east of Branciforte Creek was the location of the **Villa de Branciforte**. It was part of Spain's strategy to fortify Alta California against the territorial ambitions of other European countries. Branciforte, along with the two already established pueblos of Los Angeles and San Jose, was to be the basis of a civilian population not bound to the Church or the military.

"When [Diego de Borica, governor of California] proposed in 1796 establishing a new settlement ten leagues north of Monterey, across the San Lorenzo River from the Santa Cruz Mission, he named it Villa de Branciforte" (David W. Heron, "Branciforte: The Viceroy from Sicily," in special Branciforte edition, *Santa Cruz County History Journal*, no. 3, 1997: 59). Branciforte was named for the Viceroy of New Spain from 1794-98, Miguel de la Grua Talamanca, Marqués de Branciforte.

The first eight settlers came from Guadalajara, Mexico, where they had run afoul of the law. The ranks of these settlers were soon swelled by *invalidos*, or veterans, who received special privileges and pensions for acting as a reserve army for coastal defense in time of emergency.

"The establishment of Villa Branciforte was not an immediate success. The Franciscan fathers at the Mission opposed it, it was under-funded, and its initial resident volunteers left something to be desired. In 1803 Jose de la Guerra, sent to assess its progress, reported that of its twenty-five houses only one was built of adobe, the rest little more than thatched huts. Population fluctuated in the early years, but in 1804 Ignacio Vallejo reported that it was down to thirty one" (Heron, p. 60)

By 1831 Branciforte had a population of two hundred. Its citizens began to spread out over the county after secularization of the Mission three years later. There was plenty of land to support the large herds of cattle, which made life on the ranchos possible.

With the coming of the Americans, the Spanish lost their ranchos, and the Branciforte community disappeared. Only the Craig-Lorenzana Adobe on North

Branciforte Avenue (plotted as a combination main street and race track in 1797 by Lieutenant of Engineers Cordova) remains as evidence of this vanished village.

Ernest Otto described the area as it appeared in the nineteenth century: "In the spring in the grass were the bright yellow cups which grow in California only from Mariposa to Santa Cruz County. Another beautiful spring sight was the fields, especially at the top of the Water street hill covered with blue lupine and poppies" (*Santa Cruz Sentinel,* November 23, 1947).

(15) Zeidler House *(Joe Michalak)*

(15) 231 Isbel Drive is the Leland and Marian Zeidler house, completed in 1978 and designed by San Francisco architect Jack Reinike. The formal intentions of the exterior seem primarily sculptural, lacking in the references to vernacular buildings that one expects in Third Bay Tradition buildings and closer in some respects to East Coast work. The corrugated metal roof and greenhouse contribute to the taut look of the building. Privacy has been insured by the elimination of windows on the street-facing facades.

(16) At the far north end of Branciforte is **De Laveaga Park,** bequeathed to the city by deaf San Francisco millionaire Joseph V. De Laveaga in 1894. He acquired the property in the late 1870s for his country estate. It consists of nine similar chalk-rock hills reaching from Blackburn Gulch, where Branciforte Creek runs, to Arana Gulch.

(16) Pergola at De Laveaga Park
(Special Collections, University Library, University of California, Santa Cruz)

When De Laveaga purchased the land, it was covered with a natural growth of redwoods, buckeyes, bay, laurel, and myrtle. Along Branciforte Creek were several varieties of oak, willow and alder. On the grassy portions of the hills De Laveaga supplemented the natural groves with Monterey cypress, pine, eucalyptus, cork bark, and elm. De Laveaga was fond of horse riding and laid out many trails through his estate, which have since been overgrown.

(17) Just off Branciforte Drive was the **covered bridge** that formerly spanned the creek from Branciforte Drive to Glen Canyon Road. It was constructed in 1892. When it was replaced by a concrete span in 1939, it was moved half a block to De Laveaga Park. The bridge was dismantled in 1993.

(18) 99 Mill Road *(Joe Michalak)*

(18) 99 Mill Road is a former ranch house. Mill road is a short road running between Branciforte Drive and Glen Canyon Road, named for a brick mill once located there. The ranch once consisted of a section of land (660 acres) and the house used to be entered from a bridge across the stream to Branciforte Drive.

River—Ocean—Branciforte

Although the body of the house is a Queen Anne structure of ca. 1890, the eastern portion of the house appears to be older. The ranch house is remarkable for the bucolic splendor of its setting.

(19) 1351 North Branciforte Avenue is the **Craig-Lorenzana Adobe**, the only structure remaining from the pueblo of Branciforte period and the oldest single-family house in the city. Occupied by Judge Craig in the 1870s, its remaining adobe walls were covered with redwood when the Winchester family owned the house. Jim Hawley and Jim Hammond restored the exterior of the building including the porch and its redwood shake roof. Edna and Joe Kimbro, who owned the house in the 1980s, continued the restoration. Edna Kimbro later became a historian internationally recognized as an authority on adobe architecture and preservation.

(20) 1135 North Branciforte Avenue, ca. 1915, is the second most fully developed example of a Mission Revival style house in Santa Cruz (after the William Illif house at 314 West Cliff Drive, designed by William Weeks).

(21) 242 Berkeley Way is the 1909 or 1910 Pedro B. Chisem house. It may have been designed by William Bray, the architect for Chisem's Piedmont Court. The house was for many years the Rostron family home (*Santa Cruz Evening News*, October 18, 1934). George Rostron was a county supervisor from 1915 to 1930. Rose Rostron, his wife, was the first woman county supervisor, serving from 1931 to 1949.

(22) At the southeast corner of North Branciforte Avenue and Water Street is the **Branciforte Grammar School**. The building was designed by William Weeks and opened in 1915. Near the school is the site of "Old Chepa's" unpainted cabin. Chepa, whose name was Josefa Pérez Soto, was born in Branciforte. She was the oldest child of José Maria Pérez and Margarita Rodriguez. Once considered *La mas bonita de Santa Cruz* by many, she had fallen into dire poverty by the time she died in 1890, when she was over ninety years old.

"She made her daily pilgrimage to Pacific Avenue, passing up and down the street with sack and staff in hand, giving *Buenos Dias* to her old acquaintances and taking whatever she liked from the goods displayed in front of the stores. She was seldom refused and even money was given her in small quantities when she asked for it" *(Santa Cruz Surf,* May 19, 1890).

Merchants did not begrudge her the money, because she had aided Frémont and his company of soldiers when they were camped at Pasatiempo.

(23) Josephine Clifford McCrackin at her home
(Special Collections, University Library, University of California, Santa Cruz)

(23) At **331 Pacheco Avenue** was the home of Josephine Clifford McCrackin. McCrackin, an author and journalist, arrived in Santa Cruz County in 1880, purchasing a ranch in the Summit area of the Santa Cruz Mountains. She wrote articles for Bret Harte's *Overland Monthly* and the *Santa Cruz Sentinel*. In the *Overland Monthly* she wrote moving accounts of the horrific spousal abuse she had received from her first husband. McCrackin was a friend of Ambrose Bierce, Mark Twain, Ina Coolbrith, and other notable California authors. She was instrumental in the founding of Big Basin State Park and the Semperviren's Club.

She moved to the city of Santa Cruz after the ranch was destroyed by fire in 1890. There were several fund-raising events in 1909 to benefit the Josephine McCrackin Home-building Fund. Materials for the house were donated by local lumber companies and hardware merchants. The lot was donated by the Laveaga Realty Company. The house was built in 1909 and named "Gedenkheim" by McCrackin. Gedenkheim has been entirely re-sided, but the configuration of the house and front porch are the same as they were in her day. McCrackin died in 1920, and her will specified that the house be left as a group residence for elderly single women who were homeless.

(24) Star of the Sea Church, at **515 Frederick Street,** built in 1948, was the last prominent Spanish Colonial Revival building to be constructed in Santa Cruz until Ernest Kump's Crown College at UCSC in 1967. Its highly specific

River—Ocean—Branciforte

(25) Hagemann House *(Mrs. Charles Gunn)*

references to Hispanic architecture make it look as though it could just as easily have been built in the 1920s. The architect was Vincent Buckley of San Francisco.

(25) At **105 Mentel Avenue** is **Frederickruh,** or **Live Oak Ranch.** The house is approached by a long, gently curving private drive lined with blue gum eucalyptus and Monterey cypress.

At the end is the crisp, Stick-Eastlake design house with a crystalline coating of lathe-turned and sawn-wood trim. There is a rolling-pin-like tower at either end, with a conical roof above the crenellation at its top. In the center is a gable with spool-like spindles. The porch, with its cut-out trim of stars, is topped by iron cresting. Surrounding the house are acacia, live oak, magnolia, palm, and monkey-puzzle trees.

The front section of this house was designed by architect Emil John for Frederick Hagemann and built in 1885. The rear section may be older and could date any time from the late 1860s on.

Hagemann was a native of Hanover, Germany, who came to California in 1853 to work in the mines at Placerville. He ran a shoe store in San Francisco for a time and held an interest in Claus Spreckels's Albany Brewery from 1866-1878.

River—Ocean—Branciforte

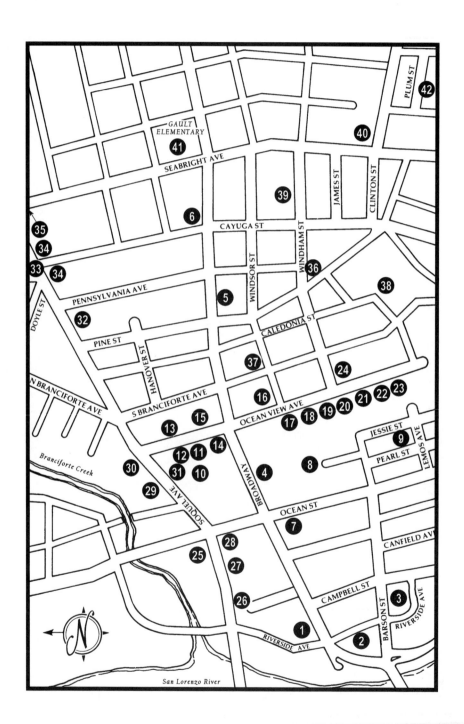

Chapter Seven

Eastside

The district east of the San Lorenzo River and south of Soquel Avenue and Water Street is made up of two main areas. On the lowlands by the river is a district of apartments, motels, and small homes, with much crosstown and beach traffic flowing through it. On the plateau to the east is a quieter residential area.

Riverside Avenue was first laid out in 1867 through the lands of Cooper, Ward, and Barker. It became a desirable residential area in 1876, when Meserve subdivided the upper portion. Many of the houses on the street date from the years 1876-77.

(1) 804 Riverside Avenue is an Italianate-influenced house with split-pedimented gables, bracketed cornices, and mansarded, one-story square bays. It was constructed in 1889 by W. W. Brown and purchased that same year by F. W. Buckley.

(2) 721 Riverside Avenue is a saltbox-shaped, clapboarded house of the 1850s or '60s with newer porch.

(3) At the end of Riverside Avenue was the **Riverside Hotel,** operated by Alfred and Mary Ellen Barson. Barson had purchased the thirty-acre property from E. H. Heacock in 1870. Seven years later he remodeled the original one-story house into a three-story, mansard-roof hotel, constructed by John Morrow. Barson raised and cured his own pork, fed and milked his own cows, and kept on hand a supply of chickens "of right age and in tip-top condition for broiling," all to supply the hotel tables. There was a large orchard of all sorts of fruit trees and a three-acre flower garden. Statuary, fountains, and an octagonal clubhouse dotted the grounds (*Santa Cruz Sentinel*, May 26, 1877).

Most of the property was subdivided by Fred Gilbert and Laurence Canfield in 1945. The hotel itself was torn down in 1960.

For an extensive history of the 700 and 800 hundred blocks of Riverside Avenue and the Riverside neighborhood, see Linda Rosewood Hooper's Web site: http://people.ucsc.edu/ ~rosewood/ riverside/neighborhood/neighborhood. html.

(4) 526 Broadway is the home of the **Santa Cruz Art League**, built in 1951 and designed by Santa Cruz architect Lynn Duckering. This site has been included not for architectural merit but rather because it is the home of an important local arts institution, the Santa Cruz Art League, which was founded in 1919. Its best known early members include artists Frank and Lillian Heath, Margaret Rogers, Cor de Gavere, and Leonora Penniman. For many years this building housed a wax reproduction of the Last Supper, now relocated to the Santa Cruz Memorial Park Mausoleum (see Chapter 6, #12).

(5) 1108 and **1114 Broadway** are twin houses with vigorous sawn-wood and spindle trim. The house at 1108 has an extra-steep pagoda-like roof.

(6) 1205 Broadway is a flashy "Barbary Coast Gothic" Eastlake house, typical of many built in San Francisco during the '80s. This house was converted to a hotel known as "The Antlers" after the turn of the century. The hipped roof is interrupted by tall, semi-detached dormers. There are two-story, mansarded, square bays and oversize Italianate brackets in the cornice.

(6) Brown House *(Museum of Art & History)*

The house was built by W. W. Brown in 1889 for Thomas L. Bell and became a "Keeley cure" sanitarium in 1893, with Dr. E. V. Jarrett in charge. "Dr. Keeley's wonderful specific for drunkenness and overindulgence in narcotics" was the "bichloride of gold" (*Santa Cruz Weekly Surf*, January 7, 1893).

(7) 363 Ocean Street has the Eastlake bent-roof silhouette common in this area of town and an elaborate sawn-wood bracket in the gable. This house was built in 1889 and designed by Daniel Damkroeger for real estate developer Elias H. Robinson.

(8) 338 Ocean Street also has a bent roofline. There are Stick brackets in the porch, a one-story mansarded bay, and sawn-wood trim in porches and gables.

(9) 206 Pearl Street has Swiss Chalet trim on the porch and large sawn-wood trim on its prominent Eastlake bargeboard.

Ocean View Avenue has been the prime residential street on the Eastside since its opening in 1871. Amenities include the cliff-top views of the town and bay, large lots, and big trees.

(10) At the head of the avenue is **Villa Perla**, the large two-story Colonial Revival house at **520 Soquel Avenue**.

There are fat, Colonial Revival garlands below the eaves, a corner tower with witches-hat roof, and a central portico with fluted Corinthian pillars. The top story is sheathed in random shingling. Below that is a band of arched shingling, and the first story is covered in narrow clapboarding. The tall chimney is exposed in the Queen Anne manner.

The ceiling of the dining room is paneled in oak. There is an oak wainscotted entrance hall, and on the second floor is a gallery around the sides of the spindle-railed staircase.

The house was built in 1893 for Fred Swanton, who named it in honor of his daughter Pearl. Edward Van Cleeck was the architect. When Pearl married, Swanton had the tracks of his trolley company brought up to the doorstep. The guests arriving from San Francisco were picked up at the railroad station and delivered straight to the house.

President Theodore Roosevelt is supposed to have stayed in the two front rooms on the night he came to Santa Cruz to dedicate a tree in what is now Henry Cowell Redwoods State Park.

Eastside

(10) Villa Perla *(Museum of Art & History)*

(11) 518 Soquel Avenue is the much-remodeled Elbert Austin house, built in 1873. Charles W. Davis designed it as a hipped-roof Italianate, with a large split-pedimented gable in each side, paired windows, and porches along at least two sides of the building.

(12) 537 Ocean View Avenue is a twin-gabled house of the late 1860s or very early 1870s that once stood on Soquel Avenue, in front of the Swanton house. It has lost the porch that once surrounded it but retains the tall openings in the gables that framed the doors to the porch. It was built for Richard Harrison Hall, a Vermont man.

"Hall had set out from Boston in 1849 for the California gold fields. By an error in ship's reckonings the vessel he was on made port in Santa Cruz (in 1850). It was said that still eager to reach the diggings he walked over the mountains and made his way to San Francisco, thence to Jackson, Calaveras County." Hall returned to Santa Cruz in 1863 and opened a butcher shop on Front Street. Prospering, he became the owner of three-hundred acres of beachfront land at Natural Bridges. His foster daughter, Stanley, married Fred Swanton.

(13) 540 Ocean View Avenue is a symmetrical Stick-Italianate house with twin corner, square bays, and squeezed-pediment cornices over the double windows.

(13) Swanton House *(Joe Michalak)*

There is a band of shingling below the eaves, Eastlake bargeboards, and stained-glass panels at the top of the windows.

This 1888 cottage was designed by Daniel Damkroeger for Fred Swanton. It was moved to its present site in 1892, when Swanton sold it to Frank Mattison and built his new and larger home on its site.

A *Courier-Item* (February 11, 1888) article describes the interior. The reception hall had walls "tinted in terra cotta and bordered with tinsel flock: a dado of Lincrusta Walton in neat design and tints of gilt and terra cotta extend to the chair rail, which like the rest of the woodwork of this apartment is of cherry."

(14) 513 Ocean View Avenue has a turn-of-the-century Colonial Revival front that was added to an Italianate house.

(15) 524 Ocean View Avenue is an early 1870s house showing a combination of Greek Revival and Italianate influences. It has corner pilasters supporting a split-pedimented gable, and a one-story slanted bay. There is a great deal of wall area relative to the window area.

(16) 412 Ocean View Avenue is an Eastlake style house with Swiss Chalet trim, bent roofline, and a change of direction in the siding below the eaves. This was the home of Gusbert Bogart Vroom DeLamater, better known as "Initials" or "Alphabet" to his friends.

Born in New York City and educated on the Indiana frontier, he came to California in 1850 in the same wagon train with Eben Bennett and future Big Four magnate Charles Crocker. Once in California, "Initials" went into the mercantile business with Crocker and later "transferred his allegiance to Michigan Bar, an almost inaccessible wealthy gold town on the middle fork of the American River, serving that community as postmaster, Wells Fargo agent, and general merchant" (Centennial edition of *Riptide*, October 19, 1950). Selling his mining camp holdings to his brother, Peter, he moved to Santa Cruz in 1868 and at once became active in promoting the growth of the community through real estate and business dealings. He was city mayor in 1871-72.

The house, constructed in 1880, originally had a three-story tower with dormers in its pyramidal roof (Margaret Koch, *Santa Cruz Sentinel,* June 2, 1963).

(17) 331 Ocean View Avenue is a standard-plan, hipped-roof, Queen Anne, raised-basement cottage constructed by A. L. Whitney for Ansel Litchfield of Stockton in 1890.

(18) 325 Ocean View Avenue is a Stick-Eastlake house remodeled with multiple parallel rooflines in the Bungalow manner. It has crisp sawn-wood trim in its porches, a band of fish-scale shingles under the roofline, and mansarded one-story bays. Designed by John Williams, it was constructed in 1886-87 by contractor L. B. McCornick for Charles Goodspeed.

(19) 317 Ocean View Avenue is a simple house with a corner polygonal bay. It was designed by LeBaron R. Olive for A. M. Johnston in 1891. As originally built, it was the twin to 250 Ocean View Avenue.

(20) 311 Ocean View Avenue is a symmetrical house with a central gable in its hipped roof and cut-away corners at the second story. It appears to have been constructed as a one-story residence in 1887 by William S. Fitch and converted the following year into a two-story house by Abram Mann.

(21) 303 Ocean View Avenue is a Colonial Revival house with slanted and rounded bays and pedimented gables. This structure was built as a one-story house in 1880 by James R. True and Mary True. The family added the second story in 1904. The house has remained in the True/Jensen/Lund family since it was built.

(22) Wilson House *(John Chase)*

(22) 245 Ocean View Avenue has a Stick-Eastlake-style front section of the 1880s that was tacked onto an existing, Italianate house of the 1870s. On either side of the not-quite-symmetrical facade there is a square bay with pitched roof poking through the eaves. One is cantilevered out and the other is a full two stories. In between is a recessed two-story porch with a latticework arch

Eastside

in the second story. The rear section has slanted bays, arched windows, and paired brackets in its cornice. The house was built by Martha Pilkington Wilson in 1877. Mrs. Wilson was a prominent businesswoman and the matriarch of the family that became the leading real estate firm in the area, now Wilson Bros. Her daughter-in-law, Emma Goodspeed Wilson in 1899 incorporated the E. G. Wilson Investment & Improvement Company with her sons David and Frank.

(24) Gray House *(John Chase)*

(23) In 1883 Mrs. Wilson built a second house, at **235 Ocean View Avenue**, to the south of her earlier house. It is a simple hipped-roof house with arched cornices and a central, recessed entranceway surmounted by a bas-relief broken pediment and urn, apparently added in the twentieth century to "colonialize" the design.

At the end of Ocean View Avenue was **Ocean Villa**, a hipped-roof Italianate structure constructed for George H. Bliss in 1870. Bliss operated it as a boardinghouse and hotel as early as 1873, gradually adding cottages.

(24) 250 Ocean View Avenue is an Eastlake home built for Captain William W. Gray of Merced in 1891 and designed by LeBaron Olive.

In a marvelous state of preservation, it even retains its carriage house. Over each of the windows in the polygonal tower is a squeezed-pediment cornice creating a zigzag effect. The Chinese-railed porch has a spindle work and sunburst pattern trim and a paneled, recessed doorway.

In 1894 it was purchased by Judge Lucas F. Smith, a former Apache Indian fighter in New Mexico. He was district attorney in the case of the notorious Texas murder of James P. Golden by Stephen Ballew. The sensational feature of the case was "the fact that Ballew returned to Illinois and married the sister of young Golden, wearing as his wedding suit the clothes he had taken from his bride's murdered brother" (Harrison's 1892 *History of Santa Cruz County*).

(25) Bausch Brewery
(Special Collections, University Library, University of California, Santa Cruz)

(25) The north side of Soquel Avenue between Branciforte Creek and Ocean Street was once the **Henry Bausch Brewery.** The main building was a ca. 1872 Italianate structure designed by Charles W. Davis.

"On the top of the building is a cupola and flagstaff with vane surmounted by a golden beer keg, gilded in the highest style of art by Mr. Gadsby" (*Santa Cruz Sentinel*, September 13, 1873).

"Following German tradition, Bausch had developed a beer garden to the west and north of the building along the banks of the creek. There were trees, gardens, paths, latticed and rose-covered summerhouses with tables, and above the creek, a bowling alley.

(26) Bernheim House
(Special Collections, University Library, University of California, Santa Cruz)

"A covered dance-platform, scene of many parties, eventually enclosed, became in 1881 a sort of variety house, where for a time one could view entertainment presented by acrobats, jugglers, singers and the like" (*Santa Cruz Sentinel*, November 21, 1954).

(27) McCann House *(Museum of Art & History)*

(26) At the southeast corner of **Soquel** and **Riverside Avenues** was the 1883 Reuben Bernheim house, a Stick Villa designed by John Williams. It had a three-and-a-half-story tower, Stick brackets in the gables, and a corner square bay. The house was torn down in 1940 for a drive-in hardware store.

(27) Next door to the east was the rambling Judge F. J. and Lucy Underwood McCann house, originally constructed in the 1870s and extensively remodeled during the nineteenth century. Known as **Ivy Lodge** for its ivy-covered entrance structure with pointed roof and built in seats, it had a circular driveway, a conservatory of tropical plants and ferns, and, to the rear, a large orchard that extended to Broadway. It was demolished in the late 1960s.

(28) A few doors down to the east of the McCann house was the Isaac H. Pierce house, an 1863 brick house with a stucco exterior. Brick homes were rarely built after the 1868 earthquake discouraged the practice, and none survives today from the nineteenth century.

213

(30) Branciforte School
(Special Collections, University Library, University of California, Santa Cruz)

(29) 519 Soquel Avenue was a Shingle-Colonial Revival house similar to 204 King Street and attributed to Edward Van Cleeck. It burned in 1973.

(30) 555 Soquel Avenue is the former Santa Cruz Hospital building, constructed in 1928-29 in a style originally termed "Italian Renaissance." Designed by San Francisco architect Alfred I. Coffey, it exhibits the controlled use of detail common in Spanish Colonial Revival buildings. This detail is concentrated in the recessed, columned second-story porch, the ironwork entrance-grill, and the large arch of the main doorway.

(30) Branciforte Plaza *(Joe Michalak)*

In 1951 the Adrian Dominican Sisters purchased the hospital, where they remained until the new Dominican Hospital on Soquel Drive was opened in 1967.

The 1976-77 pop-Spanish remodeling of the building into shops and offices known as Branciforte Plaza was by architect Gary Garmann; the landscaping was by Roy Rydell. The placement of the new circulation elements is successful in its respect for the important end and center sections of the building, though these new elements are awkward.

The building occupies the site of the first Branciforte School, constructed in 1869. Its successor was torn down in 1920.

(31) 538 and **540 Soquel Avenue** is a snappy little Moderne-tinged building built as a duplex in 1939-40 from the plans of the Santa Cruz contracting firm of Hamilton & Church.

(32) 910 Soquel Avenue has twin slanted bays and a bracketed false front, and extends far back from the street, bordered by a double porch. Originally built in the 1880s for a wagon and buggy agency, it was purchased shortly thereafter by I. G. Gebhard. As first built, it did not have the bay windows, but did have a porch out over the sidewalk.

(33) At the northeast corner of **Soquel** and **Benito Avenues** was the gem-like **Lodtman Hall**, designed by John Williams in 1889 for Justus Lodtman (Lodtmann). It had a front porch over the sidewalk and basket-handled arched windows in the second story, with all the trim picked out in dark colors. The ground floor housed the Netherton and Williams grocery and general store, and the upper floor was a hall used for dances and other social functions. Later it became the "Santa Cruz Hospital," the earliest private hospital in the city.

Next door to the east was the slightly later **Affonso Building**, with its own hall upstairs. Also designed by John Williams, it was a taller building and had paired windows under squeezed-pediment cornices.

Both were torn down in 1947 for the East Side Fire Station, designed by architect Lynn Duckering, at 1103 Soquel Avenue.

(34) 1024 and **1100 Soquel Avenue** once formed a complementary pair of Classical Revival buildings. At 1024 Soquel Avenue was the United Methodist Church. The Neoclassical Revival church was dedicated in 1923 and included six Greek columns coated with Zonolite, small bits of domolite and abalone shell. This finish material was displayed during the 1915 San Francisco Panama-Pacific Exposition. Tragically, the landmark succumbed to fire in 2000. The building at 1100 Soquel Avenue, designed by Lee Esty in 1923, opened as the East Side branch of the First National Bank.

(33) Lodtman Hall
(Special Collections, University Library, University of California, Santa Cruz)

(35) At the northeast corner of **Soquel Avenue** and **Morrissey Boulevard** was the 1885 Patrick Morrissey house. He once owned property extending to the foothills of De Laveaga Park, but he subdivided the land in 1906. The house was torn down in 1959 for a Lucky's supermarket.

(36) 406 Windham Street housed the **Windham Market**, a ca. 1900 clapboarded false-fronted building straight out of a Norman Rockwell *Saturday Evening Post* cover. This structure is now used as a private residence.

(37) The riveting feature of the house at **406 South Branciforte Avenue** is its squat tower abruptly terminated with a dome-like roof.

Chapter Seven

(36) Windham Market *(John Chase)*

(38) At the southeast corner of **Caledonia Street** and **Peck Terrace** is a two-story 1870s Italianate house with quoining, arched windows, sawn-wood trim in the porch, split-pedimented gables, and a two-story slanted bay.

(39) 519 Windham Street is a Queen Anne cottage with corner, angled square bays (unusual for this style) and patterned shingles.

(40) At the northeast corner of **Seabright Avenue** and **Clinton Street** is the Spengemann house, designed by Santa Cruz architect John Stonum and built in 1970. This board-and-batten house is simply and exquisitely detailed, appearing to be smaller than it actually is. Four bedrooms and a double-height living room have been fitted into this house, literally tucked underneath the roof. The corrugated-metal hipped roof is brought out beyond the edges of the L-shaped porch. The cupola-like box, crowning the roof, encloses a skylight, and the posts of the porch are set beyond the edges of its floor, making it appear to float. It is very similar to Moore, Lyndon, Turnbull and Whitaker's Jobson house at Big Sur of some ten years earlier.

(41) Gault School at **1320 Seabright Avenue** was designed by architects Alfred I. Coffey & Martin Rist. The school opened in January 1931. The auditorium facade on Seabright manages to achieve an austerity worthy of the California missions, and the tower takes wonderful advantage of the sculptural quality of Spanish Colonial Revival architecture.

(42) 118 Plum *(Joe Michalak)*

(42) 118 Plum Street is a Stick-Eastlake Italianate house with a very curious detail: the eye-of-the-bull window in the attic does not line up with the window of the second story below.

Eastside

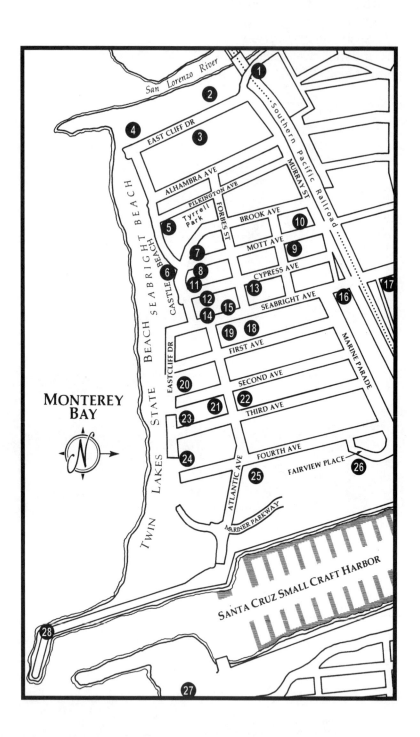

Chapter Eight

Seabright

*"Seabright is a dear little place, and if any one says to the contrary,
he simply doesn't know what he is talking about."*
Miss E. M. C. Forbes, *Reminiscences of Seabright*, 1915

Seabright can be loosely defined as the area below the railroad tracks between the San Lorenzo River and the Santa Cruz Small Craft Harbor. Part of the land was owned by Thomas Pilkington, who had purchased squatter's rights after securing United States patents on it. His property reached approximately from Pine Street to Monterey Bay, between the San Lorenzo River and the little ravine bordering Tyrrell Park.

In 1880 Pilkington developed the resort of Camp Alhambra on his property. He managed it for two years, after which it was taken over by Mr. and Mrs. Samuel A. and Rachel Hall and their daughter, Mrs. Lulu Green. The Halls leased the resort for seven years before the land was subdivided and sold.

In 1884 Foster Nostrand Mott purchased from Handley Bushnell Doane twelve acres to the east, across the ravine, and divided it into building lots, giving the tract the name of Seabright, from Sea Bright, New Jersey. "Thus was created there in a few months a most attractive little settlement composed chiefly of San Jose people of the very best class," noted the *Santa Cruz Sentinel*, September 8, 1886.

Ernest Otto described this area of Seabright prior to its development. "Not a house stood between the gulch and Woods Lagoon. The tract was a meadow of purple and gold, lupine and poppies, which was plowed for grain. There was no street except that leading to Alhambra.

"On the east side were the banks covered with spreading live oak under which ran the path, beautiful in the spring with trillium, the blue hounds tongue, red paint brush, wild hyacinths, and iris.

"Across the railroad track the banks of the lagoon were covered with thickets of azalea, under which were harebells" (Ernest Otto, *Santa Cruz Sentinel*, August 22, 1948).

In 1886 realtor Henry Meyrick, encouraged by the location of the railroad station at Seabright, laid out the easternmost section.

In keeping with the low-key, rustic atmosphere of the place, many houses were finished with board-and-batten siding, still a distinctive feature of the area today. The boards were painted white, the battens, a bright color—blue, green,

Seabright Beach
(Special Collections, University Library, University of California, Santa Cruz)

and vermillion being the favored hues (Ernest Otto, *Santa Cruz Sentinel,* May 11, 1941).

Later construction kept the Carmel-like flavor of the area, including many buildings of the 1960s and 1970s in the wooden cut-out box Third Bay Tradition.

Seabright became a cultural center in Santa Cruz through the efforts of residents such as Elizabeth M. C. Forbes and members of the Tyrrell family. Forbes was a slight wisp of a woman, who customarily dressed in black. She was responsible for the popularity of octagonal cottages in Seabright and occupied one herself. Forbes and Susan Tyrrell headed efforts to establish a library at Seabright and helped form the Seabright Improvement Society.

After his death, the home and land of Tyrrell's brother William were donated by his niece, Kate Tyrrell Peck, to the city for use as a museum, art gallery, and park. The building, known as the Arts and Crafts House, was demolished in 1954.

In 1904 Seabright was annexed to the City of Santa Cruz.

(1) 1015 East Cliff Drive was probably built for Nellie McKendry of San Jose in 1891. It is a multi-gabled Queen Anne cottage with arched windows on the riverside.

(2) At **1122 East Cliff Drive** is one of the octagonal cottages fostered by Miss Forbes. Another is located at 1183 East Cliff Drive.

(3) 1141 East Cliff Drive is a unique board-and-batten structure with a segmentally arched, recessed central porch in the second story gable.

(4) 1152 East Cliff Drive is the site of the fourteen-room **Ocean View House**, built by S. A. Hall in 1889 (*Santa Cruz Sentinel*, July 13, 1889). Daughter Lulu Hall Green was the owner, operator, and hostess of the popular hotel for many years. The plain, two-and-a-half-story structure with a two-story porch was torn down in 1967 (*Santa Cruz Sentinel*, February 19, 1967).

(5) The **Santa Cruz Museum of Natural History**, at **1305 East Cliff Drive**, was built in 1915 as the East Cliff and Seabright Library, a branch of the Santa Cruz Public Library. The Classical Revival style Carnegie library was designed by William Weeks. Artist Cor de Gavere was the librarian for twenty-five years. Her friend, Margaret Rogers, lived and worked in the Tyrrell Arts and Crafts House located behind the library. From 1954 to 1965 the building served as a joint library-museum. The library closed in 1965 and since that time the building has housed the museum.

(6) Near the entrance to Seabright Beach was the **Seabright Bathhouse** built by James Pilkington in 1899-1900. In 1920 Louis Scholl acquired the property. He later replaced the original bathhouse structures with a building that resembled a castle, which he named **Scholl-Marr**. It later housed a restaurant and art gallery. Though the building was demolished in 1967, the beach is still often referred to as Castle Beach.

(7) 101 Mott Avenue has a steeply pitched roof; the second-story porch is partially recessed and partially cantilevered out. A distinctive feature is the use of Chinese-style railing. For many years this was the home of Susan Tyrrell and later Mina Cole Unsworth. Both women were active members of the Seabright Improvement Society.

(8) At **110 Mott Avenue** is a story-and-a-half house with twin dormers and small pane windows. Though remodeled, this is one of the earliest Seabright homes.

(9) The ca. 1920 bungalow at **304 Mott Avenue** has a jerkinhead roof which gives it a thatched cottage appearance.

(10) 311 Mott Avenue is the simple two-story farmhouse of the former James and Sophia Estelle ranch. The Estelle ranch ran from the ravine to Seabright Avenue. Estelle sold wood and raised corn and other grains, vegetables, and raspberries on his property (Margaret Koch, Santa Cruz Sentinel, March 4, 1962).

Seabright

(6) Scholl-Marr Castle *(Covello & Covello Photography)*

(11) 109 Cypress Avenue *(Joe Michalak)*

(11) The Swiss Chalet-like building at **109 Cypress Avenue** features much small-pane window area and sawn-wood trim.

(12) The one-and-a-half-story board-and-batten Eastlake style house at **114 Cypress Avenue** features a corner square bay and bracket decoration in the eaves.

(12) 114 Cypress Avenue *(John Chase)*

(13) At **204 Cypress Avenue** is a simple board-and-batten house.

Seabright

HOTEL AND STATION, SEABRIGHT, CALIFORNIA.

(16) Seabright Hotel and Station with streetcar *(Judith Steen Collection)*

(14) At **207 Seabright Avenue** is a delightful cottage with built-in seats in its front portico. The battens on its boards are grooved to suggest pilasters and topped by individual, stylized capitals. The pillars supporting the porch resemble larger versions of these battens, and the windows are topped by flattened Tudor-arch cornices. The basic design motif of this cottage is the strip/batten and the circle.

(15) Next door, **211 Seabright Avenue** has a front porch out to the sidewalk. It evokes a Seabright quiet enough for sitting by the roadside, undisturbed by traffic.

(16) The Thacher & Thompson **Seabright Building**, at **500 Seabright Avenue**, is one of the most engaging commercial buildings constructed in recent years, outside downtown Santa Cruz. The massing of the building is very effective with corner tower dormers and a two-story arcade on the north side of the structure.

(17) Seabright Cash Store and Post Office *(Frank Urbancic Collection)*

Formerly on this site were the **Seabright Hotel** and the Southern Pacific Railroad's **Seabright Station**. Mrs. Fanny Hamilton Webber opened the hotel about 1900. Through her efforts, in 1906 the railroad established the ticket office with Mrs. Webber in charge (*Santa Cruz Evening News*, November 4, 1925). The station was later moved from the south to the north side of the tracks.

(17) The building at **538 Seabright Avenue** was once the **Seabright Cash Store** and the **Seabright Post Office.** The post office opened in 1899 with Mrs. Nettie Murray as postmistress.

(18) Santa Cruz architect Kermit Darrow designed **215 First Avenue**. The Third Bay Tradition house was built in 1974 for James Winfree.

(19) 203 First Avenue is a ca. 1918 Craftsman Bungalow with the box-shaped void of the porch punched into the solid facade of the house.

(20) Suggesting an English thatched cottage, **1711 East Cliff Drive** has partially hipped roofs and an arched lintel. The 1921 house was designed by the Santa Cruz firm of Walter Byrne and Allen Collins for Minnie E. Chace Hihn and her son Fred D. Hihn. Minnie was the widow of Frederick Otto Hihn, son of Frederick Augustus Hihn.

(21) The development at **310-330 Atlantic Avenue, 118-124 Second Avenue,** and **123-131 Third Avenue** creates a pleasingly variegated silhouette by the manipulation of rooflines and the inclusion of double-height windows. This complex was designed in 1982 by Thacher & Thompson.

(22) 203 Third Avenue is a Hollywood Mediterranean Revival bungalow of ca. 1925-1935. The semi-circular portico is supported by paired columns, the windows are arched, and the roofline is composed of segmental curves and notches.

(23) 1809 East Cliff Drive is a ca. 1910 bungalow shingled to within a few feet of the ground. Wide clapboards cover the bottom portion, flaring out above the foundation. Period details include the river pebble chimney and the open divider of narrow slats between the stairway and the living room. The Fourth Avenue facade is contained within a single large gable, draped with a wisteria vine.

(24) It is difficult to believe that the Russell Giffen house by Wurster, Bernardi, and Emmons at **109 Fourth Avenue** dates from 1956. The wide eaves and the placement of the entry and the picture windows are both reminiscent of some '30s and '40s work by Wurster. The house displays an affection for the Bay Area Tradition.

(25) At **210 Fourth Avenue** is the Ken and Jill Gimelli house designed by Clarke Shultes and completed in 2004. Ken Gimelli is an industrial developer in Hollister. The previous house on the site, a 1908 Craftsman house, was included by Charles

(20) Hihn House *(John Chase)*

(22) 203 Third Avenue *(Joe Michalak)*

(25) 210 Fourth Avenue *(Joe Michalak)*

Hall Page & Associates in the 1976 *Santa Cruz Historic Buildings Survey* of the city. Thacher & Thompson drew plans for alterations and additions to the house in 1994, plans that were modified by Clarke Shultes in 1995 and approved by the City's Historic Preservation Commission. Once under construction, Gimelli claimed that the structure was so deficient structurally and so termite damaged that he ordered an on-the-spot demolition without getting prior City permission.

Subsequently, he applied for permits for a new, larger house on the then vacant site. The request was denied by the Historic Preservation Commission but granted on appeal to the City Council. In an ideal world one would be able to have the original modest building on the site and the handsome new building at a different location.

210 Fourth Avenue is exquisite. It is the best period-revival building in the city since Noble and Sidney Newsom's 1921 Windy Hill Farm. The house belies the assertion that period-revival buildings are no longer possible. On the contrary, they are possible if one has an architect who has a love for, knowledge of, and aptitude for the revival style in question, has access to talented craftsmen, and an ample budget. The basement is paneled in walnut harvested from a Hollister walnut orchard that Gimelli converted to a vineyard. The house incorporates a fifty-foot tunnel leading to a hillside terrace and features metalwork by artisan E. A. Chase. A sample of Chase's work is visible in the gate to the property fronting on the yacht harbor public parking lot. The gate depicts the maritime food chain. The one shortcoming in the design is the expansive, used-brick fence. The color variations in the brick have greater contrast of light and dark than would a fence erected during the original Craftsman era.

(26) 252-256 Fairview Place are three single-family homes in the Third Bay Tradition. They were designed by the Thompson Architectural Group of Fresno, California, for Warren Thompson and built in 1972.

(27) At the **Santa Cruz Small Craft Harbor** overlook, near the Crow's Nest restaurant, is the **Joseph G. Townsend Maritime Plaza**, named in honor of the man who was the longest serving port district commissioner in state history, serving twenty-five years before retiring at the age of eighty-six. Leslie Stone Associates, of Sausalito, designed the plaza, dedicated in 2001. The great mosaic compass is effectively scaled, colored, and detailed, presenting opportunities for centering oneself and relating to the larger environment. The maritime-themed bronzes are literal minded and delightful. The rough surfaces, color,

(26) 252-256 Fairview Place *(Joe Michalak)*

and bulk of the concrete walls, however, seem jarring with the more refined elements. The plaza accomplishes the objectives for creating a monument, in terms of education and celebration, far more effectively than most contemporary monuments.

(28) At the west jetty of the breakwater of the **Santa Cruz Small Craft Harbor** is the **Walton Lighthouse**, designed by Mark Mesiti-Miller and dedicated in 2002. It is named for Derek Walton, who served in the Merchant Marines and was the brother of Charles Walton, one of the major contributors to this community-funded effort. The forty-two foot lighthouse replaces the utilitarian harbor lights that marked the entrance for forty years.

According to the Lighthouse Friends Web site, citizens wanted to replace "the unsightly harbor light with a lighthouse of classic design, adding a little more character to a community renowned for its characters"

(http://www.lighthousefriends.com).

(28) Walton Lighthouse *(Joe Michalak)*

The reason for building this structure was not to improve safety or function but rather to create a new landmark at a prominent site and to do so in a way that would be instantly recognizable to anyone as an icon of the maritime environment.

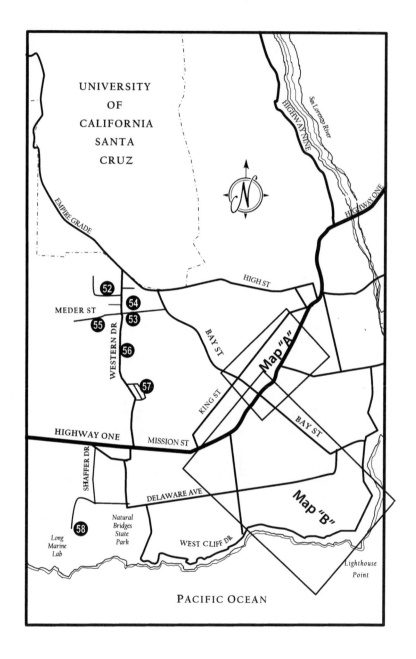

UNIVERSITY
OF
CALIFORNIA
SANTA
CRUZ

San Lorenzo River

HIGHWAY NINE

HIGHWAY ONE

EMPIRE GRADE

HIGH ST

52

MEDER ST

54

55   53

WESTERN DR

BAY ST

Map "A"

56

KING ST

57

BAY ST

HIGHWAY ONE   MISSION ST

SHAFFER DR

DELAWARE AVE

Map "B"

Natural
Bridges
State
Park

Long
Marine
Lab

58

WEST CLIFF DR

Lighthouse
Point

PACIFIC OCEAN

Inset maps are on pages 236 and 237

Chapter Nine

Westside

For the purpose of the guide, the Westside is considered to be the area west of Towne Terrace and south of Escalona Drive, extending to the city limits on the west and to the bay on the south.

(1) A steeply gabled house of the 1870s or '80s, **809 Mission Street** has classically balustraded porches containing flattened Tudor arches.

(2) 914 Mission Street is a raised-basement Colonial Revival-influenced house with a large Palladian window and a latticework arch in the central, recessed entranceway.

(3) The 1870s Gothic-influenced house at **922 Mission Street** has a Tudor-arched front porch and a finial in the gables. Ernest Otto believed this to be the first George W. Place home, moved here in 1887 to make way for his new house.

(4) In the block between **Rigg** and **Laurel Streets** on the west side of Mission was the house of "Crazy" Allan Wright. Wright started the house in 1870 but had not completed it at the time of his death in 1885, because of his continual disagreements with the carpenters. When he died, he was still living in a little shack in back of his half-built house. Mantelpieces in crates were lying there, unpacked for fifteen years.

Wright's niece, Mary Jean Greene, and her husband, Edward G. Greene, completed the house in 1885. It was torn down in the 1930s or '40s. Mary Jean Greene was the author of a well-received book on kindergartens, titled *Golden Keys*. She was also a lecturer on temperance.

(5) 1101 Mission Street is a Bungalow style house with notched rafters and multiple porch supports connected by tiny, projecting beams.

(6) On the grounds of **Santa Cruz High School, 415 Walnut Avenue,** are the locations of the first and second houses of Thomas Weeks. The first was constructed in 1850 by a Mr. Hollenbeck, then demolished in 1884 to make way

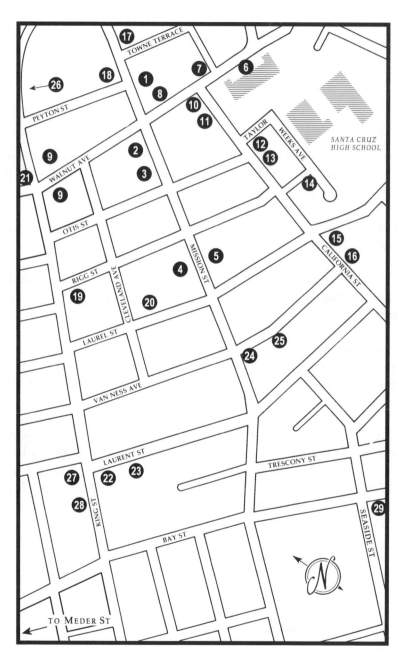

Inset map "A" from page 234

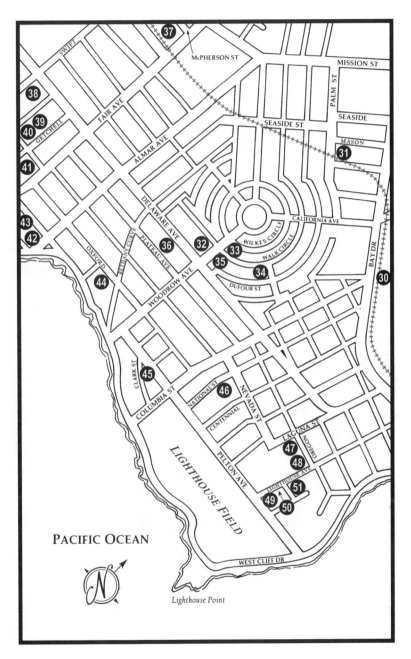

Inset map "B" from page 234

(2) 914 Mission Street *(John Chase)*

(3) 922 Mission Street *(Joe Michalak)*

for the second house, which was moved to California Street in 1914, after the school was rebuilt.

The first high school on the site was constructed in 1894-95 in a squat Colonial Revival/Queen Anne style, with a tall, stocky cupola. Designed by Edward Van Cleeck, it burned on October 1, 1913.

The present high school is a Neo-Classical Revival built in 1914-15 and designed by architect William Weeks. There are three slightly projecting pavilions, fronted by massive Corinthian columns and pilasters.

(7) North of Grover Lane on Walnut Avenue were the three eye-catching Grover residences, all designed by John Williams.

The 1887 James L. Grover house with a three-story tower and an explosion of two-story cut-away and angled square bays stood at the corner of Grover and Walnut.

Next came Stephen Grover's home, also built in 1887, with curved Eastlake brackets, patterned shingling below the eaves, and a short square tower poking through the roof. It burned in 1911.

Last was the 1877 Dwight W. Grover home, constructed with "angles and corners 'until you can't rest'" (*Santa Cruz Sentinel*, April 21, 1877). It had the richest cornices, bracketing, and trim of any one-story Italianate in the city and a strongly split-pedimented front gable over the porch. It was razed in the 1960s.

(8) 512 Walnut Avenue is a Queen Anne-influenced Colonial Revival house of the 1890s with grooved pilasters in the cut-away bay and curved brackets inset with spiral spindles. Short Ionic columns in the porch support a band of spindles.

(9) 710 and **717 Walnut Avenue** are two attractive bungalows. The house at 710 has notched rafters, and 717 has large brackets made of square beams in the eaves.

(10) The house at **837 California Street** probably was built in the 1870s and remodeled in the 1890s. It has a curved bay, and the curved porch is supported by paired columns.

(11) 827 California Street is a story-and-a-half Greek Revival-influenced house with corner pilasters supporting a split-pedimented gable. It may have been built in 1870 or '71 by James Tait, a saddle maker who later entered the plumbing and hardware business.

Westside

(7) Dwight Grover House *(Museum of Art & History)*

(12) The large, two-story house at **724 California Street** is an Italianate house with Stick-Eastlake embellishment. It has a peaked-roof, polygonal corner tower. Its entire surface is covered with moldings, brackets, and sawn-wood trim. Particularly engaging is the use of lathe-turned Eastlake columns in a structural, skeletal, Stick Style fashion in the portico over the gable.

It was erected in 1886-88 for Thomas J. Weeks by architect and contractor LeBaron Olive. According to Richard Cutts's "Victoriana Tour Guide," Olive described his design as a mixture of the Queen Anne and the Elizabethan.

Weeks had come as a '49er to California from his native state of Maine. Finding the life of a miner to be an unprofitable one, he moved to Santa Cruz around 1850, living in a former schooner cabin at the beach. Leasing land from Judge Blackburn, he raised potatoes, cashing in on the high Gold Rush prices. Eventually, he owned an orchard and farm bounded by Laurel Street, Lincoln Street, Washington Street, and California Avenue. The house was moved to this site in 1914 to make way for the new high school building.

(13) At **716 California Street** is a stucco Mission Revival bungalow with candlesnuffer corner turret and segmentally curved, false-fronted sides.

(12) Thomas Weeks House *(Joe Michalak)*

(14) At **125 Rigg Street** is a large, plain, two-story Stick-Eastlake building. It once stood opposite the entrance to the **Bayview Racetrack** on Fair Avenue. "It was a sort of hotel, and at the time of the races it was filled with jockeys, riders, and race track followers" (Ernest Otto, *Santa Cruz Sentinel*, February 1, 1942).

An 1884 account described a somewhat uncivilized day at Bayview Track: "The fox chase was not as exciting as expected. Hardly had reynard been let out of the box before the hounds had him. A rope was then tied around the fox's leg. After the hounds were taken off, Fred Moore, mounted on a horse, dragged the fox all over the field until the hounds again got hold of him and tore him to pieces" (*Santa Cruz Sentinel*, August 17, 1884).

(15) 504 California Street is the 1909 Dr. E. B. Philbrook house, a lovely shingled Bungalow style house with side eaves, central gable, and a T-shaped opening in the porch.

(16) 500 California Street, built a year later for Harry J. Bias, is another attractive bungalow.

(17) Towne Terrace is a short, narrow lane lined with small, unpretentious cottages of varying ages.

(18) 144 and **148 Peyton Street** are two houses of the '20s or '30s with columned, half-circular porticos.

(19) 427 Rigg Street is the archetypal Southern California Bungalow with wide, multiple eaves, widely spaced vertical boards below the eaves, and clustered porch supports pierced by tiny imitation beams.

(20) Collins & Byrne's own version, ca. 1922, of the Bungalow style is located at **1226 Laurel Street**. It bears the firm's trademarks of shingled walls and jerkinhead roof.

(21) The Dr. Samuel B. Randall house at **1010 Walnut Avenue** is a classic William Wurster Monterey Colonial Revival house, built in 1934.

(22) 333 Laurent Street is included for its gigantic combination bargeboard and bracket.

(23) At **325 Laurent Street** is a smaller version of architect William Weeks's Henry Wiley house in Watsonville. It has split-pedimented gables at the side, a pedimented-gable porch with spindly columns, shingled dormers curving out the roof, and a corner bay rounded at bottom and sides.

(24) The building at **157 Van Ness Avenue** isn't a native Santa Cruz landmark at all. Actually, it's one of Gilroy's landmarks that was transplanted here. The church, built in 1870, now houses the office of Boone & Low Architects and Planners. Maybe one day its steeple will be restored.

(25) At **141 Van Ness Avenue** is a raised-basement, gambrel-roofed house with Swiss Chalet porch railing. Built by Thomas Burns in 1912, it was later the home of newspaper editor, columnist, and historian, Leon Rowland and his wife, Jeannette.

(26) At **442 King Street** is the late 1920s home built by Andy Balich, developer of the Palomar Hotel.

(27) A neighborhood landmark is **1104 King Street**, a rambling, ca. 1890, Stick-Eastlake design with a polygonal, conical-roofed tower. The home was built by J. S. McPheters, who moved into this house after selling his Highland Avenue home.

(21) Randall House *(John Chase)*

(23) 325 Laurent Street *(John Chase)*

(24) 157 Van Ness Avenue *(Carolyn Swift)*

(26) Balich House, under construction
(Special Collections, University Library, University of California, Santa Cruz)

(28) The ca. 1919 house at **1120 King Street** was designed by architect Walter G. Byrne for his own home. A shingled Craftsman-influenced house, it has a partially hipped roof, no eaves, and small pane windows. The roof is brought out to the edge of the porch, making the house a single volume.

(29) According to Ernest Otto, the ca. 1904 house at **1111 Bay Street** once stood in the Circles area and was owned by Mr. Norris of the Norris & Rowe Circus (*Santa Cruz Sentinel*, October 3, 1948).

(30) La Barranca Park is on Bay Street at Columbia Street, above and to the west of Nearys Lagoon. The park is a memorial to the city's Italian community, who lived in the area of Bay Street, extending from California to Laguna Streets. A plaque, installed in 2003, gives a history of the neighborhood. Many descendants of the original immigrant families, most from Riva Trigosa, still live here.

(31) 114 Mason Street is a triple-gabled Queen Anne-Eastlake structure with lace-like, sawn-wood trim in its three-sided portico.

That marvelous planning disaster, the Circles area, was first conceived in 1889 when F. A. Hihn, E. H. Robinson and a Mr. King of San Jose offered land to the Christian Church of California as a tabernacle site to be surrounded by roads laid out in concentric circles. The church was built in 1890 from the designs of Damkroeger & Saunders. It was a boxy, irregular octagon with a tall tower poking through the roof of a shorter tower.

Westside

(27) 1104 King Street *(Joe Michalak)*

The circular street pattern has created many odd and substandard-size lots, as well as a poor circulation pattern. Developed haphazardly, the area has here and there an odd cottage with its own unusual feature. Popular was the use of angled square bays on cottages entirely too small for them.

(32) At **705 Woodrow Avenue** is the 1915 Garfield Park Library, a Carnegie library designed by William Weeks in a neoclassical vein.

(28) 1120 King Street *(John Chase)*

(33) 115 Walk Circle is an unusual little Craftsman-Shingle Style house built as a summer home, undoubtedly for one of the members of the nearby Christian Church.

Its coved eaves, saw-tooth shingle courses, and standard, Eastlake, milled doors place its date of construction in the early 1890s. The house may have been built for Alonzo Chance and his wife, Nellie Eden Chance, who owned the property by 1901. John Grinnell, who purchased the property from the Chance family and owned it from 1926 to 1978, remembered the house being there in the 1890s, when he was a small boy visiting Christian Church conferences.

This building is the best local example of the phase of the First Bay Tradition represented by designers like Ernest Coxhead, Willis Polk, and A. Page Brown, who were experimenting with a relatively simple vocabulary of forms and details.

Perhaps the ultimate Craftsman detail is the manner in which the front entry is supported; a post rests directly on a tree stump. The porches were either added or glassed in after Grinnell bought the house.

(34) The false-fronted, early-20th-century structure at **152 Walk Circle** looks like something from the set for *The Last Picture Show*. It was once the **Red Men Hall.** The Red Men were a national fraternal organization whose rituals were based on white men's perceptions of Native American ceremonies. In 1938 the Red Men bought the building, formerly known as Woten Hall, and remodeled and enlarged it.

Christian Tabernacle in the Circles
(Special Collections, University Library, University of California, Santa Cruz)

(35) The quite extraordinary building at **714 Woodrow Avenue** houses the **Santa Cruz Missionary Baptist Church**. The north wall of the structure, which begins flush with the roof at the east end, is angled in underneath the roof so that the other corner is indented. This indentation is emphasized by a lattice-framed arch on the Woodrow Avenue side. The effect underscores the skewed lines of the building. The pieces that make up the building have the quality of being utterly unrelated. Although it is hard to believe that such a combination of the perceptual architecture of Frank Gehry and the ugly, ordinary architecture of Robert Venturi could have been hit upon by accident, it seems to be the case here.

It was built ca. 1909 as a grocery store, which was owned for many years by Thomas Gillies. In 1949 it became the Santa Cruz Missionary Baptist Church, a neighborhood church serving the African American community in the Circles.

(35) Santa Cruz Missionary Baptist Church *(Carolyn Swift)*

(36) In 1890 LeBaron Olive designed **1231 Delaware Avenue** for Edward H. March. This house exhibits the Eastlake tendency to treat the facade as a kind of canvas to be adorned by surface decoration. It has an oddly placed porthole window and a Palladian window.

(37) 1211 Fair Avenue is a stone-faced, concrete-block office building, glittering with abalone shells, begun by Raymond Kitchen in 1947 and completed by a subsequent owner, carpenter Walter J. Irby, sometime during the period 1952-54. Further alterations were made by Dr. B. B. Stoller for his business, Stoller Research Company, which specialized in fertilizer research for Stoller's mushroom company. Alterations included conversion of the chimney to a small office, removal of some ornamental features, and inclusion of additional windows.

Kitchen was a skilled stonemason, specializing in fireplaces, and the building's rocket-shaped one could be the largest in Santa Cruz. Raymond worked largely at night. Some neighbors thought he was trying to avoid the building inspector, but it may have been that he had a day job. On a visit in later years to see Stoller, Kitchen told him that the inspiration for the building was a postcard he had received from India (Charlene Duval, "History of 1211 Fair Avenue–Draft," prepared for City of Santa Cruz Inventory Update, Dill Design Group, 2004; and Carolyn Swift, "Brothers Added 'Westside Bizarre' to Architectural Dictionary," *Santa Cruz Sentinel,* October 21, 2002).

(38) The house at **118 Swift Street** is long and narrow with the narrow side to the street, making it appear much smaller than it actually is. It is also notable for its landscaping, with many species of plants, including fine grasses that provide contrasting texture and color. The house, built around a large cypress tree, has energetically arched windows, finely detailed cornices, and a half-circular porch with whimsically detailed railing, containing both spindled and square balusters.

(39) At the front of **221 Getchell Street** is a gigantic hedge, possibly the largest in Santa Cruz. It is a living architectural wonder with the intertwined cypress providing a remarkable home for hundreds of spiders.

(40) As you stand at **219 Getchell Street**, just to the south of the Big Hedge, you may wonder why this modest home is included. This is a *very* simple house, which may have been remodeled by architect Mark Primack by the time you are looking at it. It was a plywood sheathed "kit" house assembled from a standardized set of parts supplied by Joseph Eichler. He is the most celebrated builder of modern tract houses in post-World War II California, working with architects such as A. Quincy Jones. Even though this house is too small to be planned around an atrium, it has one, nonetheless.

(37) 1211 Fair Avenue, Kitchen Brothers
(Covello & Covello Photography)

(41) St. Elias Orthodox Church, Kitchen Brothers *(John Chase)*

(41) At **519 Fair Avenue** is the **St. Elias Orthodox Church**, a folk-art Byzantine conglomeration of bits and pieces of tile and abalone shells in sculpted concrete. Note the unsupported arches and the elegant thin obelisk topped with what appears to be indoor-outdoor carpeting. Kenneth C. Kitchen started building the "Yogi temple" about 1946.

Following is a condensed transcript of a telephone interview by the author with someone who knew the Kitchen brothers, Kenneth and Raymond. The reader will be left to fend for himself in separating the more and less believable parts of the account.

"The yogi temple was built after dark, by the light of the moon and a lantern lamp. While erecting the temple, Mr. [Kenneth] Kitchen lived in a little shack to one side of the temple. He constructed the two obelisks as antennae, one receiving and one sending. They were used both for his radio set and as a device to stop submarines in Monterey Bay. The electrical apparatus for the submarine-stopping device was housed in a well, in the water. The well is sheltered by the smaller building to the south of the main building. Apparently, the Navy actually did begin to have some trouble with its submarines and finally shipped Mr. Kitchen off to Pensacola, Florida.

"The temple itself was constructed on a foundation of railroad bars laid in a circle, like the hub of a wheel. There are also iron-reinforcing bars embedded in the wall, as the structure was intended to be earthquake-proof.

"In the triangular plaque at the center of the entrance arch was originally a moon and a star. Kitchen believed that it was possible for them to move. When they lined up over a point on axis with the fireplace it would signal the end of the world, or at least the United States.

"Kitchen, who was something of a hermit, eventually moved out of his shack into a building or cottage on the temple grounds which doubled as a goat-milk bar. Inside were piles of books on Indian religion and philosophy.

"The temple as it stands is incomplete. Kitchen intended to add another story onto the temple. There may have been as many as three or four Kitchen brothers . . . The Kitchens were excellent stonemasons."

(42) 111 Almar Avenue *(Carolyn Swift)*

(42) Thacher & Thompson's **111 Almar Avenue** Sperbeck residence in Shingle Style Revival mode comes as close to the straight-ahead, uber-period revivalist, East Coast architect Robert Stern as one is going to find in Santa Cruz.

(43) If you wanted to know what was going on in Southern California architecture after 1980, the house at **221 Sunset Avenue** is one place you can readily get a glimpse and a glimmering from the street. A theme that resonates with post-1980 architecture is the breaking down of the box form into trapezoidal indeterminate forms. Architect Mark Primack's light hand is evident in the weightlessness of the canopies on the building. Despite the disparity in the vocabulary between this building and its neighbors, it is not a jarring element in the streetscape.

(43) 221 Sunset Avenue *(Mark Primack)*

(44) 135 Bethany Curve is a house built and designed by UCSC student Richard Van Deren in 1978. The steep gables with their 1840s Gothic Revival proportions were slanted at that angle to support solar collectors. The octagonal tower is topped by a finial patterned after LeBaron Olive's Thomas Weeks house of 1886 on California Street. Inside the tower is a living room lighted by outsize, wood, double-hung windows and a skylight. It has an appealing Shaker simplicity inside and a certain primitive quality outside.

(45) Designed by Dennis Britton in 1976, **142 Clark Avenue** once looked as though it ought to have arrows sticking out of it. Popularly known as "Fort Pelton," it clearly came out of the West Coast fantasy, Wood-Butcher tradition of the '60s. Its character has been damped down by the painting of its formerly natural wood siding. The chimney by Michael Eckerman is an archetypal piece of Santa Cruz fetishistic craftwork.

(46) The three houses at **126, 130,** and **134 National Street** constitute a little Thacher & Thompson village, designed and built by them in 1977. Perhaps the most difficult question concerning these houses is that of context. It is clear that they were meant to look as though they belonged in Santa Cruz. The problem is that there are not enough buildings nearby that relate to them.

Perhaps the neighborhood is so variegated that the only thing to do is what Thacher & Thompson did, that is, add yet more elements to the street. The most successful of the houses formally are 130 and 134 National Street. The Thacher & Thompson bungalows aren't "about" vernacular architecture, they are "of it" and would look at home in the Walnut Avenue bungalow neighborhood.

(47) 219 Oregon Street *(John Chase)*

(47) At **219 Oregon Street** is a Shingle Style house designed by Thacher & Thompson in 1975. The stern exterior of the house conceals one of the firm's most pleasant interior spaces, with a fireplace designed as an inglenook.

(48) 215 Oregon Street is a highly successful Thacher & Thompson 1975 remodel of a ca. 1890 house for Tom Thacher. In 1978 the firm's offices were housed in the little building at the back, which was originally built for Matthew Thompson.

(49) 116 Lighthouse Avenue displays an effective use of a prominent roof and roofline so that all parts of the building clearly belong to a single, highly comprehensible whole with the garage set back to prevent it from dominating the residence. It was built by and for architect Val Belli in 1994.

(50) Note that next door, at **122 Lighthouse Avenue**, the garages dominate the front facade and the dormer windows are thinly detailed. This is a Thacher & Thompson design from 1994.

(49) 116 Lighthouse Avenue *(Carolyn Swift)*

(51) 214 Lighthouse Avenue is a competent Craftsman Revival house that is true to style with the exception of the front porch. The 1992 house was designed by Jerry Allen.

(52) 100 Moore Creek Road, designed by Thacher & Thompson, has a columned portico and a walled courtyard with an outdoor fireplace facing Moore Creek Road. This is one of the largest and most original of Thacher & Thompson houses. Landscaping is by Janet Pollock.

Chapter Nine

(53) On the south side of Meder Street, between Nobel Drive and Western Drive is the **Home of Peace Cemetery.** The cemetery was founded upon the establishment of the Hebrew Benevolent Society of Santa Cruz in 1877. Moses Meder donated the land for the cemetery and is buried there.

(54) Across the street, north of the cemetery in the **300 block** of **Meder Street** are fifty-four townhouses designed by Thacher & Thompson. They were built in 1996 for the Clarum Corporation of Palo Alto. The repetition of the architectural elements of the buildings—porches, gabled roofs, and bay windows—create a strong streetscape facing the park. In good "New Urbanist" fashion, automobile access to the buildings is from the rear, eliminating the need for front driveways and front garages.

(55) 517 Meder Street was designed by Moore, Turnbull, Lyndon & Whittaker for Mr. and Mrs. Dennis McElrath in 1967. It has natural finish, weathered-board siding and shed roofs in the Third Bay Tradition of the cut-out box. The addition at the rear is from 1977-78.

(56) 810-842 Western Drive is a bucolic, exurban, 1998, co-housing development designed by architect Michael Pyatok. The dwelling units are a mix of single family and semi-detached units. "Each unit is located on a small fee simple lot with a wrap around porch, or 'outdoor room,' that overlooks the network of footpaths and open space linking the community. Parking is held to the edge of the [five-acre] site to maximize shared open area and encourage pedestrian circulation. The Common House, with broad front porch facing on the primary open space, provides kitchen and dining facilities for shared meals, a sitting room, guest room, laundry and a basement workshop" (Pyatok Architects Inc., Web site, http://www. pyatok.com).

The architecture of the buildings is pleasantly composed and detailed. This architecture is not about innovation per se but rather it is about evoking, generalized remembrances of traditional vernacular American rural and suburban, pitched-roof residential buildings.

(57) 150 Yosemite Avenue is the home of architect Mark Primack and landscape architect Janet Pollock. Primack designed the house and Pollock the landscaping. Perched on the side of a steep ravine, the residence combines vernacular charm with modernist simplicity. Various pieces of Santa Cruz landmarks, including bricks from the Cooper House and steel and glass doors from the Allegrini house, have been incorporated.

Westside

(57) Primack & Pollock House *(Mark Primack)*

(58) The UCSC **Seymour Marine Discovery Center at Long Marine Laboratory** (SRG; McHenry addition, BOORA, both 1999) is located at **100 Shaffer Road**. This old Cannery Row/warehouse-like complex is UCSC's research and education facility open to the public and well worth a visit.

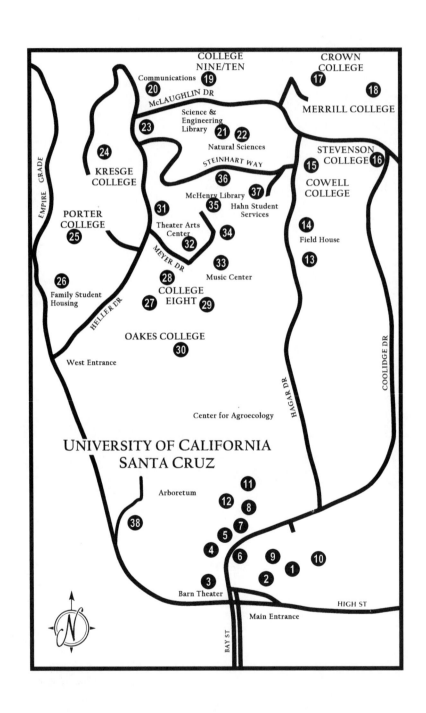

Chapter Ten

UCSC

The University of California at Santa Cruz (UCSC) property was once owned by Albion P. Jordan and Isaac E. Davis for their lime manufacturing business because of its large deposits of limestone, its abundance of trees to fuel the lime kilns, and its proximity to Monterey Bay and shipping vessels. Henry Cowell, who had come to California from Massachusetts during the Gold Rush, bought Jordan's interest in the property in 1865 and Davis's interest after his death in 1888. Lime making was discontinued on the ranch in 1946.

Establishment of a new campus in the central-coast counties was authorized by the University's Board of Regents in 1957, and the Cowell Ranch site was selected three years later. The site was purchased by the University in 1961 from the S. H. Cowell Foundation.

University administrator and politics professor Dean McHenry was selected as UCSC's chancellor in 1961 by his old Stanford University roommate, UC president Clark Kerr. The campus McHenry set out to build was to be "a large high-caliber university, composed of small, intimate collegiate units, with the same budget allocated to other state schools" (David Talbot and Barbara Zheutlin, 1973 *Sundaz!*). The pass/no record grading system, the cluster colleges, and the beautiful campus attracted the second-most affluent and the most liberal student body in the state.

Although the Santa Cruz community, the *Santa Cruz Sentinel*, the city council, and the chamber of commerce all welcomed the campus for the student dollars and the prestige it would bring, they got more than they bargained for. The students registered to vote in Santa Cruz rather than in their home counties and voted in ninetieth-percentile blocs for some candidates and on many issues. Their impact changed Santa Cruz politically from a conservative, sleepy, vacation town to a liberal enclave. Skewing leftward, the city has sometimes matched the People's Republic of Berkeley in its leftist iconoclasm. In the last decade, however, the UCSC population has become more conservative.

Because UCSC was designed to be a major campus, it originally had the same maximum enrollment figure (27,500) as did UC Berkeley and UCLA. Enrollment in 2005 was about 15,000, and the increasing number of students has made a significant impact on housing in Santa Cruz County.

UCSC is located on 2,000 acres of rolling meadow and forestland overlooking Monterey Bay and is the most spectacularly scenic college campus in California. The site plan for UCSC was developed in 1962 by architect John Carl Warnecke (b. 1919) and landscape architect Thomas Church (1902-1978). The original campus architect, Jack Wagstaff, was a member of William Wurster's architectural firm in the 1930s. Wagstaff afterwards became an architect for the University of California, working at several campuses before taking charge of construction at UCSC in 1961.

There are two main architectural themes on the campus. One of them is the participation in the evolution of traditional vernacular and modern themes known as the Bay Area Tradition. This tradition includes concepts, such as the shed roof or the simple porch or veranda supported by pillars, that date back to William Wurster and before him Bernard Maybeck. The second theme is the dialogue between the last strains of neoclassicism evident in the New Formalism of the 1960s and the Brutalism of exposed concrete, popular at the same time. Building type plays a role in the individuation of the structures, with lab and classroom buildings in exposed raw concrete while dorms are of wood-stud, Type-5 construction, sheathed in combinations of wood siding and stucco.

The basic site plan of the University is concentrated in the middle, upper section of campus; the rolling meadows up to the tree line are kept free of structures. However, within these limits, development is still decentralized, a decentralization reinforced by the hills. The rapidly growing redwoods have the capacity to enfold and screen most buildings. In preparation for writing this chapter, I returned with trepidation after a twenty-five year absence for a tour by long-time campus architect Frank Zwart. With relief I found that the considerable number of new buildings disappeared into the trees, and the magic feeling of being contained within and traversing through a sylvan grove remains.

The sheer density and height of the redwoods and the variation in campus topography (there is a variation of 891 feet in altitude) allow the landscape to surround and soften the buildings. Because of the hills, ravines, and trees, the relationship between buildings and building complexes is highly individual and site specific, limiting conventional right-angled building placement. The building height-limit is seventy-five feet, due to fire-safety constraints, the four-story maximum in the construction of wood frame buildings, and the need to stay below the redwood treetop line. The idea of clustering, a timeless concept in campus planning, was first adopted for the residential structures of each college and has become a UCSC standard.

Though the idyllic quality of the campus remains, the Bay Area Tradition in architecture is fading. The original colleges had individually defined architectural vocabularies. The new colleges appear more interchangeable, despite laudable attempts on the part of campus architects to give the buildings every distinction that budget allows.

It is not reasonable, of course, to think that each residential college and each classroom building should be a new and entirely different animal in a Noah's ark concept of campus building. There is something to be said for a commonality of building vocabulary. At UCSC this consistency lies in four-story residential buildings where wall mass predominates over window area, windows are centered in wall areas and regularly placed, and there may or may not be projecting eaves. Similarly, many labs and classrooms employ exposed concrete construction.

At the base of the campus are the historic ranch structures.

(1) Cardiff House *(John Chase)*

(1) The home of landowners Albion P. Jordan and Mary Perry Jordan (later Fagen) was built in 1864 by Mary's father, John B. Perry. Later, Henry and Harriet Cowell occupied the house with their five children until the family moved to San Francisco in 1879. Henry's son, S. H. (Harry) Cowell, was head of the Cowell Company from 1911 until his death in 1955, at the age of 93. The last of the Cowell family, in his will he established the S. H. Cowell Foundation.

Now known as **Cardiff House**, named for George Cardiff, who lived there and was manager of Cowell operations in Santa Cruz before UCSC, the building houses the **Women's Center**. The Cardiff Gate, visible from High Street, was restored in 2002. The grape-stake design gate and columns were built in the 1960s to replicate the original.

(2) At the northeast corner of Bay and High Streets are the one-story **granary** and the **stonehouse** buildings. Now the **Child Development Center**, the granary was used to store the seed and cattle feed made from the oats and barley grown on the ranch. The stonehouse was the paymaster's house in the days when Henry Cowell paid his men only once a year. Later they were paid monthly, and a commissary for the ranch workers was established in the building.

(3) Across Glenn Coolidge Drive, named for the California State assemblyman who was influential in the establishment of UCSC, is the old **horse barn**, now known as the **Barn Theater**, converted into a 250-seat theater in 1968. Project architect for the conversion was Henrik Bull.

(4) The red-painted wood and stone **cookhouse** north of the barn was one of several cookhouses on the Cowell Ranch property, but the only one inside the portion that makes up the UCSC campus. The cookhouse is on the site of the first quarry on the ranch.

(5) The long frame building elevated on stone piers is half of the old **cooperage building**, where the lime barrels were assembled. The other half was removed in 1965 to make way for road expansion.

(6) The **cabins** on the hillside above Coolidge Drive once housed the ranch workers.

(7) North of the cooperage are the wood burning, stone **lime kilns,** which were constructed in the 1850s and 1860s and were used until 1920. In 1946 lime burning was discontinued at Rincon, but the property continued as a cattle ranch.

(8) North of the juncture of the bicycle path and Coolidge Drive is the **blacksmith shop**, in use until the early 1950s.

(9) The **bull barn** housed the ox teams used for hauling cordwood, limerock to the kilns, and barrels of lime to the wharf. This building, now called the H Barn, is home to the UCSC Police Department.

(5) Cooperage *(John Chase)*

(6 and 9) Workers' cabins and bull barn *(John Chase)*

(10) The **carriage house** once sheltered the Cowell riding horses and carriages. This building has been adaptively reused for the UCSC University Relations Division offices.

(11) North of the blacksmith shop, along the bicycle path, is the **powder house**, where blasting powder, used to quarry lime, was stored.

(12) Further north is the **slaughterhouse**, where a bull was slaughtered every week to provide meat for ranch workers.

(13) Wellness Center *(John Chase)*

(13) The **Wellness Center** (BOORA Architects, 2000; landscape architect, Joni Janecki & Associates) is one of the handsomest smaller buildings on campus. Its standing seam metal roof overturning into wall is sympathetic to the neighboring Field House with its period Japanese-lantern-like, pointed-edge roofs.

(14) East Field House (Callister, Payne & Rosse, 1965) is largely sunk into the hill with a great roofscape of building components, such as vents, treated as sculptural objects. Although it is an operational necessity, the fencing that now encloses the project diminishes the integration of the roof form into the landscape.

(15) Cowell College *(Carolyn Swift)*

UCSC

(15) Cowell College (Wurster, Bernardi & Emmons [William Wurster, 1895-1973]; landscape architect, Lawrence Halprin, b. 1916), built in 1966, was the first college at UCSC to be constructed, and it received the choicest site. The architectural use of trellises and wisteria, the alternately red- and green-stained boards used in the ceilings of the corridors, and the sturdy open-beams in the roof of this entrance breezeway are reminiscent of the work of Bernard Maybeck. The view of the town and the bay, framed by the breezeway and the pagoda-like dining hall, is strikingly dramatic.

(16) Adlai Stevenson College (Joseph Esherick [1914-98], 1966; landscape architect, Lawrence Halprin) dormitories are planned around central cores that contain bathrooms and stairwells, in contrast to the more linear dormitories of the other colleges.

The **Stevenson College Apartments** (Backen, Arrigoni & Ross, 2000-02) are too stripped down to be sited at the edge of the tree line.

(17) Tile-roofed **Crown College** (Ernest Kump & Associates, 1967 [Ernest Kump, 1911-99]; landscape architect, Lawrence Halprin) managed to achieve the most traditional feeling of any of the colleges on campus. A warm, modern adaptation of the twentieth-century favorite style, the Spanish Colonial Revival, it puts the visitor at ease immediately. The human scale of Crown has been achieved by the emphasis of the sections of its buildings as semi-detached elements, such as the stairwells of the preceptors' houses.

(17) Crown College *(Joe Michalak)*

Much of the reassurance and strength that Crown exudes is illusory, however. The thick walls that mimic masonry construction are actually built up of stucco over a wooden framework. Curving the walls around corners has rendered the stucco vulnerable to cracks. These cracks let in moisture, which warps and decays the wooden framework.

(18) The placement of buildings at **Merrill College** (Campbell & Wong, 1968-69; landscape architect, Robert Royston) has resulted in a poor circulation pattern, with landscaped areas cut up by paths. An intimately scaled core is juxtaposed with a long, high wall of dormitories.

Because the narrow knoll slopes off steeply on both sides, the dormitories have been placed so that the bottom floors on one side look out on a mural-covered concrete retaining wall. The advantages of the below-grade site are the lessened apparent height of the buildings and the increased feeling of spaciousness. Because the knoll is on a level with the midpoint of the dormitories, bridges are employed, eliminating the need for expensive elevators.

The present sites of both Crown and Merrill were selected in order to reserve space at the center of the campus. In the early years of UCSC the cluster college concept was experimental, and this space was set aside in case it should become necessary to revert to a traditional central-plan campus.

(19) Off McLaughlin Drive are the **Central Heating Plant** (Spencer, Lee & Busse, 1966) and the **Communications Building** (Spencer, Lee & Busse, 1968; landscape architect, Roy Rydell). Two steep, hipped roofs float on a band of windows above the heating plant's concrete walls.

Communications is a similar building. It is quite serene, with much wall space and arched windows slightly recessed.

(20) Engineering 2 Building (*Joe Michalak*)

(20) Baskin Engineering Building (Reid & Tarics, 1971; landscape architect, Anthony Guzzardo) is a Brutalist monolith. The central, open stairwell is treated as a juxtaposition of strong vertical, horizontal, and diagonal elements. The interior of the building, originally occupied by Applied Sciences, was remodeled to accommodate the Engineering Department. The 2004 **Engineering 2**

Building is by Anshen & Allen. This firm is an architect's architect, who gets it right all the way down to the smallest of details. One side of the building confronts the Brutalism of the original engineering building with a sheer wall of sleekly designed high-tech glass to minimize the heat gain on this southerly facade.

The panels for the building were made in a factory in San Jose and trucked over the hill to be joined together on site. The back of the building is sheathed in a gorgeously soft "Rheinzink" brand of zinc alloy metal horizontal cladding, with extruded windows appearing as openings punching out of the building.

(21) Interdisciplinary Sciences (2004) and **Physical Sciences** (2004) are both designed by the firm of Moore Ruble Yudell (MRY). EHDD (Esherick, Homsey, Dodge, and Davis) is the executive architect on the Interdisciplinary Sciences building (landscape architect, Pamela Burton) and Anshen & Allen is the executive architect for Physical Sciences (landscape architect, Joni Janecki & Associates). One of the principals of Moore Ruble Yudell (MRY) was Charles Moore (1925-1993), who was also a principal in Moore Lyndon Turnbull (along with William Turnbull [1935-1997]), the firm that designed Kresge College. (Charles Moore enjoyed being associated with several architectural offices simultaneously.) Moore was famous as a post-modernist who introduced quotations from history, symbolic references, and whimsy and irony. At this point MRY has moved on to modernist territory in these science buildings.

(22) Natural Sciences 2 (Anshen & Allen, 1969; landscape architect, Doug Baylis) is the most monumental building complex on campus, if viewed from the level of the lecture hall, looking upward at the **Science & Engineering Library** (EHDD, 1991).

(23) In order to fit into the surrounding redwoods and not disturb their root systems, the structural columns of the **Core West Parking Structure** (Watry Design, 2000; landscape architect, Merrill & Befu) are inset about five feet from the edge. As a result, when you park here you feel like you are floating in the redwoods, a far more ethereal feeling than you would expect from a parking garage.

(24) Kresge College (MLTW/Moore Turnbull, 1973; Faculty Office Additions A and B, K+CZL, 1991; landscape architect, Dan Kiley with Mai Arbegast) is the most innovative complex of buildings on campus. This is one of the seminal buildings in American architecture. Conceived around the idea of the Italian hill town with a unifying main street, it follows the twists and turns of a narrow ridge.

(22) Natural Sciences 2 *(John Chase)*

(24) Kresge College *(Joe Michalak)*

At one end of the ridge are Kresge's ceremonial entrance arch and college offices; at the other end are the meeting hall (called the Town Hall) and deli, giving the street significant destinations in both directions.

Many of the building elements at Kresge, such as the arches and colonnade/sun baffles, appear as symbols for these elements rather than actual elements in themselves. It is not the buildings that are treated as plastic forms in this curiously one-dimensional village but the space they enclose. Evidence of the firm's preference for complex buildings is the use of layered space created by the arches and colonnades.

Some noteworthy Kresge features are the row-house stoops, ziggurat-like ramp, telephone booths turned into outsized structures, and the suggested "collapsed dome" of the polygonal enclosure in front of the meeting hall. Note also the domestically scaled interior of the Women's Studies Library and study lounge, the light baffle in the meeting hall, and the dynamic vertical interior of the provost's house.

Kresge does not have traditional dormitories with one- or two-person bedroom units nor does it have the usual college dining hall. Instead, the living units are equipped with kitchens and their own small communal spaces.

Important among the intentions of the architects of Kresge was the establishment of a sense of community through the metaphor of the street and a set of "trivial monuments," like the phone booths. They are meant to substitute for more conventional civic monuments and to act as place-markers in the passage along the street.

(25) At **Porter College** (Hugh Stubbins & Associates [Hugh Stubbins b. 1912] 1971 and 1973; Music Building, Del Campo Associates, 1978; landscape architect, Thomas Church), dormitories are grouped in two massive buildings facing each other across a courtyard filled with live oaks. Buildings are banded in pale-yellow stucco and grey concrete. The facades have been very methodically ordered and grouped, giving them a tight, controlled appearance.

Stubbins's design is a compromise between East Coast and West Coast building styles. A modified Brutalism (particularly evident in the office buildings) has been tempered by the tile roofs and bands of stucco. Elements borrowed from California architectural tradition include the use of trellises and the open air corridors and courtyard of the office building.

(26) The apartments at **Family Student Housing** (Ratcliff, Slama, Cadwalader, 1971; landscape architect, Casey Kawamoto) have been built in smaller units than the other building complexes at UCSC. Because of their diminished height and bulk, they approximate more closely non-institutional housing types, such as the townhouse condominium, than do the colleges.

(27) The strong point of **College Eight** (Simon Martin-Vegue Winkelstein Moris, 1990 [these architects were responsible for everything except the two apartment buildings]; landscape architect, Wallace Roberts & Todd) is a lavishly designed series of central public space, both hardscape and lawn, stepping down the hills. The student commons at the heart of the complex is an ingratiating small building in the Bay Area Tradition, appearing as though it should be a completely symmetrical, rather than an almost symmetrical, structure.

(28) The **College Eight Apartments** (Palmer & Rahe, 1990; landscape architect, Thomas Scherer) are a low point at UCSC, especially in the use of aluminum false-mullions. The University Architect's Office had less control over these apartments than it normally would have because they were built by the design/build method. This means that one entity or set association of firms is jointly involved in both the design and the construction of a project. Here the process has produced buildings that are basically flimsy developer boxes that happen to be built on a University of California site. They are not worthy of the setting. The University should always set an example in the quality of all its architecture for pedagogic value and as a point of institutional pride.

(29) The **West Field House** (Bull, Field, Volkmann & Stockwell, in cooperation with the UCSC Office of Physical Planning and Construction, 1977) occupies its site like an enormous barn. The interior is one of the best major spaces on campus, due in part to the beautiful metal and wood trusses. Making a building of this size fit so well into the landscape is a major achievement.

(30) Oakes College (McCue, Boone & Tomsick, 1976; landscape architect, Royston, Hanamoto, Beck & Abey) is a puzzling combination of successful interior spaces and lackluster exteriors and siting. The best of the buildings at Oakes is the laboratory-restaurant building on the brow of the hill, in the cut-into box mode of Caudill-Rowlett-Scott. The square grid of the trusses in the laboratory and the excellent vertical integration of space in the college offices and lounge are worth seeking out. The "color corrected, mercury vapor" light fixtures in the college building look capable of blasting the entire college into orbit.

(31) The **Theater Arts Center** (Ralph Rapson, 1971 [b. 1914]; landscape architect, Thomas Church) is dominated by the heavy cornice roof of the main theatre. The building is as much a theatrical event as any of the productions it houses. This massive slab, the pillars that support it, and the hooded stoop entranceways with their supergraphics are the main elements in the design. The slab over the theatre was originally designed to be both higher and thicker, but budget cuts dictated otherwise. Because the slab extends out to the edge of the

UCSC

(30) Oakes College *(John Chase)*

pavement, it defines the space surrounding the theater as an indoor/outdoor room, which doubles as the theatre's lobby.

The interior of the theater is somber, simple, and elegant. Some major difficulties are created by the stage, a cross between a thrust and a proscenium. If the entire stage is employed, seats at the far sides cannot be used because load-bearing walls block the view.

(32) The **Elena Baskin Visual Arts Center** buildings are by Marquis Associates, 1984, except for the Plaster Studio by Santa Cruz architect Gary Garmann, 1990; the Photography Studio by Herbert Kahn, 1992; and the Storage Studio and Visual Arts Studio by Paulett Taggart, 1993; landscape architect, Richard Vignolo.

The most distinctive feature of this complex is the shed-roof articulation which creates a saw-tooth ridgeline of individual building blocks of art studio spaces. Both sides of the shed roof are transparent, with vision glass on the tall north side and translucent material on the sloping side to the south. At the bottom of the complex, open towards Monterey Bay, is a simple courtyard.

(33) The **Music Center** (Antoine Predock, 1999 [b. 1936]; landscape architect, Joni Janecki & Associates). Architect Predock has brought the austerity of the desert to the verdant UCSC hills. As originally conceived, the building was going to have a sod roof. It would have appeared more as a continuation of the landscape rather than an interruption in it. At the point at which the sod roof was eliminated the whole design concept should have been reconceived.

(31) Theater Arts Center *(Carolyn Swift)*

Apparently, a University poo-bah saw an article about Antoine Predock in an airline magazine and decided that the architect's talent was needed here. However, the belief that hiring a famous architect and letting him do whatever he wants is misguided. Even the most talented of architects, such as Predock, can nonetheless have foibles. The architect did not want any foliage around this maximum-security prison for music. This building is a bunker that needs to be screened. The sunken garden in the complex also needs rethinking. Looking down on it from above, your eye inevitably comes to rest on a drainage grate, which could have easily been sunken and covered with the river-rock used next to it. In a Zen-like contemplation garden all the details need to be right.

(32) Elena Baskin Visual Arts Center *(John Chase)*

(34) Academic Resources Center (ARC) (Fernau & Hartman, 1989) is the most traditional building of recent years on campus. The center partakes of the first generation of Bay Area Tradition buildings. It has overhanging eaves, exposed rafters, wisteria covered pergolas, and other iconic Bay Area elements. Its small scale and its detailing make it seem like a building that could have somehow been associated with the original Cowell Ranch, pre-dating rather than postdating the development of UCSC.

(35) The **Dean E. McHenry Library** (John Carl Warnecke [b. 1919] & Associates, 1966 and 1975; landscape architects, Thomas Church and Michael Painter) is noted for its sky-lighted, concrete, spiral staircase, sky-bridge magically suspended in mid-air over the lobby, and sunken courtyard resembling a giant terrarium. The courtyard is named for founding University Librarian Donald T. Clark. Now that the New Formalism of the 1960s has passed into history, it is possible to see the calm and majesty of Warnecke's execution of the style here, merged with the then fashionable Brutalism of exposed concrete.

(33) Music Center *(Carolyn Swift)*

(34) Academic Resources Center *(Carolyn Swift)*

(36) UCSC's rugged terrain makes pedestrian bridges a necessity. The **McHenry/ Hahn Bridge** (Stefan J. Medwadowski, 1966) was the first one to be built, and more wood was employed here than in later bridges. The projecting beams and rounded edges recall the exquisite frame detailing of Southern California architects Charles and Henry Greene.

(37) The copper roof, battered walls, spreading eaves, and Gothic lancet windows give the **Hahn Student Services** building (Ernest Kump & Associates, 1965; landscape architect, Lawrence Halprin) building the appearance of a hilltop shrine. It was partially rebuilt after it had been damaged by fire in 1970.

(38) Arboretum Docents Building and **Building #2** (Thacher & Thompson, 1994) These are the only Thacher & Thompson buildings on campus.

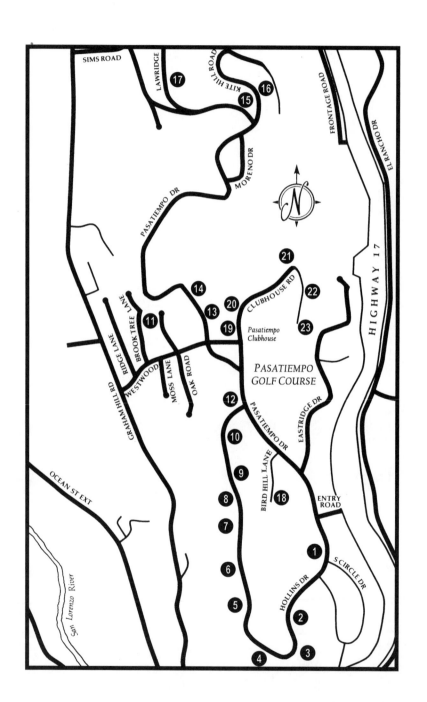

Chapter Eleven

Pasatiempo

by Daniel P. Gregory

Pasatiempo is a residential golf club development planned in the late 1920s to provide a setting for elegant country living rivaling that of Pebble Beach. Indeed, its developer, Marion Hollins, felt that Pasatiempo surpassed the other resort because, as she maintained, Pasatiempo lay on the sunny side of Monterey Bay. Situated on the oak- and redwood-studded hills above Santa Cruz, with a spectacular view of the bay, Pasatiempo can claim an impressive design pedigree. The landscape architecture firm of Olmsted Brothers (successors to Frederick Law Olmsted) drew up the master plan, and Scottish golf-course architect Alister MacKenzie laid out the course. Architects Clarence Tantau and William W. Wurster designed the club structures and the first houses, and landscape architect Thomas D. Church designed the original gardens.

Pasatiempo is an early monument to the tenets of modern San Francisco Bay Region architecture: that is, to an architecture which combined open floor-plans and plain, undecorated surfaces with natural materials, emphatic indoor-outdoor relationships, and a tradition of borrowing from vernacular architecture. Like other exclusive subdivisions before it, such as Palos Verdes, Hope Ranch at Santa Barbara, or Pebble Beach, Pasatiempo was designed to project an image of refinement and taste. But here that image did not depend on imported styles. Instead, Pasatiempo produced a new style of its own, based on elements loosely derived from old Monterey buildings and indigenous California barns and farmhouses. Wurster employed thick, whitewashed walls, shingle roofs, double-hung windows, and an occasional pair of shutters to make a modern or new architecture that somehow still looked familiar. The almost stark simplicity of the early houses stood out in the architectural press of the time and brought national recognition: six received AIA and House Beautiful awards. The houses looked modern because they appeared so simple, and yet they did not do away with traditional style altogether. They seemed to capture the ideal image of a modern California where every living room lay outdoors

View of Pasatiempo, ca. 1935.
In the foreground is the first clubhouse of 1930. In the background is the main clubhouse of 1935.
One of the early guest homes can be seen between the clubhouses.
(Pasatiempo Clubhouse)

and where Helen Hunt Jackson's "Ramona" owned a house near the second tee.

Pasatiempo was the brainchild of Marion Hollins, a latter-day forty-niner from New York. A famous golfer, she had come to California to work for the Del Monte Properties Real Estate Company at Pebble Beach. She immediately fell in love with the coast landscapes along Monterey Bay and dreamed of creating her own golfing community across the bay at Santa Cruz.

Hollins was famous for her flamboyant style. In the early 1920s she had made a bet with two New York friends that the first to make a million dollars would give $25,000 to each of the other two. Shrewd speculation in oil-rich Southern California land (the Kettleman Hills) soon produced her quota. She officially opened her new resort by giving a large dinner party in the first Pasatiempo clubhouse, 34 Clubhouse Road (#23). Toy oil derricks lined the table; under the salad plates of her two friends lay checks for the full amount of the wager.

More than just another vivid character out of the Roaring Twenties, however, Hollins was a conservation-minded visionary who wished to preserve the beauty of the land she was developing. No tree could be removed to make way for the golf course without her personal permission. She established small parks along the creek beds and in the heavily forested sections. With Wurster, Church, and her business manager, she drew up a list of protective restrictions which, according to the advertising brochure of 1930, "will go with the land, assuring maintenance to the purchaser of the character of the surroundings as to trees, shrubs, and individuality." She even persuaded Church to live at Pasatiempo in order to oversee the homeowners' landscaping needs. He and his wife lived at 5 Clubhouse Road (#20), in a house designed for them by William Wurster. This concern for total environmental planning was rare at the time.

In fact, the landscape had taken on such importance for Hollins because that is what she was selling. As Wurster wrote in the *San Francisco Call Bulletin*, "It was Miss Hollins' idea that there should be created here a place for those to live who desire to enjoy the out-of-doors." Outdoor enjoyment meant golfing, hiking, riding, swimming, and tennis. Hollins wanted to create the image of a gracious, recreational way of life. This image, though largely unattainable during the Depression, would capture the imagination of the affluent post-War era and become synonymous with the popular notion of "Western Living."

She had not idly chosen the Spanish word Pasatiempo as the name for her resort community. The property had been part of the Rancho la Carbonera, one of the original Mexican land grants, and Hollins was quick to associate her enterprise with the traditions of hospitality and informal, leisurely country living which she felt to be the hallmarks of California's earlier age. Since she imagined that many of the houses would be vacation homes, she was interested in setting Pasatiempo apart from the city and making it a "country" resort.

Pasatiempo

Marion Hollins knew what kind of architecture she wished to see at Pasatiempo, and Wurster was chosen to be the architect for the development because Hollins admired the Scotts Valley house he had designed for the Gregory family in 1927. She felt that early California architecture ought to have some influence on the house designs. But, to Hollins and Wurster, "early California" did not mean Mission Revival. Wurster preferred instead what he called the "early California warehouse buildings," such as the simple, board or whitewashed adobe, shingle-roofed structures in Monterey, the Spanish capital of California. The desire to make use of an early-California style of architecture soon crystalized into a definite policy when, in drawing up the building restrictions, Hollins finally decided to follow Wurster and Tantau's recommendation that fireproof roofs not be mandatory. Thus it was possible to use shingles on the houses. Wurster had written to Robert Howes, the Pasatiempo business manager, that if fireproof materials were required, "your thought of an 'early California' must go by the boards as so much of this depends upon the split wood roofs." Even before the lots were sold, both client and architect were thinking in regional terms.

Wurster's houses at Pasatiempo were done for clients who held similar convictions about the importance of ". . . living in touch with the out-of-doors and being able to secure privacy for outdoor life." More than just an isolated development, Pasatiempo helped spawn the California ranch house type, perhaps the ultimate post-war symbol of suburban "arrival." Though buried in relative obscurity since the late 1930s, Pasatiempo demonstrated that planned suburban development could be done with great sensitivity, achieving a level of quality rarely matched since.

(Note: William Wilson Wurster has been abbreviated WWW in this section. The reader is asked to remember that all the residences listed are private.)

(1) 2 Hollins Drive, Spec house, 1936, WWW. A graceful trellis-arched entry, luxuriant plantings, and bridges across a modest ravine set this house apart from the ordinary house built on speculation.

(2) 19 Hollins Drive, H. W. Bradley house, 1939, WWW. A two-story rectangular box with horizontal siding. The living room is on the second floor. Originally, several Murphy beds were built into the open ground-floor gallery on the south.

(3) 21 Hollins Drive, D. Palmer house, 1939, WWW. This two-story house on a steep slope was built for respected and successful Santa Cruz contractor Darrow Palmer and his wife, Nina Palmer. Palmer built many of the Pasatiempo structures when he became a partner in the Palmer and Balsiger Construction Company. Palmer and Wurster enjoyed a unique working relationship throughout their lives, and Palmer often influenced the design of a house by advising on the choice of woods or other materials.

(4) 23 Hollins Drive, E. Berry house, 1935, WWW. A long, low elegant ranch house which won first prize in the *House Beautiful* competition of 1936. A later owner added a wing to the southeast, designed by Theodore Bernardi, one of Wurster's partners.

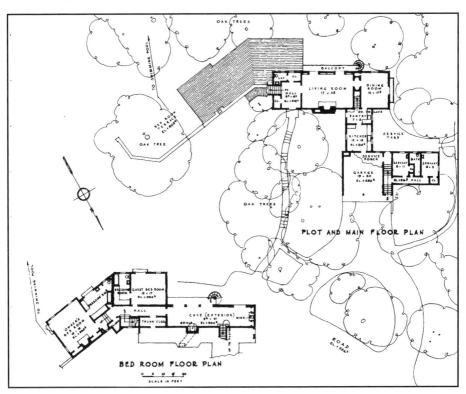

(5) Plans for Hollins House *(Daniel Gregory)*

(5) 33 Hollins Drive, Marion Hollins house, 1931, WWW. The exquisitely sited house built for the Pasatiempo developer. This house almost disappears into the gentle, oak-covered southern slope. Only the generous front door and a small round window punctuate the north side. Here Marion Hollins gave her guests, who were often prospective lot owners, a glimpse of the kind of informal but highly civilized life she envisioned for Pasatiempo. This introduction to the development often occurred at alfresco luncheons in the "cave," a room burrowed into the house and the hillside on three sides and open on the fourth.

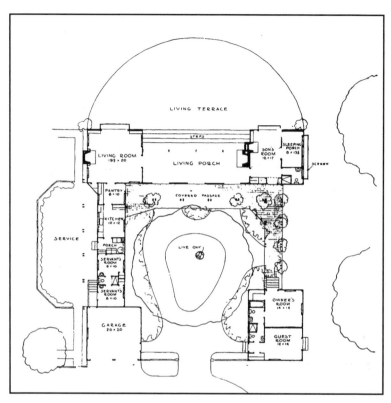

(7) Plan of Butler House *(Daniel Gregory)*

(6) 39 Hollins Drive, M. Cowden house, ca. 1958, Wurster, Bernardi & Emmons. An elegant shingled box. Not visible from the public road.

(7) 41 Hollins Drive, Butler house, 1935, WWW. Vincent and Lucy Butler wanted a house which expressed the greatest possible contrast to urban and professional life. Wurster used four detached, more or less square pavilions, arranged around an existing specimen oak tree to establish the four corners of a rectangular inner courtyard. Since it was a summer house, Wurster could do away with interior hallways altogether, providing a "covered passage" to link the pavilions instead. He could also make the central living space into an outdoor "living porch," the true summer living room complete with fireplace. The corner living room was to be used only in inclement weather. The outdoor living-room/entrance-courtyard, with its triple set of large double barn doors, recalled the imagery of the Gregory ranch house. (Editor's note: The Butler House was torn down due to "irreparable termite damage" and rebuilt to echo original plans.)

(7) Living Porch of Butler House *(Rob Super)*

(8) 51 Hollins Drive, W. Gallwey, 1932, WWW. A miniature ranch house with a V-shaped courtyard plan and a slate floor in the living room. Its understated, simple, cottage-like street front sports familiar Wurster ingredients: generous front door, vertical board siding, double-hung windows, a hint of tradition. It was originally intended as a summer house.

(9) 70 Hollins Drive, MacKenzie-Field, 1931-4, WWW. Built for the golf course architect Alister MacKenzie and shortly thereafter sold to the Field sisters, who enlarged it by adding a new living room, also designed by Wurster, in 1934. The house was meant to float at the edge of the golf course so that the owner might claim the fairway as his lawn, which it was in a sense. Wurster treated it in a modified Monterey style.

(10) 80 Hollins Drive, Grunsky, 1939, WWW. A simple, refined two-story box.

(11) 10 Brooktree Lane. Dennis Britton designed this house in a manner developing out of the Wood-Butcher houses of the 1960s. It was completed in 1976.

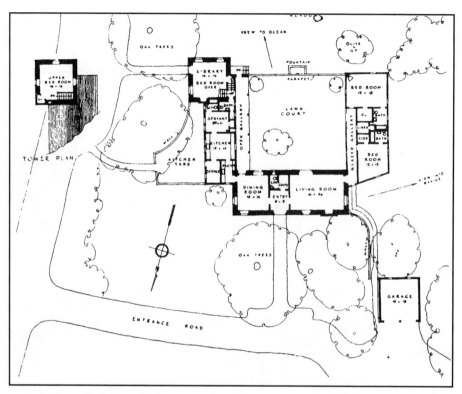

(12) Plan of Howes-Kaplansky House *(Daniel Gregory)*

(12) 17 Pasatiempo Drive, Howes-Kaplansky, 1930, WWW. This is the classic Pasatiempo house, built to set the keynote for the entire development. It symbolized the new life of the Rancho la Carbonera, the land grant in which Pasatiempo lies. The client was Robert Howes, Marion Hollins's general business manager. This house was designed to evoke the image of simplicity, without being all that simple.

The Howes residence is a grouping of separate units—bedroom wing, living room and dining room, kitchen wing, office—about the central court. Since each wing is never more than one room wide, there are windows on at least three sides of every major room, which makes the rooms appear, from inside, to be set in their own landscapes. This autonomous quality of the wings is reinforced by the use of contrasting materials, such as glass walls next to clapboards.

(13) 30 Pasatiempo Drive, West, ca. 1953, R. L. Byrd. Built for the owners of West Foods mushroom company, this estate is remarkable for its theatrical integration of house and landscape. The house and its outbuildings are treated as a series of events in a garden: its half-hidden outline of wood and brick reflects the irregular contour of the slope; the garage executes a daring leap over a

(12) Gallery of Howes-Kaplansky House *(Rob Super)*

(12) Howes-Kaplansky House, side entrance to library *(John Chase)*

fern-draped ravine; the timbers still have their bark; and the roof is a lush, sod hanging garden. Byrd's design is one of the few buildings in California which appears to be related both to the pre-World War II Hansel-and-Gretel tradition of architects like W. R. Yelland, Carr Jones, and Hugh Comstock and to the Wood-Butcher aesthetic of the 1960s.

(14) 32 Pasatiempo Drive, R. L. Byrd also designed the Anzalone house next door, ca. 1968, a smaller version of the West house, with a flagstone living room and a kitchen conservatory.

(15) 76 Pasatiempo Drive, Maridon, 1977, Brian Maridon. A simplified version of the current 1920s Le Corbusier revival, as popularized by New York architect Richard Meier. This tasteful house is unusual for Santa Cruz in the spareness of its modernity.

(16) 36 Kite Hill Road, Schwartz house, 1977, Gary Garmann. A tribute to the Moore, Lyndon, Turnbull & Whittaker cut-out vertical box of the '60s and the curved forms of the New York architect Charles Gwathmey by a young Santa Cruz architect who had lived in MLTW's McElrath house on Meder Street The interior has the large volume of vertical space one associates with MLTW houses,

(15) Maridon House *(John Chase)*

but the organization, configuration, and relationship of the spaces lack the refinement, complexity, and style of MLTW houses.

(17) 12 Lawridge Road, Dunmire, 1972, Tom Williamson. The Dunmire house consists of a series of boxes arranged on several levels around a central three-story tower. It was designed to accommodate the wood-frame doors and windows collected by the family. The exterior mimics the turn-of-the-century work of Berkeley architects such as Bernard Maybeck and John Galen Howard.

(18) 7 Bird Hill Lane, Scott, 1935, WWW. A modified French-style house with hipped roofs and distinctive formal entrance portico framed by symmetrical pavilions. The house occupies one of the most important sites at Pasatiempo: on the knoll between the second and third fairways, directly in front of the main entrance. Marion Hollins had intended to sell the entire knoll as one lot for one grand estate. The effects of the Depression forced her to subdivide it into what is now Bird Hill Lane. The Scott house shows that the aristocratic restraint of Wurster's Pasatiempo work had the potential for hauteur. It is important to remember that Wurster received some of his training at the distinctly upper-

(16) Schwartz House *(John Chase)*

(17) Dunmire House *(John Chase)*

crust Eastern firm of Delano & Aldrich, and that the restrained Regency-style Smith house at Berkeley is contemporaneous with the masterful simplicity of the Gregory ranch house.

(19) 3 Clubhouse Road, Randall, ca. 1960, Wurster, Bernardi & Emmons. A late example of the modernized board-and-batten tradition and the second Wurster house for this Santa Cruz family.

(20) 5 Clubhouse Road, Church, 1931, WWW. Built for the resident landscape architect and his wife, this house has a frontier-style fireplace in the kitchen, conversation pit in the living room (one of the very first), and a large shed-roof studio, which was Church's office.

 (21) 20 Clubhouse Road, Pasatiempo Clubhouse, 1935, Clarence Tantau. A large, rambling house in a modified Monterey style, commanding a spectacular view over the golf course to the bay. The main room is a grandly proportioned salon with a fireplace at each end.

The entrance facade has the same concern with arrival and entrance that characterized the more consciously pretentious houses built in Los Angeles

(21) Pasatiempo Clubhouse of 1935 *(John Chase)*

during the 1960s. The separation of the building into hipped-roof pavilions in the French manner and the emphasis on, and height of, the entry have become the hallmarks of this Beverly Hills Regency look.

(22) 28 Clubhouse Road, Caddy House, 1930, WWW. Though completely altered, this residence contains the original caddy house, once an extremely simple two-room, whitewashed board structure. According to photographer Roger Sturtevant (whose photos made Pasatiempo famous), the architecture was either praised for its refreshing simplicity or damned as a shack. Not visible from the road.

(23) 34 Clubhouse Road, 1st Clubhouse, 1930, Clarence A. Tantau. A simplified Monterey-style, two-story house distinguished on the south by a finely proportioned two-story verandah. The garden was designed by Thomas D. Church. Not visible from the road.

Pasatiempo

Appendix A

Biographies of Local Architects/Designers/Builders

William Bagnall (b. 1932) William Bagnall was born in Long Beach. He attended Menlo College Business School and Cal Poly, graduating in 1959. He worked for the San Jose architectural firm of Goodwin Steinberg from 1962 to 1970 and has been in independent practice in Santa Cruz since then.

Dennis Britton (b. 1940) Dennis Britton is one of the most accomplished Santa Cruz designers to have emerged from the Wood-Butcher movement. He was born in San Jose and graduated from San Jose State University as an art major in 1966. Britton, who was already building in his last years at school, was dissatisfied with how sterile construction in the area had become. The buildings constructed in the Wood-Butcher style exhibited a love of craftsmanship and elaborate detailing of materials, while tending to ignore more basic architectural qualities of structure, space, function, and the overall unity of the building. "They tended to look good for the same reason a patchwork quilt looks good," Britton has said. Britton's later work moved closer to the Craftsman-revivalist spirit of Thacher & Thompson and Clarke Shultes. (Additional information in 2nd edition, 1979)

William Henry Burrows (1838-1908) William Henry Burrows was born in Montreal. From 1868-78 he was in Gilroy, where he designed, contracted, and supervised construction of structures, including water tanks. However, no architectural survey of Gilroy has identified any of his designs. Burrows's 1887 Columbia County Courthouse is the oldest continuing operating courthouse in the state of Washington. He died in Dayton, Columbia County, Washington. (Research contributed by Stanley D. Stevens)

Walter Graves Byrne (1891-1949) Walter Graves Byrne was born in San Francisco, the son of George Griffin Byrne and Helen Graves Byrne. Approximately three years later, the Byrne family, formerly of Jackson, Michigan, settled in Santa Cruz.

Walter Byrne attended the University of California, Berkeley, when the Craftsman aesthetic was prevalent there, graduating in the class of 1914. While a student, he did drafting work for Julia Morgan and John Galen Howard. The Craftsman preference for simplicity, a preference which allows material to become important as design elements, is evident in the buildings in Santa Cruz which can be assigned to him: the Walter Charles Byrne house, 1912, and his own home, 1919.

On returning to Santa Cruz, Byrne found that there were not enough commissions available to support him as an architect. Consequently, he became a teacher of mathematics and mechanical drawing at Santa Cruz High School in 1918. During the years 1921 to 1923, he was the junior partner of architect Allen C. Collins. Their office was located in the New Santa Cruz Theatre Building at the northwest corner of Pacific and Walnut Avenues.

In 1923 Byrne moved to Los Angeles, where he was associated with the firm of Ross Montgomery and that of John C. Austin, architect of Los Angeles City Hall, Shrine Auditorium, and the Griffith Park Observatory. Byrne's most important project was the California State Building in the Los Angeles Civic Center. Byrne left Southern California for Oakland in 1942 and worked for Kaiser Industries during the war. He was afterwards employed by John J. Donovan, architect of Oakland Technical High School, the Ina Coolbrith Library, also in Oakland, and a consulting architect for the San Francisco-Oakland Bay Bridge. At that time Byrne also designed an addition to the building which housed Oakland's Little Sisters of the Poor. He continued to practice until three years before his death in 1949.

Allen C. Collins (1888-1950) Allen Clark Collins was born in San Jose. "In 1919 he was listed as a draftsman in San Jose. He formed a short-lived partnership in 1911-1912 with Delbert H. Main as Collins and Main, Architectural Designers, after which he worked alone until 1915." He then went to work, both before and after service in World War I, with architect Warren Skillings in San Jose. "Their design for a home for Dr. Lincoln Cothran of San Jose was published in *Architect & Engineer* in 1919." After being licensed as an architect he partnered with Walter Graves Byrne. "When Byrne moved to Los Angeles in 1923, Collins continued working in Santa Cruz. In 1928 he moved to Watsonville to form a partnership with J. H. De Lange. It ended when De Lange relocated to Aptos that same year. In 1936 Collins accepted a position with Fresno builders Taylor and Wheeler as a 'captive architect,' designing custom homes throughout the Central San Joaquin Valley. Collins moved to Oakland in 1940," possibly because his case study house "Felton Gables," built in Menlo Park, had received wide publicity in *Pencil Points*, *Architectural Forum*, and *American Home*. "In the mid-1940s Collins returned to Watsonville, where he maintained an office until his death" (John Edward Powell, biography of Allen C. Collins: http:// historicfresno.org/bio/collins.htm).

Nelson Alanson Comstock (1851-ca. 1920) Nelson Comstock is notable in Santa Cruz history for his design work on the County Courthouse of 1894, later known as the Cooper House. He was the son of Edwin Comstock and Sylina Dibble and was born in Jackson, Michigan. From around 1886 to 1891 he practiced architecture in San Diego with his partner Carl Trotsche, and together they designed many important buildings.

Comstock moved to San Francisco in 1891, where his career was apparently less successful than his stint in San Diego. In 1913 his name appears in the city directory for El Paso, Texas, as an assistant building inspector. Three years later his status had improved to building inspector. In 1916 he is listed as vice-president and secretary-treasurer of the El Paso Composition Tile and Terra Cotta Company.

Earlier, Comstock had married Amanda Wright. Since his wife in El Paso is listed as Gertrude Comstock, it is likely that he married twice. Comstock had two daughters, Jessie and Alice.

Daniel A. Damkroeger (ca. 1856-1931) Daniel A. Damkroeger was born in Minnesota. His father, Carl Friedrich Gottlieb Damkroeger, was born in Holzhausen, Westphalia, arriving in the United States in 1850. Daniel Damkroeger opened his office in Santa Cruz in 1887, according to the October 21, 1887, *Santa Cruz Sentinel* article, which mentioned that he was building an office on Elm Street. In 1887 he was assisted by Warren Clark. In 1888 he made a map of Santa Cruz with H. E. Makinney. The firm of Damkroeger & [A. E.] Saunders was formed in mid-1889. Damkroeger probably left Santa Cruz in 1891 or 1892, as this is the date at which references to him and his firm are no longer found in local newspapers. He died in Alameda County.

Charles Wellington Davis (1826-1897) Charles Wellington Davis was born in Newburyport, Massachusetts. He began his architectural career in Boston. He left for California in 1849, landing in San Francisco, where he practiced with distinction for twenty years. During the four years that he was in Santa Cruz, 1871-1874, he was the city's most accomplished architect. Charles sometimes designed projects for his brother, **Calvin Withington Davis** (1829-1912), who lived in Santa Cruz from the 1870s into the 1890s and worked as a carpenter and contractor. Because newspapers often referred to each of them as C. W. Davis, it is difficult to determine who was responsible for the design of a particular building. There is also some confusion over the relationship of Charles and Calvin.

During the 1870s, both Charles and Calvin Davis worked for Frederick A. Hihn, designing and building not only passenger and baggage cars but also the critical dump cars used in the construction of rail lines of the Santa Cruz Rail Road. According to railroad historian Bruce MacGregor, "Charles Wellington Davis encouraged diversification in the local lumber industry, which until this point in time was dominated by production of coastal redwood. Davis envisioned increased local production of a raw material basic to railroad construction: Oregon pine, commonly known today as Douglas fir." MacGregor states that "before coming to Santa Cruz County, Davis had worked as master car builder for the Market Street Railway in San Francisco and later as car builder for the Southern Pacific. He came to Santa Cruz as an architect primarily in Hihn's employ, developing his commercial properties and in 1873 completing his Santa Cruz residence. When Davis gave an interview to the *Sentinel* in 1872, railroads, not homes, were the focal point of his search for commercial potential" (Bruce MacGregor, *The Birth of the California Narrow Gauge* [Stanford, CA: Stanford University Press, 2003], 251). MacGregor states that Calvin Davis with a partner, the carpenter Charles Kaye, provided contract car construction (p. 252). In fact, MacGregor believes that the "Davis family was in many ways the unsung hero of the railroad revolution in Santa Cruz County . . . especially its manufacturing overtones" (personal communication, February 15, 2005). He

299

states that the manufacture in Santa Cruz of "the Davis dump car was a little like the construction of a small, crude nuclear weapon by a Third World country" (p. 263).

Charles Davis's first wife was Caroline Collins, who died, leaving three children. In 1879, at the age of fifty-three, he married twenty-year-old Frances Parks Tuttle and started a new family, naming one of his sons Calvin W. After leaving Santa Cruz, Charles opened an office in Los Angeles. At the time of his death in Gardena in 1897, he was the second oldest architect in Southern California (*An Illustrated History of Los Angeles County, California* [Chicago: Lewis Pub Co., 1889], 730; Henry F. Withey and Elsie Rathburn Withey, *Biographical Dictionary of American Architects, Deceased* [Los Angeles: New Age Publishing Co., 1956; Reprint, Omnigraphics, 1996], 164). Calvin Davis, after the death of his second wife, Mary, in 1894, left Santa Cruz and died later in Los Angeles.

Lee Dill Esty (1875-1943) Lee Dill Esty was born in Maine and came to Santa Cruz as a young boy in 1879. He was the son of J. D. Esty, who served as Santa Cruz County Supervisor from 1897 to 1904 and 1909 to 1915. In the *Santa Cruz Sentinel*, September 15, 1931, there was an announcement that Lee Dill Esty along with D. M. McPhetres and C. J. Ryland had announced the opening of a new firm to be known as Ryland, Esty and McPhetres (note: D. M. McPhetres, not earlier architect, J. S. McPheters).

Gary Garmann (1942-2005) Gary Garmann was born in Toppenish, Washington. He graduated from the University of Washington in 1967 and went to work for Fred Bassetti and Company the following year. From 1970 to 1972 he was employed by Calvin/Gorasht , another Seattle firm. Garmann is best known for creating a mylar wall calendar in 1971, a project which liberated him financially. (Additional information in 2nd edition, 1979)

Emil John, a San Francisco architect, briefly had an office in Santa Cruz, beginning about 1884. By 1885 he was again spending most of his time in San Francisco.

Kitchen Brothers. Raymond Sylvester Kitchen (1894-1973) and Kenneth Claire Kitchen (b. 1888) came from Five Points, Clearfield County, Pennsylvania. "Grover Cleveland Kitchen [d. 1939], a building contractor, and a sister, Hazel, were the first to arrive in Santa Cruz, staying briefly in 1923. Their brother Kenneth–known then as Claire–showed up a while later, working as a carpenter and bricklayer. They were among the 11 children of William Kitchen and his second wife, Sarah. Another 11 half siblings were born earlier to William and first wife Hannah. In 1929 the youngest brothers also came to work in construction. A fifth brother Raymond, pulled into town last and rented a place of his own on Walnut Avenue, a few doors from Kenneth. The six Kitchens spread out to different towns when the Depression hit and jobs were tough to find. Kenneth and Ray left, too, but were back in 1934 with cash to buy the Fair Street properties," where the Kitchens built their famous folk art masonry buildings. One of the Kitchen sisters, Sarah Jane, married local eccentric

William Daglish, who was infamous for crackpot campaigns and was suspected of murdering her (Carolyn Swift, *Santa Cruz Sentinel*, Oct. 21, 2001).

John Marquis (1834-1911) John Marquis was born in Glasgow and studied architecture in Scotland, moving to Wisconsin where he spent thirty-two years as a prominent architect. He later relocated to Santa Cruz, to a vineyard on Blackburn Drive, where he lived for fifteen years. The last seven years of his life he practiced as an architect in Santa Cruz, responsible for both residential and commercial work (*Santa Cruz Sentinel*, May 14, 1911).

Lila Sweet Martin (1860-1948) Dr. Lila Sweet Martin was born in New York. Although she was a graduate osteopath, she never practiced, preferring to devote her time to architectural designing. She was living in San Francisco by 1900, and by 1910 she was a building contractor in Santa Cruz County. She consulted on the design of the C. C. Moore residential buildings at 660 High Street, working with a second architect, Edwin Symmes. She had worked with Symmes on architect Bernard Maybeck's renowned Palace of Fine Arts in San Francisco, built for the Panama-Pacific International Exposition of 1915.

She was hired as consulting architect to Wood Brothers Lumber and Mill Company's Home Building Service in the 1920s. The *Santa Cruz Evening News* ad announcing her employment (May 19, 1922) stated: "Many of the most beautiful and unusual residences of Santa Cruz have been designed by Mrs. Martin. Her work is so well known that it needs no comment." In the 1920s, she owned the Forest Farm summer resort in Scotts Valley, off today's Highway 17.

Martin also built her own homes on High Street and on California Street. (Dill Design Group [Leslie A. G. Dill, Kara Oosterhous, Charlene Duval, and Franklin Maggi], "Historical and Architectural Assessment: Historic Resource Design Review, prepared for Louis Rittenhouse, July 5, 2002; additional research contributed by Judith Steen).

Henry A. Minton (1883-1948) Henry A. Minton formed a partnership with Wilton Smith in San Francisco in 1934. Minton designed St. Brigid's and St. Francis Xavier Mission for Japanese, both in San Francisco, the Alameda County Courthouse, and together with well-known theater specialist Thomas W. Lamb, the Fox Theater in San Francisco. One of his largest buildings is the Bank of Italy building at the corner of First and Santa Clara Streets in San Jose. Minton did much work for A. P. Giannini and his Bank of Italy prior to 1931.

LeBaron R. Olive (1850-1942) LeBaron R. Olive was trained by his father, George Olive, as a carpenter in his native town of St. John's, New Brunswick. He left home at age nineteen and settled in New York, where he worked as a construction supervisor. From 1886 to about 1906, he practiced as a contractor-architect in Santa Cruz. In 1892 he was afflicted by two grievous personal blows. His wife, Sarah Anne, succumbed to pneumonia, leaving him the sole parent of five children. A week later his house, located near the corner of Pacific Avenue and Sycamore Street, was partially destroyed by fire.

Said Harrison's 1892 *History of Santa Cruz County* of Olive, "He endeavors to adapt his buildings to their surroundings. His style is light and airy, and his work as a whole has given this young man a desirable and enviable reputation as an architect in Santa Cruz County."

Mark Primack (b. 1952) Mark Primack received his undergraduate degree in architecture from the Rhode Island School of Design in 1973. His 1974 master's degree in architecture is from the Architectural Association of London. He came to Santa Cruz in 1976.

In addition to his professional work, he has been involved in community housing and preservation activities. Some of these include serving on the Santa Cruz City Council, the City's Zoning Board, for eleven years, and on the Historic Preservation Commission; saving the Tree Circus of Axel Erlandson; and working to oppose the destruction of the Allegrini house, the Cooper House, the Yogi Temple, and the Pogonip Clubhouse. After the 1989 earthquake, he served on the City's Vision Santa Cruz committee. His particular interests are affordable housing, housing for the homeless, and building neighborhoods. He contributed one of the seven prototype plans published in *Accessory Dwelling Unit Program Plan Sets, Santa Cruz, California* (City of Santa Cruz, Office of Planning and Community Development, 2003). The Santa Cruz Art League named him "Distinguished Artist of the Year" in 2001, the first architect to receive such an honor, in acknowledgment of twenty-four years spent combining art and public service. He shares an office with landscape architect and wife, Janet Pollock.

Roy Rydell (1915-2000) Landscape architect Roy Rydell was born in Minneapolis, Minnesota, and moved to Los Angeles at the age of thirteen. He graduated from the University of Southern California with a B.F.A. in 1937 and did graduate work at the University of California, Berkeley, in 1940. He also attended Chouinard's in Los Angeles and Atelier 17 and L'Academie de la Grande Chaumiere, both in Paris.

In his active career as a designer, Rydell created a wide variety of objects: buildings, costumes, furniture, and jewelry. At Santa Cruz he was involved in community affairs of both a cultural and a political nature.

Among his most noted landscapes are those at the Communications Building at UCSC, Deer Park Center, Santa Cruz City Hall Annex, and the Alfred Hitchcock estate.

One of his most successful designs was his own house on Pine Flat Road in Bonny Doon, a nineteenth-century schoolhouse that he and his wife, Frances, remodeled and expanded, beginning in 1948. The Rydells were far ahead of the times in this example of adaptive re-use. Their home can be said to be the symbolic birthplace of historic preservation in Santa Cruz. Rydell wrote on gardens and landscaping for Sunset Books and *Sunset* magazine. He was a mentor to local architects and landscape architects, including Mark Primack and Janet Pollock.

Columbus J. Ryland (1892-1980) Columbus J. Ryland was born in San Jose and educated at the Normal School (San Jose State) and the School of the California Guild of Arts and Crafts (California College of Arts and Crafts). Ryland went overseas with the army during World War I. He took courses in architecture, engineering, and art at the University of Toulouse. From 1919 to 1931 he was a partner in the firm of Swartz and Ryland with offices in Fresno, Monterey, and Salinas. Ryland and Fred Swartz designed many houses in San Joaquin Valley towns like Hanford, Coalinga, Corcoran, and Chowchilla. Although Ryland is listed in the 1962 *American Architects Directory* as having been in independent practice since 1931, the firm of Ryland and Miller appears on the drawings for the Santa Cruz County Building remodeling of 1950. In 1928 Ryland designed the Catholic Chapel Car St. Therese, used to visit agricultural camps. It resembled a bus, with clamshell backdoors that opened to reveal an altar (Brother Larry Scrivani, e-mail to Stanley Stevens, August 22, 2005).

Clarke L. Shultes (b. 1948) Clarke L. Shultes was born in Everett, Washington. In 1970 he graduated from San Jose State University with a B.A. in Fine Arts. Shultes began his architectural design career with an apprenticeship to Danish architect Stanley E. Yorke and Associates in El Granada, California. From 1972 to the present he has designed custom residences in San Mateo, Santa Cruz, and Monterey counties. Shultes's early work in Half Moon Bay was representative of the commercial variant of the Third Bay Tradition as practiced by contractors and building designers on the central California coast. Shultes and the firm of Thacher & Thompson are responsible for most of the better period-revival inspired buildings in the city. In 2005 he is the chair of the City's Historic Preservation Commission. (Additional information in 2nd edition, 1979)

Wilton Smith (1903-1966) Wilton Smith was born in Wisconsin and attended the University of California, Berkeley, in the 1920s, although he never graduated. He went to work for the Capital Company in 1925, an architectural firm which did the construction work for the Bank of Italy (now the Bank of America). The firm, which was just beginning to expand at that time, had Henry A. Minton as architect. Smith designed gymnasiums at St. Emydius Parish and St. Vincent de Paul Parish and the rectory of St. Brigid Church in San Francisco.

Smith became a partner in the firm in 1934 and eventually took charge after Minton's death. Minton's son, John, was Smith's partner in 1952-53. From 1946 to 1948 Smith operated his firm with Fred Keeble as partner. Keeble was later the senior partner of Keeble and Rhoda in Monterey. Houses built during this partnership include those for Dr. Nelson in Pasatiempo, Mr. Winette on Graham Hill Road, and for Dr. Anthony E. Allegrini, also in Pasatiempo.

Other work by Smith includes St. Hilary's Catholic Church in Tiburon, St. Agnes's Catholic Church in Stockton, and a house for Mr. Bacigalupi on Dewey Boulevard in San Francisco (1963). His biggest commission was for an addition to Lone Mountain College of San Francisco.

Biographies

John Stonum (1932-1995) Born in San Francisco, Stonum began college at San Francisco State in 1956 and graduated from the University of California, Berkeley, in 1961. After his arrival in Santa Cruz in 1969 to supervise the construction of the Spengemann house, John Stonum's practice was composed of small residential commissions. Their basic concepts and detailing place them in the late second phase of the Bay Area Tradition rather than in the third phase. Stonum was influenced by two of the firms that he worked for, Warren Callister, and Marquis & Stoller. In at least one instance, the Lloyd Kahn house, the influence of Bernard Maybeck's work is apparent.

Firms he worked for included Roy Starbird, 1956; Ira Beales, 1960; Walker & Moody, 1961; Self-employed, 1962-63; Callister & Payne, 1963-64; Marquis & Stoller, 1964-65; and Pacific Architects & Engineers, 1966-68. (Additional information in 2nd edition, 1979)

Thomas Thacher (b. 1947) and **Matthew Thompson** (b. 1948) Thomas Thacher and Matthew Thompson, along with Clarke Shultes, represent what might be considered a fourth phase of the San Francisco Bay Tradition in Santa Cruz. Their residential work emphasizes strong domestic house types taken from a variety of late nineteenth- and early twentieth-century English and American styles.

Thomas Thacher was born in 1947 in Portsmouth, Maryland, and graduated with a Bachelor of Architecture degree from the University of Minnesota in 1972. While in college he worked for the firm of Miller, Melby, and Hanson in Minneapolis. He next worked for Hodne and Stageberg, also in Minneapolis. He moved to Santa Cruz in April of 1973 to join Matthew Thompson in the formation of Thacher & Thompson.

Matthew Thompson was born in 1948 in Minneapolis and graduated with a Bachelor of Architecture degree from the University of Minnesota in 1972. He, too, worked for Miller, Melby and Hanson, as well as Setter, Leach, and Lindstrom; and Haarstick and Lundgren. The firm has often employed revivalist-period vocabularies. Thacher & Thompson sometimes acted as both architect and developer/ and or builder for some early projects but has not done so for the past twenty years. Some of Thacher & Thompson's larger recent commissions include the Horticultural Center for Cabrillo College and the Aptos Village Town Center, as well as mixed-use projects in Hercules and a twenty-eight townhouse project in Santa Clara. (Additional information in 2nd edition, 1979)

Edward LaGrand Van Cleeck (1849-1925) Edward Van Cleeck was born in New York and raised in North Carolina, arriving in California in 1885. Before 1889 he was a partner in the contracting firm of Kaye, Knapp & Co. in Santa Cruz. He probably contributed more to the city through his many designs than did any other single architect. Among the designs are Villa Perla, Rutherglen Terrace, the Haslam, Deming, and Wessendorf houses, and the Trust and Elks buildings.

At the time of his death, he had been retired from practice for several years due to poor health and was living in the Santa Cruz mountain community of Ben

Lomond. His obituary described him as "a southerner and a southern gentleman, always courteous, obliging, and most generous" (*Santa Cruz Sentinel*, October 27, 1925).

William Henry Weeks (1866-1936) The son of a Canadian builder-architect, William Henry Weeks was born in Charlottetown, Prince Edward Island. He studied architectural design at the Brinker Institute in Denver. He was a member of the Christian Church and came to Watsonville to design a church building for them in 1892. By 1894 he was well established there, and three years later opened a branch office in Salinas. The opening of his San Francisco office in the James Flood building came in 1905, just in time to be ready for all the building jobs created by the earthquake of 1906. Following his business up the peninsula, Weeks left Watsonville in 1911 for Palo Alto and moved again to Oakland in 1915 and to Piedmont in 1924. At one time he had thirty people working in his office, including his brother Hammond Weeks, his son Harold, Robert Orr, and Ralph Wyckoff. The office closed during the Depression.

"It was said of Mr. Weeks that practically every city and town in Northern and Central California claimed one or more buildings which he had designed," reported his obituary in *The Architect and Engineer of California*. "All told Mr. Weeks is said to have designed more than twelve hundred school houses, besides about fifty churches, as many banks, and at one time, all of the Carnegie libraries in this part of the State."

Although his Watsonville commissions of the 1890s are probably his most interesting work, with their novel combinations of Queen Anne, Colonial Revival and Mission Revival motifs, his school buildings could be remarkably straightforward.

Thomas J. Welsh (1847-1918) Thomas J. Welsh was a member of the San Francisco firm of Welsh and Carey. For a number of years he was the architect for the San Francisco Board of Education.

John H. Williams (ca. 1829-1891) John H. Williams was a Pennsylvania-born architect who arrived in Santa Cruz about 1868. He first had his office in architect John Morrow's home on Pacific Avenue. He resided on Branciforte Avenue.

Biographies

Appendix B

Supplementary List of Buildings

Following is a list of buildings not included in the body of the book because of insufficient documentation, lack of a known location, or divergence from the selection criteria of the book. They were all either designed by Santa Cruz firms or firms active in Santa Cruz or were located in Santa Cruz County.

Solon Blodgett Abbott (1832-1911)
1890 Twin Lakes Baptist Church Building, Seventh Avenue and Second Street (now Bonnie Street), demolished

Clay N. Burrell (1881-1958)
1914 D. S. Dunphy, one-story residence

William Henry Burrows (1838-1908)
1877 City Hose Cart; County Hospital addition; Nathaniel Manson house, Walnut Avenue
1877-78 Murdock Young's Candy Store, Ice Cream Saloon & Candy Manufactory, Pacific Avenue
1887 Columbia County Courthouse, Dayton, Washington
Date unknown: First Baptist Church and parsonage, Dayton, Washington

Walter Graves Byrne (1891-1949)
1927 Seventh place winner in the small brick house competition sponsored by the California Common Brick Manufacturers Association

Russell B. Coleman
1931 H. E. Murray house, two-story, eight-room stucco

Allen C. Collins (1888-1950)
1926 First Church of Christ Scientist, Ocean Street and Dakota Avenue

1927 C. D. Sheerin house, Walnut Avenue Extension

Collins & Byrne (Allen C. Collins & Walter Graves Byrne)
1921 Two- and three-bedroom apartments for E. C. Lerock, Watsonville

Mario Corbett (1901-1977)
1932 Dudley Sales house, one-story, board & batten

Daniel A. Damkroeger (1857-1931) and **Damkroeger & Saunders**
1887 Fred and Albion Paris Swanton, plans for stable, Pacific Avenue, demolished; E. Warren house; Damkroeger office, Elm Street; Gottlob Zeigler house, Pine Street; R. H. Hall house, Branciforte; Santa Cruz Mountain Winery Building, Market Street, demolished
1888 C. N. Mann, houses at Vine Hill and Mel's Vineyards; Soquel School, demolished; Mary Wakeman house, Ocean Street, one hundred feet south of Soquel Avenue; John R. Chace house, Walnut Avenue, between Center Street and Pacific Avenue, demolished; William Kerr house, Old San Jose Road; J. F. Holloway house, Soquel Avenue; A. Dias Pena house, 227 Walnut Avenue, demolished

1889 C. T. Sutphen house, east side of Garfield Street, demolished; W. Hamilton house, Old San Jose Road; R. Schaeffer house, Merced; Branciforte School Annex, demolished; Captain Short residence, corner Broadway and Ocean Street; Dr. Whitney Sanatorium, Pacific Avenue; Mrs. H. M. Blackburn house, corner Pacific Avenue and Sycamore Street; A. E. Crane house, Laurel Street; Judge Logan house alterations, Mission Hill; H. H. Blood and Fred Swanton, Palace of Pharmacy interior, Pacific Avenue; George Campbell residence, Watsonville; Richard Thompson house, Mission Street and Saint Lawrence (Highland Avenue); A. L. Whitney house, Newman's addition to East Santa Cruz; A. P. Swanton Building (housing Woods Machine Shop), Pacific Avenue; James Phelan, Phelan Park improvements, West Cliff Drive; J. H. Sinkinson house addition, Cedar Street; E. L. Fitch, six cottages, near Garfield Park

1890 Henry Curtner house, 231 Wilkes Circle; Hopkins house remodel, Locust Street; M. Hoyt cottage, Circles area

1891 John S. C. Stevens house, St. Helen's Ranch, Soquel; Michael McMenomy, additions to two houses

Charles Wellington Davis (1826-1897)
1873 Levi K. Baldwin house, located on a portion of the former Morgan farm; William Ely house, Sunnyside Farm; Ryan house, Coast Road (now Highway 1)
1876 Mr. Ely, two houses (might also be assigned to Calvin W. Davis)

Lynn R. Duckering (1895-1968)
1941 Gault Elementary School, reconstruction

1946 Jay Dickerson, motel, 211 Water Street
1948 Farrar-Halbach, one-story, L-shaped steel and concrete-block garage, Spruce and Front Streets
1952 Valencia Elementary School, Aptos

Edwards & Schary
1932 Royal Order of Moose, three-story lodge, 306 Pacific Avenue

Lee Dill Esty (1875-1943)
1911 Pogonip Golf Club
1912 Women's Exchange and Decorative Art Society Building, remodel, 125 Walnut Avenue
1915 Bank Building, 1100 Soquel Avenue
1923 Santa Cruz County Hospital
1924 Hanly Hospital, Bay Street and West Cliff Drive
1925 W. H. Crowe & Sons, one-floor, concrete garage, Walnut Avenue
1926 Odd Fellows Lodge, Soquel
1927 C. H. Griffen house, High Street near Storey Street
1929 J. V. Toscano residence, two-story, stucco, Beach Hill
1930 Concrete ship remodel and wharf, Seacliff; Society of Mary, Chaminade Boys School, two-story stucco Mission style, Laveaga park; A. D. Chance residence, one-floor, seven-room, stucco, upper Van Ness Avenue
1936 J. D. Wagner, apartments, five, two-story stucco, four-room with tile roof, East Cliff Drive between First and Second Avenues

John E. Fennacy (1904-1979)
1937 Pasatiempo Club, one-story guest cottage, early California style

John J. Foley (d. 1946)
Date unknown: School, one-floor concrete, Mission Street

Henry Geilfuss (1850-1922)
1888 Claus Mangels house, Aptos

Hamilton & Church (Robert H. Hamilton & John M. Church)
1921 Patrick Neary, stucco house, Mission Street
1929 Bernard Clark, garage, one-story concrete, Front and Cathcart Streets
1931 Garage, auto service station, one-story concrete
1932 Building, southwest corner Vine and Locust Streets, Dr. Clyde C. Carmean, one-story office and laboratory, concrete

William C. Hays (1873-1963)
1926 S. W. Coleman, et. al., forty-seven bungalows, First Street, Main Street, and Westbrook, Beach Hill

Samuel Heiman
1933 Palomar Hotel, new cocktail lounge

Hertzka & Knowles (Wayne S. Hertzka [1907-1973] & William Howard Knowles)
1935 Palomar Hotel, new or remodeled cocktail room

William E. Higgins (d. 1936)
1935 Live Oak School, add two stucco classrooms with shingle roof

Emil John
1892 Hagemann Hotel (with Mieczislas Balczynski) on Pacific Avenue
1893 Alonzo Coffin steamboat-shaped house, Tamalpais Avenue, Mill Valley, California

Earl Thomas Kerr
1921 Realty Building Exchange, nine bungalows, Morrissey Boulevard, Soquel Avenue, and Water Street

Kenneth Claire Kitchen (b. 1888) and **Grover Cleveland Kitchen** (d.1939)
1924 House of concrete blocks made to look like bricks at King and Laurent Streets

Raymond Sylvester Kitchen (1894-1973)
1940 House addition, southeast corner McPherson Street and Fair Avenues
Date unknown: Wall at Civic Auditorium parking lot

Francis E. Lloyd
1940 One-story, three-bedroom house, Pasatiempo

Lewis B. McCornick (often incorrectly spelled as McCormick)
1889 J. R. Briggs house, Branciforte Avenue and Windham Street; B. C. Gadsby house, Elm and Cedar Streets; Spec house, Minnesota (Soquel Avenue) and Branciforte Avenues

George E. McCrea (1871-1943)
1916 A. H. Munsell house, two-story
1922 L. T. Bachman house, remodel, Third Street

Charles S. McKenzie
1920 J. A. Rachal house, two-story stucco

Henry A. Minton (1883-1948)
1926 Holy Cross School, two-floor concrete, opposite Sylvar Street

Minton & Smith (Henry A. Minton [1883-1948] & Wilton Smith [1903-1966])
1948 Anthony E. Allegrini house, 33 Eastridge Drive, Pasatiempo

John Morrow (1830-1914)
1867 Homes for E. Bender, Captain Orville Root, C. O. Cummings, John

Langenbeck, Captain Hobron, William Effey, Andrew Trust, Samuel Sharp, Samuel Winans, A. A. Phillips, B. P. Kooser, Reverend C. G. Ames, and Mr. Colby; Frame building for William Anthony
1876 William Vahlberg house
1878 Glora F. Bennett house
1885 House on Spruce Street

William A. Newman
1909 Church of Christ Scientist

LeBaron R. Olive (1850-1942)
1887 A. A. Terrill house, addition, Ocean View Avenue; E. J. Swift cottage at Pope House, Mission Street
1888 Elise McClure Gregory (of Oakland) ranch house near Soquel
1889 Josiah S. Green house, west side of Washington Street; J. McLeary, plans for three houses, Water Street; Soquel School, Soquel
1891 Soquel IOOF Lodge, Soquel; Howard W. West, plans for hotel, Boulder Creek
1892 James L. Dutton house, Mission Street, east side between Otis and Rigg Streets
Date unknown: Mrs. H. M. Blackburn, Thomas Dorsey (San Jose), residences

Percy & Hamilton (George W. Percy [1847-1900] & Frederick F. Hamilton [1851-1899])
1886-1889 Greystone Cellars (Christian Brothers Winery, now Culinary Institute of America's West Coast campus), St. Helena
1889 Mrs. Henry P. Bowie (of San Mateo), plans for a tile-roofed, stuccoed, and colonnaded Italian or Spanish Villa at Seabright

John Bourne Perry (1811-1871)
1865 Frank Waterman house,

Center Street
1867 Houses for J. W. Brown, T. W. Brown, Mrs. Mary (Perry) Jordan, Peter Wilkinson, and James Howe
1868 Two houses on Union and Green Streets for Mrs. Jordan

Keith Ponsford
1936 House, one-story stucco with shake roof, Pasatiempo

Walter H. Ratcliff (1881-1973)
1916 W. H. Heywood house, one story

Columbus J. Ryland (1892-1980)
Before 1931: Oakland stage depot; American Legion, Civic Center, Hanford; Elks Building, Visalia; Modesto Hotel; Salinas National Bank building; Monterey Union High School; Library, California State College at Fresno
1931 Sunset School, Carmel; E. A. Williams Jr. house adjacent to the Monterey Peninsula Country Club
1936 Monterey City Hall
1938 Dr. Philbrook house, two-story, three bedroom, stucco
1948 La Plaza Apartments, 515 Riverside Avenue; Thrash Motor Company, salesroom and garage
Unknown Christian Science Church, Monterey

Ryland, Esty & McPhetres (Columbus J. Ryland, Lee Dill Esty & D. M. McPhetres)
1932 Hiram Gosliner house, Escalona Drive; Dr. Frederick Shenk house

Henry A. Schulze
1892 Morris Thompson, country cottage, Wright's Station

Wilton Smith (1903-1966)
Before 1940 in Santa Cruz County:
Santa Cruz: William C. Cober house, modified early California style; Dr. W.

K. Shulte house, Laurent Street; Frank T. Carroll house, 209 Laurent Street
Bonny Doon: Don Staffler ranch house
Pasatiempo: Dr. A. B. Diepenbrock house
ca. 1938 Lee Monroe house, Huntington Road, Aptos
1948 Anthony E. Allegrini house, 33 Eastridge Drive, Pasatiempo

Edwin Lewis Snyder
1954 Large apartment complex adjacent to West Cliff Drive

Robert Stanton
1937 Monterey County Courthouse, Salinas
1949 Bayview School, Bay and Mission Streets
1950 Branciforte Junior High School, two-story addition and one-story wings

Joseph L. Stewart
1930 Recreation building, swimming pool, and bowling alley, two-floor concrete

Clarence A. Tantau (1884-1943)
1922 Mrs. E. W. van Antwerp house, 101 Eighteenth Avenue

Rollin S. Tuttle (1886-1931)
1926 Eastside Methodist Episcopal Church, community home, three-floor

Edward LaGrand Van Cleeck (1849-1925)
1888 Joseph Kenney Building, northwest corner Pacific Avenue and the Pacific Avenue Street Railroad; John W. and Elizabeth Towne, two-houses, Marine Parade, north side between First and Second Avenues
1889 Henry Uhden house, Third Street and Riverside Avenue; James

F. Simpson house, north side Mission Street near Highland Avenue
1891 Catholic Ladies Aid Society building, Santa Maria del Mar
1892 Building for Santa Cruz, Garfield Park and Capitola Electric Railway
1895 Capitola Hotel, Capitola, destroyed by fire, 1929
1897 Ranch house for D. D. Wilder
1900 Design of Beach Street (project)
1905 House on Escalona Drive and Jordan Street
1910 Knights of Pythias Hall, Locust Street, north side near Pacific Avenue, demolished
1912 House on High Street; Hotel Dickinson, Ben Lomond **1914** Frapwell's Live Oak Dairy barn, Scotts Valley, demolished, 1991
1923 Edward Frapwell house (in 2005, Scotts Valley Sprinkler and Pipe Supply), 5010 Scotts Valley Drive, Scotts Valley

Van Siclen & Haynes (William D. Van Siclen & Charles Layman Haynes; partnership dissolved, 1895)
1894 A. L. McCandless house, Salinas; High School in Sutter County, California

Benjamin C. Viney
1928 California State Automobile Association, east of 330 Soquel Avenue, demolished
1929 Mary Antonelli, hotel and two stores, concrete, Spanish style, Front Street

Walker & Eisen (Albert R. Walker & Percy Eisen [1886-1946])
1928 County Offices (project), Church and Locust Streets

Ward & Blohme (Clarence R. Ward [b.1876] & J. Henry Blohme [b.1878])

1910 W. T. Sesnon house, Aptos

William Henry Weeks (1866-1936)
List adapted from Betty Lewis,
W. H. Weeks: Architect, 1985, see
bibliography. Santa Cruz except
where noted.
Date unknown: Grammar School,
Aromas
1898 Christian Church
1904 Chittenden residence
1905 Catholic Church, Capitola,
demolished; High School, Boulder
Creek, southwest corner of Azalea
Lane and Lomond Street
1906 Becker residence; John Cooper
residence; Courthouse remodeling;
King residence
1907 Hawes Flats addition
1908 All Souls Church; Bayview
Grammar School; Gault School
addition; Big Creek Power Station; Cox
residence; Field and Cole Block
1910 County Bank remodel; Peoples
Bank addition, second-floor, 1515
Pacific Avenue
1911 Fred Swanton summer home
1914 Grammar School, two-floor
concrete
1917 Hotel Waldo remodel
1920-21 Eastside Branch Library, one-
floor, Soquel Avenue and Water Street
1927 Masonic Hall remodeling
1929 A. O. Goldstein, stores and
offices, two-story, Soquel Avenue and
Branciforte Avenue
1930 Farmers & Merchant's Bank,
remodel, Pacific Avenue and Locust
Street

Weeks & Day (Charles Peter Weeks
[1870-1928] & William P. Day)
1928 T. S. Montgomery house with
keeper's cottage, two-story stucco
with tile roof

Thomas J. Welsh (1847-1918)
Date unknown: San Francisco: St.
Mary's Cathedral, Girl's High School;
Supreme Court Building, destroyed
by 1906 quake; Paulist Church (old St.
Mary's), California and Dupont Streets;
the Buckley Building, Spear and
Market Streets; Italian American Bank

John H. Williams (ca. 1829-1891)
1876 Samuel Winans house, remodel,
Broadway
1877 Mrs. Morgan house; Isaac
Thurber double tenement, Pacific
Avenue; J. J. Hug, plans for building,
Pacific Avenue
1883 Branciforte School, demolished
1885 O. J. Lincoln, plans for cottage,
Laurel Street; Knowles house,
Broadway; George Staffler house,
Church Street
1887 William Degener, plans for
building, Pacific Avenue; Santa Cruz
Sentinel, improvements on the office
block occupied by the newspaper;
D. F. Gardner, cottage on Boston
Tract; L. H. Brannack, plans for house,
Branciforte Avenue and Broadway;
Andrew Trust house, Lincoln Street;
Peter V. Wilkins house, northeast
corner Ocean View Avenue and
Windham Street, demolished; George
Ford house, Highland Avenue,
demolished; F. M. Becker cottage,
Elm Street.; W.H. Martin house,
Washington Street; Patrick Fisher
house, east side Garfield Street,
demolished; Werner Finkeldey house,
Front Street, north of the lot of Mrs.
Peck, demolished; Michael O'Keefe
house, northeast corner Elm and
Washington Streets; D. T. Stribling
house, Van Ness Avenue and Grant
Street; William H. Rose house, lot in
back of Uhden Street and Leibrandt
Avenue

1888 Charles S. Johnson house, Seabright; Building at Bay State Cottages, Third Street; G. W. Place house, Ocean Street, Russell Tract; Mark W. Whittle house, Beach Hill; Frederick A. Hihn, plans for cottage, Fern Street; F. Koehn house, Ocean Street and Branciforte Creek; Louis Wenks house, Soquel Road
1889 J. Conran boardinghouse, Walnut Avenue, demolished; Henry Willey, plans for house, Walnut Avenue; John Carney, plans for house, River Street; Peter Woesselhoft house, Soquel Avenue and Cayuga Street; A. Doyle house, west side Branciforte Avenue; Mr. White, building, Soquel Avenue; D. Younglove house, Church Street; August Peter house, south side Soquel Avenue
1890 Mark A. Buckley, printing office
1891 William Baird house, south side Soquel Avenue; A. J. Hinds house, lots 9 and 10, Block D, Map of Boulder Creek; Ferdinand Koehn house, lot 7, Block D, Map of Boulder Creek
1892 Martha Wilson house, east of the northwest corner of Second and Main Streets, demolished

Wing & Beebe (Engineers)
1921 Soquel Avenue Bridge over the San Lorenzo River

Wood Brothers
1931 Auto repair shop, one-story concrete, Vine Street between Locust and Church Streets

William J. Wright
1928 Civic Center on lower Pacific Avenue (project)

William Wilson Wurster (1895-1973)
1927-28 Warren and Sadie Gregory ranch house, Scotts Valley
1930 Marion Hollins, swimming pool, concrete, Pasatiempo; Marion Hollins, stables, Scotts Valley
1933 Eiskamp house, 523 Brewington Avenue, Watsonville; Donald Gregory house, Scotts Valley
1935 Cowgill beach house, Aptos (unrealized project)
1936 Blaisdell house, Watsonville
1937 Clark beach house, Aptos
1938-1939 Construction and remodeling of shops and shop fronts on Walnut Avenue between Pacific Avenue and Cedar Street for Frederick C. Benner, including space leased by J. J. Newberry store
1963 John H. Gregory house, Scotts Valley

Wilson J. Wythe
1912 First Methodist Church, Walnut Avenue and Church Street, demolished

Architectural Styles in Santa Cruz

The Ohlone Indians, who populated the San Francisco Peninsula and the coast south to Carmel, built three types of structures. Circular houses of poles, covered with brush and about twelve feet in diameter, were inhabited by the women and children. For the men there was the *temescal,* a combination clubhouse and sauna. During camping trips, small circular bark structures were erected for temporary shelter.

When the Spanish and Mexicans arrived, they tried to reproduce as best they could the late baroque architecture familiar to them in Mexico, which had in turn been imported from Spain. The limitations of the adobe building material and the unskilled Indian labor reduced the buildings constructed to very simple adobe structures with thick walls and a roof of thatch, brea (the natural tar found in California), or tile. Plastering the wide eaves protected the adobe from being washed away by the rain. Floors were almost always of tamped earth, and glass was not used for windows until the 1840s (Armas and Rodriguez adobes).

The earliest frame buildings in Santa Cruz were simple clapboarded saltboxes of one story or story-and-a-half, such as the Francisco Alzina house. In a short time, building resources and carpentry improved to the point where John B. Perry could build the comfortable board-and-batten house at 114 Escalona Drive.

Gothic Revival

Gothic and Greek Revival were the major styles of the 1850s and 1860s in Santa Cruz. Modeled after the temples of ancient Greece, Greek Revival buildings were characterized by the temple form—portico, pedimented gable, entablature, and pillared portico.

Gothic Revival buildings have steep gables, lacy bargeboards, delicate split-pilasters, Tudor-arched porches, cornices, and doorways, and pointed-arch windows. Gothic Revival derives its origin from the nineteenth-century desire for the picturesque, the romantic, and the medieval, using Gothic cathedrals as its inspiration.

Italianate

In the 1860s and 1870s the Italianate style was popular for homes and continued to be used into the 1890s for business buildings. The style was derived from fifteenth- and sixteenth-century Italian architecture, characterized by bracket-supported cornices, pedimented or split-pedimented gables, pedimented windows, corner pilasters or quoining, and slanted bays. Several different types of arches were used, including the round arch, the flat-topped arch, and the straight-sided arch.

Stick and Eastlake Styles

In the 1880s a move away from the classical forms was embodied in the Stick and Eastlake styles, usually found in combination.

The Stick Style is characterized by high, steep roofs, prominent framework at the corners, and continuations of the window frames beyond the windows. There are stickwork brackets in the gables, irregular plan and outline, and extensive verandas. The dominant motif is the stick, expressing the balloon-frame method of construction.

Eastlake ornament is characterized by bold use of geometric shapes, three-dimensional pattern, curved brackets, rows of lathe-turned spindles, incised carving, grooved moldings, circular perforations, sunburst-motif panels, bent roofline, and stained glass.

Queen Anne

The Queen Anne style appeared in the late 1860s in England. The term "Queen Anne" is really a misnomer, as the style is more reflective of the Elizabethan or earlier period. While the form of the building often had boldly articulated large volumes, these volumes were often highly adorned with small-scale ornaments. Queen Anne buildings have pedimented gables, corner turrets with candle-snuffer roofs, curved, slanted, and square shallow bays, elaborate exposed chimneys, cut-away corners, and irregular plans and facades.

Shingle Style

The idea of the facade as a skin for the building was even more apparent in the stripped-down Shingle Style of the 1890s, dominated by unornamented primary shapes. The hipped and gabled roofs were often swept low to the ground; the siding was either shingle or clapboard and often stained rather than painted. Banded windows contributed to a general horizontal emphasis. In Santa Cruz, the Shingle Style is always found mixed with other styles.

Richardsonian Romanesque Revival

The Richardsonian Romanesque Revival came into vogue for business and public buildings in the 1890s. It is distinguished by multiple overlapping arches, Syrian arches, short, clustered columns, rock-faced masonry, usually rusticated, and foliage ornament of carved stone or terra cotta. The 1894 Santa Cruz County Courthouse is a good example of the style.

Colonial Revival

The Colonial Revival style, indicative of the twentieth-century preference for more traditional period styles and an awakening sense of America's history, became prevalent during the 1890s and early 1900s. Its features include hipped or gambrel roofs, multiple columned porches, eaves detailed as classical cornice, Palladian windows, and doors with pilasters, pedimented gables, classical balustrades or delicate spindles, colonial swags, and diamond pane windows.

Mission Revival

Around the turn of the century Californians began to realize that they had a rich heritage of their own to explore, and the Mission Revival Style was the result. Attributes of the style are low-pitched tile roofs, hipped or edged by segmental curved gables, smooth-plastered walls, arched windows, arcades, balconies, and towers topped with pyramidal roofs. The style lasted into the early 1920s when Spanish Colonial Revival, a more formal Hispanic style, replaced it.

Spanish Colonial Revival

The Spanish Colonial Revival came to include a wide range of sub-styles from the restrained Monterey Revival Style and the formal Italian-inspired examples to the informal Andalusian-inspired style. The style was popular in Santa Cruz from 1920 to 1948 and was revived again with somewhat less conviction in the 1970s. Spanish Colonial Revival is characterized by decorated multiple arches, arcaded cornices, wooden balconies with turned wood ornament, and red tile roofs with curbed cornices. Also used are fountains, glazed and unglazed tiles, and arcades supported on columns. There is a preponderance of walls and frequent use of courtyards and fountains.

In the Monterey Colonial Revival sub-style, a mixture of Spanish Colonial Revival, East Coast Colonial Revival, and California pioneer architecture, the house is treated as a single two-story volume. The rafters are carved and exposed, and the eaves have a broad overhang. A balcony on the second story runs the length of the house. Much Colonial Revival detailing is employed, especially for interiors.

Bungalow Style

Sharing the Mission Revival's concern for the California environment, the Bungalow style emphasized the natural rather than the historic aspects of that environment. Both stressed a return to simple handcrafted workmanship, and the Bungalow style also stressed the integrity and beauty of materials in their native state. Characterized by rustic exteriors, and open, comfortable interiors, bungalows were most popular in the growing suburbs of Los Angeles.

Bungalows are often stained, rather than painted, covered with clapboards or shingles, have broad spreading eaves supported by large brackets, and broad flat bays. The multiple gables have parallel eaves lines, and the projecting beams are exposed. Windows may be small paned or are often divided into a large lower pane and a small upper pane. Spacious front porches are supported by squat posts atop chunky river boulder or clinker brick piers.

Moderne

In the 1930s the influence of an increasingly machine-dominated society and the utilitarian "form follows function" ethic manifested itself in Santa Cruz in the Moderne. The Moderne is the pop version of the International Style pioneered in the 1920s by Gropius, van der Rohe, Le Corbusier, and others. Both styles share the use of banded windows set flush with the surface and directional emphasis that would be expressed either horizontally or vertically. The Moderne allowed greater freedom of detailing,

315

particularly in the use of cylindrical and zig-zag forms. While Moderne homes were often painted white, as dictated by the International Style, commercial buildings often employed a dazzling polychrome and sometimes neon.

Characteristic of the style is the use of glass-brick, pipe railings, and flat, projecting, cornices and door and window hoods. As the style progressed from the late 1920s to the early 1940s it became increasingly streamlined. It encompassed both the black and gold Gothic of early Moderne skyscrapers and the WPA Neo-Classicism of late Moderne government buildings.

Third Bay Tradition

In the 1960s and '70s the Third Bay Tradition reflected a continuing interest of the San Francisco Bay region in lucidly expressed volumes covered by rustic wooden surfaces. This interest is more evident in the First Bay Tradition of Shingle- and Craftsman-influenced architecture than in the carefully understated ranch style-inspired homes of the Second Bay Tradition. In the 1960s architects working in the Third Bay Tradition turned from the ranch house to the ranch barn, borrowing the shed roofs and the plank siding. The shed roofs opened up dimensions of vertical space in the interiors. Windows are placed flush to the surface and overhanging eaves have been eliminated, so that the buildings appear to be constructed of two dimensional planes.

In the 1970s the Third Bay Tradition was enriched by a more "complex and contradictory" approach to design. This approach expresses the conflict between the various demands of program, site, and interior and exterior space.

Glossary

Baluster. A vertical support for a hand-rail on a stair.

Balustrade. A row of balusters supporting a rail.

Bargeboard. Decorative boards placed perpendicular to the eaves and concealing the rafters.

Barrel Vault. A vault which is a simple continuous arch in section.

Belvedere. An open tower to take in the view.

Bent Roofline. A roofline which changes slope from a low pitch at the ends to a steep pitch at the center.

Bevelled Glass. Glass which has been cut on the slant for the sake of the faceted effect thus produced.

Board-and-Batten. A type of siding consisting of wide boards set vertically whose joints are covered by raised, narrow strips of wood (battens).

Bracket. A small supporting or decorative brace-like element under the eaves or in the gable ends.

Broken Pediment. A pediment that is divided at the bottom.

Brutalism. An architectural philosophy that sought to expose the methods of a building's construction, functions, and service components by using symbolically massive and powerful forms. A movement popular in the 1950s and '60s.

Bull's Eye Window. A round window.

Bungalow Brackets. Triangular brackets composed of stick-like members.

Buttress. A vertical support extending out from a wall.

Casement Window. A window which is hinged at the sides.

Chinese Railing. A wooden railing with an interlocking pattern of posts defining a checkerboard pattern.

Clapboard. Overlapping horizontal boards used as siding.

Clerestory. A wall containing windows extending above the space defined by the first story.

Clinker Brick. Brick which has been fired longer than is customary. It is characterized by dark color and irregular forms.

Coffered Ceiling. A ceiling treatment composed of sunken panels.

Corbel. An element extending from a wall and supporting an exterior weight.

Cornice. A decorative molding or projection at the top of the eaves or over a window or door.

Craftsman. A general term for the artists, architects, and workmen interested in the merits of hand labor, personal involvement in the work, and the use of materials for their intrinsic value and in their natural state.

Glossary

317

Crenellated. Finished with a gap-tooth-like motif.

Cross Vault. *See* **Groin Vault**.

Cut-away Bay. *See* **Slanted Bay**.

Dentil Course. A small cubic block employed in Ionic, Corinthian, and, less commonly, Doric cornices.

Doric. The classical order that employs columns with simple capitals composed of moldings.

Double-hung Window. A window mounted in an upper and lower frame which can slide up and down by means of balanced weights or, later, springs.

Dunce-cap Roof. A pointed, conical roof shape.

Encaustic Tiles. Glazed and decorated earthenware tiles.

Entablature. The broad flat part of a classical temple below the pediment.

Fenestration. The design and placement of windows in a facade.

Finial. A decorative spike or bulb at the top of a building.

Fishscale Shingles. Small shingles ending in a half-circle.

Gable. The topmost triangular portion of an exterior wall.

Gambrel Roof. A roof whose gable ends are slanted back toward the ridge line part way up the side of the roof.

Garland. *See* **Swag**.

Giant Order. A term for a column, pillar, or pilaster which extends for more than one story.

Groin Vault. A four-part vault composed of the intersection of two tunnel vaults.

Half-Timbered. A type of timber construction in which the spaces between the timbers consist of brick or plaster infill.

Hipped Roof. A roof in which the roof sides slope back on all four sides.

Ionic. An order of classical architecture in which the capital, or uppermost part of a column, ends in spirals, called volutes.

Jerkinhead. A roof having a sloping, or hipped end, cutting off a gable.

Keystone. The central stone of an arch or vault.

Lancet Windows. Long narrow windows terminating in a point.

Lincrusta Walton. Heavy fabric coated with linseed oil. Usually pressed into patterns. Used in late-nineteenth-century interiors for decorative friezes.

Lintel. The beam over a doorway or window.

Lunette. An arch shaped like a lintel.

Mansard Roof. A roof that is almost vertical, appearing as an additional story.

Moorish Arch. An arch which completes more than half a circle.

Neo-Classical. A variant of the revived use of architectural forms of antiquity, known as classicism, which emphasized the strongest and most primitive elements in classicism. It is characterized by a rigid and "rational" ordering of elements.

Newel Post. The main support at the end of a stair.

Ogee Arch. A pointed arch which reverses from convex to concave near its apex.

Palladian Window. A window with a large central light and two smaller side lights.

Parti. The underlying concept of a work of architecture.

Pavilion. A portion of a building which has been set off as a semi-independent mass.

Pediment. A triangular gable or cornice treated like the gable end of a classical temple.

Pendant. A decorative bulb or spike extending down from the top of a gable.

Pier. A vertical support, usually quite substantial in appearance.

Pilasters. Pillars attached to or embedded in a wall.

Portico. An entrance porch.

Post-Modern. A term popularized by Charles Jencks beginning in 1976 to indicate architecture which attempts to communicate by use of imagery, symbolism, iconography, and sometimes irony.

Quatrefoil. A symmetrical figure composed of four circular lobes.

Quoining. The decoration of a building's corners with materials in shapes other than those used for the walls.

Raised-Basement. A basement largely above ground level, allowing access to plumbing, heating, as well as providing space for storage.

River Rock, River Pebble. Rounded stones found in streambeds and gullies.

Rustication. The treatment of a surface to indicate that it is composed of cut stone or intended to simulate cut stone.

Segmental Curve. A curve which is broken into parts, with the possibility that the shape of the curve will vary from part to part.

Shed Roof. A roof which slopes in only one direction.

Shingle Style Gable. A gable which projects out from the body of the building and is interrupted by a recessed arch.

Shiplap. *See* **Tongue and Groove.**

Slanted Bay. A bay with sides at a forty-five degree angle to the front side of the bay.

Spandrel. The space above an arch.

Split Pediment. A pediment which is divided at the top.

Split Pilasters. Pilasters divided into vertical members.

Square Bay. A bay window with a rectangular or square configuration.

Squeezed Pediment. A pediment which slants up toward the center, beginning at a point inset from the ends of the pediment.

Story-and-a-half. A building configuration in which the roof of the second story begins at a point below head height.

Swag. A festoon shaped like a piece of cloth or chain of foliage as though it was hung between two supports.

Swiss Chalet Trim. A type of decorative sawn wood ornament with folk motifs.

Glossary

Tongue and Groove. Horizontal board siding with the boards milled to interlock with each other.

Truss. An openwork structural member composed of wood or metal to support a roof.

Tudor Arch. A low flattened arch terminating in a blunted point.

Vault. An arched structure that supports a ceiling or roof.

Vernacular. Architecture whose appearance and layout has been determined largely by custom and popular usage rather than architecture designed by architects.

Wainscot. Rectangular or square wooden paneling on walls.

Window hood. A projection over the window for decorative or sun-shading purposes.

Glossary

Bibliography

The author's reference card files used in preparation of the three editions of *The Sidewalk Companion to Santa Cruz Architecture* are available in the Archives, The Museum of Art & History, Santa Cruz. For hours, see "History Resources" at http://www.santacruzmah.org/ or for an appointment, email archives@ santacruzmah.org. Additional information or corrections related to specific buildings included in this book may be sent to the Archivist, The Museum of Art & History, 705 Front Street, Santa Cruz, CA 95060.

A primary reference for anyone doing research on the history of a Santa Cruz building is *Every Structure Tells a Story: How to Research the History of a Property in Santa Cruz County*. It was published in 1990 by the Publications Committee of the Santa Cruz County Historical Trust (now the Museum of Art & History), under the direction of Stanley D. Stevens. This 111-page book is not only a "how to" manual and a guide to county and city government records but also a comprehensive, local-history reference work with lists and locations of newspapers, census, birth, and death records, maps, city directories, telephone directories, and other useful information.

Newspapers

The best sources of information about architecture in Santa Cruz are back issues of local newspapers. The *Santa Cruz Sentinel* is the most important of these, as it has been published continuously since 1856. The twentieth-century historical articles of reporters Ernest Otto (1871-1955) and Leon Rowland (1884-1952) supplement contemporary accounts of building activity.

Ernest Otto grew up in the Santa Cruz of the 1870s and '80s. With his knack for observation and his keen memory, he could recall the smallest detail of days past. The location of the various circus lots in town, the taste of an apple plucked from a particular tree, and the description of the carriages of prominent families were all fit subjects for his "Old Santa Cruz" column. Throughout his writing he expresses a love of life's small pleasures, an enjoyment of people, and a relish for the details of daily life.

Leon Rowland's column, "Circuit Rider," appeared first in the 1930s in the *Santa Cruz Evening News* and after 1941 in the *Santa Cruz Sentinel*, when that paper acquired the *Evening News*. Rowland's articles are generally more formal and less familiar than the "Old Santa Cruz" columns and were based on Rowland's research. Rowland also authored five monographs on Santa Cruz history, which were collected and reprinted as *Santa Cruz: The Early Years*. Rowland's scrapbooks and his 8,000 cross-referenced research card-file are in Special Collections, University Library, University of California, Santa Cruz. The card file can be searched at: http://library.ucsc.edu/speccoll/rowland/.

Also published in the *Santa Cruz Sentinel* were historical local photographs collected by Preston Sawyer (1899-1968), a *Sentinel* employee. Beginning in 1948, a weekly "Santa Cruz Yesterdays" column featured his photos. By 1955, over 350 of his photos with descriptive text had been published. The University Library, UCSC, later purchased his photo collection.

Because structures are described in different newspapers in varying degrees of detail, it is important to check as many papers as possible for information. The building descriptions in the *Santa Cruz Surf*, which was published from 1883 to 1919, were often more detailed than those of the *Santa Cruz Sentinel*.

The newspapers listed below were those primarily used for this book.

> *Santa Cruz Evening News.* November 1, 1907-December 1941. The News was acquired by the *Sentinel* and became *Santa Cruz Sentinel-News*, January 1, 1942.

> *Santa Cruz Sentinel.* June 14, 1856-1914 as a weekly or semi-weekly; since 1884 as a daily.

> *Santa Cruz Surf.* 1883-1918, weekly; 1883-1919, daily.

Also cited is the newspaper *Riptide*, 1942-1953. The centennial edition was published October 19, 1950.

For a comprehensive listing of Santa Cruz County newspapers, see *Every Structure Tells a Story*, pp. 36-45. Alternative newspapers that are not listed in *Every Structure Tells a Story* are also essential resources for anyone researching life, politics, and culture in Santa Cruz after the arrival of UCSC. Included among these are: *City on a Hill Press* (the UCSC newspaper), *Free Spaghetti Dinner, Good Times, Metro, Morning Star, People's Press, Santa Cruz Independent, Santa Cruz Times, Sundaz!* and *Town Crier*.

Newspaper Indexes

Invaluable indexes to Santa Cruz newspapers have become available since the earlier editions of *The Sidewalk Companion*. With these indexes, research that formerly took days can now often be accomplished in minutes. The indexes are compiled and organized by volunteers from the Friends of the Santa Cruz Public Libraries and the Genealogical Society of Santa Cruz County, with Sara Bunnett as chair of the team effort. The local news indexes provide access to selected articles published from 1856 through 1954 (as of 2005). Indexes to the *Santa Cruz Sentinel, Santa Cruz Daily Surf*, and *Santa Cruz Evening News* are available in print format for varying periods. These indexes are being computerized by the Santa Cruz Public Library. The first one available is the index to the *Santa Cruz Daily Surf* from 1883 to 1900, in the *Santa Cruz Local News Index* database available at the library's Web site: http://www.santacruzpl.org/history/oldnews/. Another online access to local newspaper articles is the index to the public library's newspaper clipping file.

Photographs

Nothing conveys a clearer idea of a building's former appearance than an old photograph. Photographs also establish locations of vanished landmarks. A prime source is the photograph collection in Special Collections, McHenry Library, UCSC. The photograph collection of the Museum of Art & History has also become a valuable resource. The Santa Cruz Public Library's photo collection is available online at: http://www.santacruzpl.org/history/photos/index.html. The commercial source for historical photographs is Covello & Covello Photography, which was founded by the late Santa Cruz photographer Ed Webber in 1938. Webber's was the news photography service that provided photos for the *Santa Cruz Sentinel* from 1938 to 1969. The business was sold to Vester and Esther Dick in 1960. The *Sentinel* began its own photography department in 1966. There are thousands of negatives in the Covello & Covello stock photograph collection. The firm also has a collection of many hundreds of historical photographs dating from the middle of the nineteenth century through the 1920s and 1930s.

Maps

Equally specific, but less graphic than photographs, are the Sanborn Fire Insurance Maps in the Map Room at the Science and Engineering Library, UCSC. Sanborn maps show the position, dimensions, materials, number of stories, and use of buildings. Because they were revised every few years, they are helpful in dating buildings. Maps for the City of Santa Cruz are available for the following years: 1877, 1883, 1886, 1887, 1888, 1892, 1905, 1917, 1928, 1929, 1934, 1936, 1939, 1950, 1952, 1960, 1965, and 1988.

Land ownership maps, available in the Map Room, can also provide useful information in determining names of property owners. They show who owned what land at the time that the map was prepared.

Directories

Polk's Santa Cruz City Directories, published by R. L. Polk and Company, beginning in 1925, list residents and businesses by name and address. Earlier directories with various titles and publishers provide similar though usually much less comprehensive listings. Included in *Every Structure Tells a Story* is "Chronological Tables of Holdings" of city and business directories for Santa Cruz.

County Records

County records can be profitably searched for dates of purchase and former owners. If a newspaper article mentions a house being built by an owner who recently purchased a lot, the Grantee-Grantor indexes can be consulted. There will probably be an entry for approximately the same date, referring to a deed book describing the location of the lot. Unfortunately, the descriptions are often confusing and occasionally incomprehensible.

Bibliography

Among the vital statistics records maintained by the county, death certificates prove the most useful in researching local owners and architects. Access to these records has become very restricted.

At the county building was the most obscure source of information used for the second edition of this book, the bundled packets of building contracts between architects, clients, and contractors. These were invaluable for the years between 1887 and 1894. These records now cannot be located.

City Records

The researcher will find that much of the data in the two-volume *Santa Cruz Historic Building Survey* is drawn from *The Sidewalk Companion to Santa Cruz Architecture*. However, these two volumes contain about 650 photos of the city's historic structures.

City building permit information may be available from the City Planning Department. Master-list records since the 1930s-1940s are on microfilm.

Biographical and Historical Reference Sources

The subject of your research, of course, will determine which, if any, biographical or historical reference sources will be useful for information on owners and occupants. Of the biographical and historical books concerning Santa Cruz County, Elliott's, *Santa Cruz County, California*, authored by Rev. S. H. Willey, Dr. C. L. Anderson, Edward Martin, and others, published in 1879, is the earliest and perhaps the most important architectural history source. Its many engravings provide an extensive record of the town's appearance at the time. The Museum of Art & History 1997 reprint, with its extensive indexes and especially Jill Perry's guide to illustrations, is essential. Also valuable for their illustrations are E. S. Harrison's 1892 *History of Santa Cruz County* and Phil Francis's 1896 *Beautiful Santa Cruz County*. Although only a few local architects are mentioned, all of the histories contain a good deal of biographical information, though often inaccurate.

Two indispensable Internet sources for biographical and genealogical information are www.ancestry.com and www.vitalsearch-ca.com.

Three books essential for an understanding of California's architectural history are listed in the bibliography. Harold Kirker's *California's Architectural Frontier* discusses the architectural development of the state in the nineteenth century as a long period of colonial domination by Eastern styles. Kirker concentrates on individual buildings and architects as examples. Joseph Baird's *Time's Wondrous Changes* discusses San Francisco's nineteenth-century architecture in terms of styles. Helpful in placing Santa Cruz architecture in relation to that of other towns is *The Guide to Architecture in San Francisco and Northern California*.

Santa Cruz—General

"Alfred Baldwin: A Biography." Compiled by Charles N. Edmonston. San Francisco: 1967. Includes reminiscences of Baldwin. Typewritten copy in Genealogical Society of Santa Cruz County, Local Family Collection, Santa Cruz Public Library.

Building Permits in the City of Santa Cruz: Reported in Newspapers 1909 through 1924. Compiled by the Early Santa Cruz Newspaper Indexing Committee of the Friends of the Santa Cruz Public Libraries. Santa Cruz: Genealogical Society of Santa Cruz County, 1994. Permits listed by street and name. Supplemented by *Santa Cruz, California, Building Permits from Early Newspapers (ca. 1910-1954)*, compiled by Sara A. Bunnett (Santa Cruz: Genealogical Society of Santa Cruz County, 2004).

"Charming Santa Cruz." *Los Angeles Tribune*, March 26, 1887, 3.

Clark, Donald Thomas. *Santa Cruz County Place Names: A Geographical Dictionary*. Santa Cruz: Santa Cruz Historical Society, 1986.

Coope, J. F. "Santa Cruz: The City of Mountain and Shore." *Sunset*, September 1900, 227-238.

Dunn, Geoffrey. *Santa Cruz is in the Heart*. Capitola, CA: Capitola Book Company, [1989]. Collected essays and newspaper and journal articles, including "The Confessions of Old Chepa: Josefa Pérez Soto and the Spirit of Old Santa Cruz;" "A Historian for All Time [Ernest Otto]." Additional chapters are on African American, Chinese, Italian, and other local ethnic groups.

Elliott's 1879 *Santa Cruz County, California*, see *Santa Cruz County, California . . . 1879.*

Every Structure Tells a Story: How to Research the History of a Property in Santa Cruz County. Compiled by members of the Santa Cruz County Historical Trust Publications Committee. Santa Cruz: Santa Cruz County Historical Trust, 1990.

Farnham, Eliza W. *California, In-doors and Out: or How We Farm, Mine, and Live Generally in the Golden State.* New York: Dix, Edwards and Co., 1856.

Fehliman, Clinton. "Economic History of Santa Cruz County, California, 1850 to 1947." Unpublished student report, Summer 1947. Copy at Santa Cruz Public Library.

Feldstein, Kenneth. "The Demographic and Spatial Development of Santa Cruz." Unpublished paper, University of California. Santa Cruz, 1969.

Fenyon, W. J. "The Story of the Hills." *Land of Sunshine*, July 1891, 66-70.

Foote, Mary Hallock. "A Sea-Port on the Pacific." *Scribner's* 16 (August 1878): 449-460.

_____. *Reminiscences of Mary Hallock Foote: A Victorian Gentlewoman in the Far West*. Edited by Rodman Paul. San Marino, CA: The Huntington Library, 1972.

Francis, Phil. *Santa Cruz County, A Faithful Reproduction in Print and Photography of Its Climate, Capabilities and Beauties.* (Cover title: *Beautiful Santa Cruz County*). San Francisco: H. S. Crocker Co., 1896.

Gandolfi, Daisy Rose. *Living and Loving: Santa Cruz in the Fifties*. [Santa Cruz]: The Author, 2001. Biographies contributed by ninety Santa Cruz High School graduates of the Class of 1951, with historical photos of Santa Cruz in the 1950s.

Guinn, J[ames] M[iller]. *History of the State of California and Biographical Record of Santa Cruz, San Benito, Monterey* and *San Luis Obispo Counties*. Chicago: Chapman Publishing Co., 1903.

Hallett, Richard. "Never a Dull Moment: Fred Swanton and Santa Cruz." Master's thesis. San Jose State University, 1976.

Harrison, E[dward] S[anford]. *History of Santa Cruz County, California*. San Francisco: Pacific Press Publishing Co., 1892.

_____. *Santa Cruz County*. Santa Cruz: Published for the Santa Cruz County Board of Supervisors, 1890.

Hoover, Mildred Brooke, Hero Eugene Rensch, and Ethel Grace Rensch. *Historic Spots in California*. 5th ed. Revised by Douglas E. Kyle. Stanford, CA: Stanford University Press, 2002.

Houston, J. D. "View from Santa Cruz." *Holiday,* May, 1967, 18+.

Jones, Donna. *Santa Cruz County: A Century*. Santa Cruz: Santa Cruz Sentinel, 1999.

Judah, H. R., Jr. "At Santa Cruz by-the-Sea." *Sunset,* June 1905, 171-177.

_____. "Santa Cruz: The Home City of the Pacific Coast." *Out West,* August 1906, 183-192.

Kirby, Georgiana Bruce. *Georgiana, Feminist Reformer of the West: The Journal of Georgiana Bruce Kirby, 1852-1860.* With biography based on research of Helen Giffen, Carolyn Swift, and Judith Steen; edited by Carolyn Swift and Judith Steen. Santa Cruz County Historical Trust, 1987.

_____. *Years of Experience*. Putnam, 1886.

Koch, Margaret. *Going to School in Santa Cruz County: A History of the County's Public School System*. Santa Cruz: Santa Cruz County Office of Education, 1978.

_____. *Santa Cruz County: Parade of the Past*. Fresno: Valley Publishers, 1983.

_____. *They Called It Home: Santa Cruz, California*. Fresno: Valley Publishers, 1974.

_____. *The Walk Around Santa Cruz Book: A Look at the City's Architectural Treasures*. Fresno: Valley Publishers, 1978.

Lehmann, Susan. *Fully Developed Context Statement for the City of Santa Cruz*. Prepared for City of Santa Cruz Planning and Community Development Department. Santa Cruz: The City, October 20, 2000.

Lewis, Betty. *Monterey Bay Yesterday: A Nostalgic Era in Postcards*. Fresno: Valley Publishers, 1977. Features the works of architect William H. Weeks.

_____. *Watsonville: Memories That Linger*. 2 vols. Fresno and Santa Cruz: Valley Publishers, 1976, 1980.

"A Look at Some California Resorts." *Sunset,* December 1899, 46-55.

Lydon, Sandy. *Chinese Gold: The Chinese in the Monterey Bay Region*. Capitola, CA: Capitola Book Co., 1985.

Martin, Edward. *History of Santa Cruz County, California, with Biographical Sketches*…. Los Angeles: Historic Record Co., 1911.

Mead, G. S. "Santa Cruz, California." *National Magazine* 4:573.

MacGregor, Bruce. *The Birth of the California Narrow Gauge: A Regional Study of the Technology of Thomas and Martin Carter.* Stanford: Stanford University Press, 2003.

McCaleb, Charles S. *Surf, Sand* and *Streetcars: A Mobile History of Santa Cruz, California*. Glendale, CA: Interurbans, 1977. Reprinted with author's addenda. Santa Cruz: History Museum of Santa CruzCounty, 1995.

McDonnell, Terry. "The Greening of Santa Cruz." *San Francisco*, May 1974, 46-52.

O'Hare, Sheila, and Irene Berry. *Santa Cruz California*. Chicago: Arcadia, 2002.

Olin, L. G. "The Development and Promotion of Santa Cruz Tourism." Master's thesis. San Jose State University, June 1967.

Pfremmer, Patricia. *Santa Cruz, 1850-1976: A Selective Bibliography Based on Resources in the Library of the University of California, Santa Cruz*. Santa Cruz: University Library, University of California, Santa Cruz, 1976.

Phelan, J. D. "Santa Cruz, California." *Harper's Weekly*, July 28, 1894, 708.

Proctor, Harriette Jessup. "Full Life, Empty Pockets: A Personal Account of Living in Santa Cruz During the Great Depression, 1930-1935." *Santa Cruz County History Journal*, no. 2

(1995): 35-47. The author worked for the Hihn family, for Judge Cerf at his home on Beach Hill, for Sally Field at Pasatiempo, and at the Guest House at Pasatiempo.

Raymond, I. H. *Santa Cruz County, Resources, Advantages, Objects of Interest*. Santa Cruz, Calif.: Santa Cruz Development Association, 1887.

Reader, Phil. *To Know My Name: A Chronological History of African Americans in Santa Cruz County*. http://www.santacruzpl.org/history/culdiv/know1.shtml

Rowland, Leon. *Santa Cruz: The Early Years; The Collected Historical Writings of Leon Rowland*. Santa Cruz: Paper Vision Press, 1980. Includes *Old Santa Cruz Mission, Villa de Branciforte, The Story of Old Soquel, The Annals of Santa Cruz*, and *Los Fundadores*.

Santa Cruz (City) Planning Department. Historic Preservation Plan, 1974. Santa Cruz: 1974.

"Santa Cruz." *Grizzly Bear,* September, 1927, 10.

Santa Cruz, Cal.: Illustrated in Photogravure. New York: A. Wittemann, c1894.

Santa Cruz (City). Parks and Recreation Department. *City of Santa Cruz Heritage Trees*. Brochure prepared by the City's Urban Forester Leslie Keedy lists forty-nine trees with site addresses. Includes many color photographs.

Santa Cruz County, California: Illustrations Descriptive of its Scenery, Fine Residences, Public Buildings…. San Francisco: Wallace W. Elliott & Co., 1879. Reprinted with guide to illustrations by Jill Miller Perry; alphabetical list of "Officers of Santa

Bibliography

Cruz County from 1850 to 1879" arranged by Stanley D. Stevens; indexed by Leonard A. Greenberg and Stanley D. Stevens. Santa Cruz, CA: Museum of Art & History, 1997.

Santa Cruz Historic Building Survey. [Vol. 1] Prepared for the City of Santa Cruz by Charles Hall Page & Associates, Inc. San Francisco: 1976. Preface by Mayor John G. Mahaney, M.D. Historic Preservation Commission: Willard Morris, Chairman; Harold Steen, Vice Chairman; Margaret Lezin, Virginia Sharp, Bruce Seivertson.

Santa Cruz Historic Building Survey. Vol. 2. Department of Planning and Community Development. City of Santa Cruz. Santa Cruz: May 1989. Selections and research by John Chase. Architectural writing by Daryl Allen. Designed and produced by Jeanne Gordon.

Santa Cruz Sentinel. *5:04 P.M.: The Great Quake of 1989.* Santa Cruz: Santa Cruz Sentinel Publishers, 1989.

Santa Cruz: The Whole Thing Catalog, 1974 [by Tom Bean, Richard Curtis, and Robert Page]. Santa Cruz: Santa Cruz Publishing, 1974.

Society of California Pioneers of Santa Cruz County, with Biographies and Portraits. Edited by Stanley D. Stevens. Special Issue, *Santa Cruz County History Journal*, no. 4 (1998).

Stein, Benjamin. "At Rainbow's End–A Gang of Bikers." *Wall Street Journal*, January 10, 1975.

"A Summer Idyll of Santa Cruz." *Sunset*, July 1909, 70.

Tennyson, Mildred. "Miss Skeen's Outing at Santa Cruz." *California Illustrated*, March 1894, 421-437.

Torchiana, Henry Albert van Coenen. *Story of the Mission Santa Cruz.* San Francisco: Paul Elder and Co., 1933.

van Gorder, Harold J. *Now and Then.* Santa Cruz, CA: 1995. The reminiscences of Van Gorder, who arrived in Santa Cruz in 1905 at the age of four.

Verardo, Jennie Dennis, and Denzil Verardo. *Santa Cruz County: Restless Paradise.* Northridge, CA: Windsor Publications, Inc., 1987.

Watkins, Rolin, ed. *History of Monterey and Santa Cruz Counties, California.* Chicago: S. J. Clarke, 1925.

Weyburn, Cynthia, and Peter Scott. *In the Ocean Wind: The Santa Cruz North Coast.* Felton: Glenwood Press, 1974.

Chapter 1

Beal, Chandra Moira, and Richard A. Beal. *Santa Cruz Beach Boardwalk: The Early Years—Never a Dull Moment.* [Austin, TX] Pacific Group, 2003.

Dormanen, Susan. "The Golden Gate Villa." *Santa Cruz County History Journal*, no. 2 (1995): 122-135.

"F. H. Davis House." *Architect and Engineer of California*, February 1918, 18.

Hyman, Rick. "Early History of the Carmelita Cottages." In *Every Structure Tells a Story: How to Research the History of a Property in Santa Cruz County.* Santa Cruz: Santa Cruz County Historical Trust, 1990: 80-102.

For a revision of this article, see the Santa Cruz Public Library Web site, http://www.santacruzpl.org/history/arch/. For the later history of the cottages, see the author's article "Saving Carmelita Cottages," *California Coast and Ocean*, Winter/Spring 1993, also reproduced on the Santa Cruz Public Library Web site. An exhaustive history of the cottages, their owners, and the neighborhood.

Iliff School of Theology. [Iliff and Warren biographies]. Web site, http://discuss.iliff.edu/meidson/archives.

[Koch, Margaret]. *Towards Artistic Development: Frank Heath, Lillian Heath*. [Santa Cruz]: Santa Cruz Art League, [1987]. An eight-page pamphlet with photos and examples of their paintings.

Kraft, Jeff, and Aaron Leventhal. *Footsteps in the Fog: Alfred Hitchcock's San Francisco*. Foreword by Patricia Hitchcock O'Connell. Santa Monica, CA: Santa Monica Press, 2002. In addition to suggesting that the Hotel McCray/Sunshine Villa may have been Hitchcock's inspiraton for the Bates Mansion in *Psycho*, the authors say that the Bernheim house, now demolished, resembled the film's mansion.

McCrackin, Josephine Clifford. "The Country Home of the Frank J. Sullivan Family at Santa Cruz." *Overland Monthly*, July 1914: 89-91.

Norris, Frank. "The Santa Cruz Venetian Carnival." *The Wave*, June 27, 1896. Available at http://scplweb.santacruzpl.org/history/19thc/norris.shtml

Orlando, Alverda. "Davenport and Its Cement Plant: The Early Years, 1903-1910." *Santa Cruz County History Journal*, no. 1 (1994): 49-60. Includes information on William J. Dingee and his proposed cement plant in the city.

Perry, Frank. *Lighthouse Point: Illuminating Santa Cruz*. Santa Cruz: Otter B Books, 2002. An outstanding, thoroughly researched book not only on Lighthouse Point and the lighthouse but also on the Adna and Margaret Hecox family, including daughter Laura, lighthouse keeper from 1883 to 1916. The book also provides information on prominent people who lived on West Cliff Drive. Includes an extensive bibliography.

[Ryan, Micki]. *Walking Tour of the Historic Santa Cruz Beach Boardwalk*. Santa Cruz: Santa Cruz Seaside Co., 1999.

"Santa Cruz Casino." *Architect and Engineer of California*, June 1907, 44 and September 1907, 83.

Walsh, James P., and Timothy J. O'Keefe. *Legacy of a Native Son: James Duval Phelan and Villa Montalvo*. Los Gatos, CA: Forbes Mill Press, 1993. Though there is no information on Phelan's Santa Cruz estate, the book chronicles his life and homes in San Francisco and at Villa Montalvo, in Saratoga, California.

Yudelson, Jerry, and Lynn Nelson. *Desolation Row: The Proposed Lighthouse Point Convention Center Complex. Part One: History and Description of the Project. A Report to the People of Santa Cruz*. Santa Cruz: Save Lighthouse Point Association, [1972].

Bibliography

Chapter 2

Dunn, Geoffrey. "More Than a Name: London Nelson's Living Legacy." *Good Times*, February 22, 1996, 10.

Edgerton, Wanda Misbach. *From These Beginnings, 1866 to 1986: The First One Hundred Twenty Years for Santa Cruz Unitarian Universalists*. Santa Cruz: Unitarian Universalist Fellowship of Santa Cruz County, 1993.

Marshall, Franklin. *Louden Nelson: From Slavery to Philanthropy*. Illustrated by Maricela Marshall. Santa Cruz: Children's Learning Museum, 2003. Children's book "Dedicated to [Louden Nelson's] Love for Education."

Spalsbury, Edgar. *The Place on Laurel Street: The Diary of Judge Edgar Spalsbury*. Introduction by Viola Washburn. [Santa Cruz: privately printed, 1971].

Chapter 3

A Century of Christian Witness: History of First Congregational Church, Santa Cruz, California. Prepared under the supervision of the Church Historical Committee. Santa Cruz: 1963.

"Doctor's Office." (Randall-Phillips-Cowden Building by Wurster). *Architectural Record* 89:62-63.

Hihn, Frederick Augustus. "How I Came to Santa Cruz." Introduction and End Notes by Stanley D. Stevens. *Santa Cruz County History Journal*, no. 1 (1994): 72-81.

Hihn-Younger Archive. Available at UCSC and through the University Library Web site: http://library.ucsc.edu/ Zope/hihn/about/index_html The archive contains correspondence, biographies, business records, artifacts, maps, memorabilia, and photographs of the Hihn and Younger families.

Pitts, ZaSu. *Candy Hits*. New York: Duell, Sloan and Pearce, 1963.

Chapter 4

Allen, Rebecca. *Native Americans at Mission Santa Cruz, 1791-1834: Interpreting the Archaeological Record*. Perspectives in California Archaeology, vol. 5. Los Angeles: Institute of Archaeology, University of California, Los Angeles, 1998.

Allen, Rebecca, Glenn J. Farris, David L. Felton, Edna E. Kimbro, and Karen Hildebrand. "Restoration Research at Santa Cruz Mission State Historic Park: A Retrospective." In *Archaeological, Cultural and Historical Perspectives on Alta California*. Proceedings of the 20th Annual Conference of the California Mission Studies Association, Santa Cruz, California, February 14-16, 2003, 1-20.

Burton, Robert, and Thomas L. McHugh. *Samuel Leask: Transplanted Scot, Citizen Par Excellence*. Felton, CA: Village Print Shop, 1964.

Dietz, Stephen A. *Report of Archaeological Investigations of a Mission Santa Cruz Tanning Vat Located at 126 Escalona Drive, Santa Cruz, California*. Prepared for Gregory Hendee. Santa Cruz: Archaeological Consulting and Research Services, Inc., November 1986. Copy in Museum of Art & History Archives.

Dill Design Group. "Historical and Architectural Assessment, Historic Resource Design Review (abridged), 660 High Street, Santa Cruz,

California." Los Gatos, CA: Dill Design Group, July 5, 2002. Leslie A. G. Dill, Historic Architect; Kara Oosterhous, Architectural Historian. Property History by Charlene Duval, Consulting Historian; Evaluation for Significance by Franklin Maggi, Architectural Historian.

Gebhard, David. "William Wurster and His California Contemporaries: The Idea of Regionalism and Soft Modernism," in *An Everyday Modernism: The Houses of William Wurster*, edited by Marc Treib. San Francisco: San Francisco Museum of Modern Art, 1995.

Kimbro, Edna. "Construction Chronology of the Site of Holy Cross Church, Santa Cruz, California." This document was originally prepared for the City of Santa Cruz Historic Preservation Commission as part of Holy Cross Parish's application to build a new parish hall. Available at the Santa Cruz Public Library's Web site: http://www.santacruzpl.org/history/spanish/kimbro.shtml.

Kirby, Georgiana Bruce. *Georgiana, Feminist Reformer of the West: The Journal of Georgiana Bruce Kirby, 1852-1860.* With biography based on research of Helen Giffen, Carolyn Swift, and Judith Steen; edited by Carolyn Swift and Judith Steen. Santa Cruz: Santa Cruz County Historical Trust, 1987.

Logan, Mary E. *The Loganberry*. Oakland, CA: privately printed, c1955.

McCrackin, Josephine Clifford. ["Article on Torchiana Estate"]. *Overland Monthly*. 1912.

_____. "The Beautiful Garden Surroundings of C. C. Moore." *Overland Monthly* 59 (1912).

Patten, Phyllis. *Santa Cruz Mission: La Exaltacion De La Santa Cruz*. Santa Cruz: Published by the author, 1974.

Pokriots, Marion Dale. *McPheters House, 203 Highland Avenue, Santa Cruz, California*. 2004. Unpublished report prepared for the owners.

Rowland, Leon. *Old Santa Cruz Mission*, in *Santa Cruz: The Early Years; The Collected Historical Writings of Leon Rowland*. Santa Cruz: Paper Vision Press, 1980, 1-24. Originally published in 1941.

Silvers, Dean A. *A Brief History of the Creeks of Rancho Tres [o más] Ojos de Agua*. Santa Cruz: the author, 1992.

Torchiana, Henry Albert van Coenen. *Story of the Mission Santa Cruz*. San Francisco: Paul Elder and Co., 1933.

Chapter 5

California Emergency Design Assistance Team. *Downtown Santa Cruz Urban Design Workshop*. Santa Cruz: CEDAT, 1990. Presented by Architects Association of Santa Cruz County, California Council of the American Institute of Architects, and Santa Cruz Tomorrow.

Chinatown Dreams: The Life and Photographs of George Lee. Edited by Geoffrey Dunn; with contributions by Lisa Liu Grady, Tony Hill, James D. Houston, Sandy Lydon, Morton Marcus, and George Ow Jr. Capitola, CA: Capitola Book Co., 2002.

Duval, Charlene. "History of 1534 Pacific Avenue." Draft. Prepared for the City of Santa Cruz Inventory Update, Dill Design Group, 2004.

Ellmore, Titus, Architects. *Feasibility Study of Upper Floor Renovations on the Pacific Garden Mall*. Prepared for the City of Santa Cruz. Santa Cruz: 1977.

Bibliography

Friends of the Del Mar. Web site: http://friendsofthedelmar.com.

Gandolfi, Daisy Rose. *Theatre Del Mar: Now Playing in Santa Cruz.* [Santa Cruz]: The Author, 2002. A history of the theatre, with contributed stories of former ushers and usherettes who worked there; heavily illustrated with historical photos.

Lydon, Sandy. *Chinese Gold: The Chinese in the Monterey Bay Region.* Capitola, CA: Capitola Book Co., 1985.

MacGregor, Bruce. *The Birth of California Narrow Gauge.* Stanford: Stanford University Press, 2003.

Patten, Phyllis B. "The Italian Hotels of Santa Cruz." *Santa Cruz Historical Society News and Notes*, nos. 51 and 52, October 1972 and March 1973.

"Post Office Building for Santa Cruz." *Architect and Engineer of California*, April 1908, 45.

"Santa Cruz County Office Building and Courts by Rockwell & Banwell." *Architectural Record*, August 1968, 105-110.

Chapter 6

Giffen, Barbara. "The Tannery on the San Lorenzo." Unpublished report, 1968. Copy at Special Collections, UCSC, Santa Cruz.

Holland, Michael R. *The Origins of the Santa Cruz Wine Industry*, in *Late Harvest: Wine History of the Santa Cruz Mountains*. Santa Cruz: [Late Harvest Project, 1983]. Includes a history of the Santa Cruz Mountain Wine Company.

Kaufman, Dan. "Primary Sash Mill Historical Summary." Typewritten manuscript, 1974.

McCrackin, Josephine Clifford. "Auto-Biography" and "Forest Idyl and Forest Fire." *Santa Cruz County History Journal*, no. 2 (1995): 87-100.

_____. *The Woman Who Lost Him and Tales of the Army Frontier.* With an introduction by Ambrose Bierce. Pasadena: George Wharton James, 1913.

McInerney-Meager, Colleen, and Catherine Graham. "Comin' Thru: The Untold Story of the Pogonip Women's Polo Team," 2004. Unpublished manuscript in Museum of Art & History Archives, Santa Cruz.

Reader, Phil. "The Tales of Old Mother Chapar." *Santa Cruz County History Journal*, no. 1, 1994: 91-97. Article on Josefa Pérez Soto.

Rowland, Leon. *Villa de Branciforte: The Village that Vanished,* in *Santa Cruz: The Early Years; The Collected Historical Writings of Leon Rowland.* Santa Cruz: Paper Vision Press, 1980, 25-56. Originally published in 1941.

Santa Cruz County History Journal, no. 3 (1997). Branciforte Issue. "Dedicated to Starr Pait Gurcke and Leon Rowland." Gurcke translated thousands of documents relating to Branciforte and Rowland was a pioneer researcher and writer of Spanish Colonial history and the genealogy of Branciforte pioneers. Includes contributions by twenty authors, including David W. Heron, "Branciforte: The Viceroy from Sicily": 59-61, cited in Chapter 6.

Chapter 7

Duval, Charlene. "History of 555 Soquel Avenue [Santa Cruz Hospital]." Draft. Prepared for the City of Santa Cruz Inventory Update, Dill Design Group, 2004.

Hooper, Linda Rosewood. *The Riverside Neighborhood*. For an extensive history see: http://people.ucsc.edu/~rosewood/riverside/neighborhood/neighborhood.html. Includes photos and maps.

[Rogers, Margaret E.] *History of the Santa Cruz Art League Galleries*. Santa Cruz, 1974. Reprint.

Wilson, Tanner G. *Yesterday and the Day Before: Part II*. Santa Cruz: T. G. Wilson, 1984.

Chapter 8

Forbes, E. M. C. *Reminiscences of Seabright*. Seabright, CA: 1915. 2nd printing by Dorothy C. Miller, 1968.

Larson, Ed. *Gaff-Rigged Remembrance: Writings from the Santa Cruz Harbor*. Santa Cruz: Fly By Night Graphics, 2000.

Rogers, Margaret E. *Eighty years in California*. Xerox copy of typescript, prepared by nephew Eugene B. Reid in 1977. Copies at Santa Cruz Public Library and in Special Collections, UCSC.

Chapter 9

Dunn, Geoffrey. "Male Notte, Santa Cruz-Italian Relocation and Restrictions, During World War II." *Santa Cruz County History Journal*, no. 1 (1994) 82-91.

_____. *Santa Cruz is in the Heart*. Capitola, CA: Capitola Book Company, [1989].

Lydon, Sandy. "Walk the West Side to Find 'Real' Santa Cruz." *Santa Cruz Sentinel*, July 1, 1990.

Reader, Phil. *To Know My Name: A Chronological History of African Americans in Santa Cruz County*.

http://www.santacruzpl.org/history/culdiv/know1.shtml

Chapter 10

Calciano, Elizabeth Spedding, and Ray Collett. *The Campus Guide: A Tour of the Natural Environment and Points of Historical Interest*. Santa Cruz: University of California, Santa Cruz, 1969.

Chase, John. "Kresge: Architecture for the Hell of It." *City on a Hill Press*, November 8, 1973, 6-7.

"Cowell College." *Progressive Architecture* 45:34-35.

"First Year at Santa Cruz." *Time*, May 13, 1966, 56.

Fischer, J. "Different Kind of Campus." *Harper*, July 1969, 124+.

Grant, Gerald, and David Riesman. *The Perpetual Dream: Reform and Experiment in the American College*. Chicago: University of Chicago Press, 1978.

Herbert, Frank. "Beachhead School, the Small Worlds of UC Santa Cruz." *San Francisco Chronicle*, California Living Section, September 22, 1968, 16+.

Janssen, P. "Groove with the Redwoods." *Newsweek*, November 18, 1968, 86.

Jarret, J. L. "Santa Cruz after One Year: Report on Cowell College." *Saturday Review*, January 21, 1967, 67.

Kirk, R. "Academic Order and the Human Scale." *National Review*, March 23, 1965, 241.

"Kresge College." (MLTW). *Progressive Architecture*, January 1970.

"Merrill College." (Campbell & Wong). *Architectural Record*, May 1969.

Bibliography

"Merrill College Interiors, UCSC." *Interiors*, December, 1969.

"Moore Is Moore." *L'Architecture d'Aujourd'hui*, no. 184 (March-April 1976).

"New and Spacious Campus Inspires a Fresh Approach." *Architectural Record*, 145:146-148.

Niblett, Roy. "Santa Cruz Colleges Under Attack." *London Times*, Higher Education Supplement, June 23, 1972, 15.

"Outdoor Theater." (Royston, Hanamoto & Beck). *Progressive Architecture*, December 1970, 60.

"Provost's House, Merrill College." *Architectural Record*, May 1972, 46-49.

"Santa Cruz Campus; with a Statement by D. E. McHenry." *Architectural Record*, November 1964, 176-85.

"Santa Cruz, Crown College." (Ernest Kump). *Architectural Record*, May 1969, 146-50.

"Santa Cruz, Lecture and Demonstration Building." (Marquis & Stoller). *Architectural Record*, July 1972.

"Santa Cruz Library, University of California at Santa Cruz." (John Carl Warnecke). *Architectural Record*, April 1967, 202-5.

"Santa Cruz Performing Arts Center, University of California." (Ralph Rapson). *Progressive Architecture*, January 1968.

Smith, Page. "Some Advice on Sex, Dress, and Manners: Cowell College." Excerpts from a memorandum. *U.S. News and World Report*, June 6, 1966, 14-15.

Solomon's House: A Self-conscious History of Cowell College, [by members of the Cowell History Workshop]. Felton, CA: Big Trees Press, 1969.

Stookey, B. "Starting from Scratch: the University of California at Santa Cruz." *Harvard Review*, Winter 1965, 22-34.

Tracy, Stephen. "Potato Baron and the Line." (Fictional account of student life in the Thomas Weeks house). *New Yorker*, February 26, 1972, 32-39.

Treib, Marc. "Mastery & Reflection," in *Thomas Church, Landscape Architect: Designing a Modern California Landscape*, edited by Marc Treib. San Francisco: William Stout, 2003.

"U. C. Fieldhouse: Bold Solution + Size, Space Problems." *Architectural Record*, December, 1966, 146-8.

"The University of California at Santa Cruz." *AIA Journal* (August 1979). Includes: Daniel Gregory, "U.C. Santa Cruz: Site and Planning," 34-41; John Pastier, "U.C. Santa Cruz: The Architecture," 42-47; John Pastier, "U.C. Santa Cruz: Kresge College," 48-54; and Glenn Robert Lym, "Kresge Postscript," 55, 70.

Woodbridge, Sally. "How to Make a Place." *Progressive Architecture*, May 1974, 76-83.

"Works–Kresge College." *Architecture and Urbanism*, May 1975, 44-45.

Chapter 11

Houses of William Wurster, edited by Marc Treib. San Francisco: San Francisco Museum of Modern Art, 1995.

Imbert, Dorothee. "Byways to Modernism: The Early Landscapes of Thomas Church," in *Thomas Church, Landscape Architect: Designing a Modern California Landscape*, edited by Marc Treib. San Francisco: William Stout, 2003.

Koch, Margaret. *The Pasatiempo Story*. Los Gatos, CA: Pasatiempo, Inc.: 1990.

Outerbridge, David E. *Champion in a Man's World: The Biography of Marion Hollins*. Chelsea, MI: Sleeping Bear Press, 1998.

"Santa Cruz Home of E. S. Berry." (A Wurster house). *American Architect* 150:36-37.

Architects and Architecture

Andersen, Timothy J., Eudorah M. Moore, and Robert W. Winter, eds. *California Design 1910*. Pasadena: California Design Publications, 1974.

Baird, Joseph Armstrong, Jr. *Time's Wondrous Changes: San Francisco Architecture, 1776-1915*. San Francisco: California Historical Society, 1962. Reprint, Santa Barbara: Peregrine Smith, 1980.

Freudenheim, Leslie Mandelson, and Elisabeth Sussman. *Building with Nature: Roots of the San Francisco Bay Region Tradition*. Santa Barbara: Peregrine Smith, 1974.

Gebhard, David, and Susan King. *A View of California Architecture: 1960-1976*. San Francisco: San Francisco Museum of Modern Art, 1976.

Gebhard, David, Eric Sandweiss, and Robert Winter. *The Guide to Architecture in San Francisco* and *Northern California*. Rev. ed. Salt Lake City: Gibbs Smith, 1985.

Gebhard, David, and Harriette Von Breton. *Architecture in California, 1868-1968*. Santa Barbara: University of California at Santa Barbara, Art Gallery, 1968.

Gregory, Daniel. "The Nature of Restraint: Wurster and His Circle," in *An Everyday Modernism: The Houses of William Wurster*, edited by Marc Treib. San Francisco: San Francisco Museum of Modern Art, 1995.

Jones, Tom, William Pettus, and Michael Pyatok. *Good Neighbors: Affordable Family Housing*. Foreword by Chester Hartman; edited by Sally D. Woodbridge. Melbourne, Australia: Images Publishing Group, 1995.

Jordy, William H. *American Buildings and Their Architects: Progressive and Academic Ideals at the Turn of the Twentieth Century*. New York: Doubleday, 1972.

Kirker, Harold. *California's Architectural Frontier: Style and Tradition in the Nineteenth Century*. 3rd ed. Salt Lake City: Peregrine Smith, 1986.

_____. *Old Forms on a New Land: California Architecture in Perspective*. Niwot, CO: Roberts Rinehart, 1991.

Lewis, Betty. "W. H. Weeks, Watsonville Architect." *Santa Cruz County History Journal*, no. 2 (1995): 1-4.

_____. *W. H. Weeks: Architect*. Fresno: Panorama West Books, 1985.

Lyndon, Donlyn. *MLTW: Houses by MLTW, Moore, Lyndon, Turnbull & Whitaker*. Edited and photographed by Yukio Futagawa. Tokyo: A.D.A. Edita, 1975.

McAlester, Virginia, and Lee McAlester. *A Field Guide to American Houses*. New York: Knopf, 1984.

Bibliography

Moore, Charles, and Gerald Allen. *Dimensions, Space, Shape and Scale in Architecture.* New York: Architectural Record Books, 1976.

Moore, Charles, and Donlyn Lyndon. *The Place of Houses.* New York: Holt, Rinehart & Winston, 1974.

Pierce, Nona Prettyman. "Roy Rydell's International Medley." *Garden Design* 4, no. 2 (Summer 1985): 22, 56-59.

Scully, Vincent, Jr. *The Shingle Style and the Stick Style: Architectural Theory and Design from Richardson to the Origins of Wright.* Rev. ed. New Haven: Yale University Press, 1971.

_____. *The Shingle Style Today: or, The Historian's Revenge.* New York: George Braziller, 1974.

Venturi, Robert. *Contradiction and Complexity in Architecture.* New York: The Museum of Modern Art, 1966.

Whiffen, Marcus. *American Architecture Since 1780.* Rev. ed. Cambridge, MA: MIT Press, 1992.

Withey, Henry F., and Elsie Rathburn Withey. *Biographical Dictionary of American Architects* (*Deceased*). Los Angeles: New Age Publishing Co., 1956. Reprint, Omnigraphics, 1996.

Woodbridge, Sally, ed. *Bay Area Houses.* New ed. Salt Lake City: Peregrine Smith, 1988.

Index of Street Addresses

Index of Street Addresses

Index

Index

The Sidewalk Companion

Index

Index

Index

Index

Index

Index

Index

Index

Index

Index

Index

Index

Index

Index

John Chase has a BA in art history from UCSC and a master's in architecture from UCLA. He has worked as a journalist, architectural designer, critic, and Disney Imagineer. He is currently the urban designer for the City of West Hollywood. His previous books include *Everyday Urbanism; Las Vegas: The Success of Excess; Exterior Decoration;* and *Glitter Stucco & Dumpster Diving: Reflections on Building Production in the Vernacular City*.

Daniel Gregory received his doctorate in architectural history from UC, Berkeley. He is Senior Home Editor for *Sunset* magazine and the author of numerous articles and essays on architectural subjects, including those on William Wurster and Thomas Church.

Judith Steen holds a master's degree in librarianship from the University of Portland. She retired from UCSC after a career in academic, public, and research libraries. She has edited numerous books in the fields of history and women's studies.